Cambridge
Lower Secondary

Computing 8

Ben Barnes
Margaret Debbadi
Pam Jones
Tristan Kirkpatrick
SERIES EDITOR:
Lorne Pearcey

HODDER EDUCATION
AN HACHETTE UK COMPANY

Hachette UK's policy is to use papers that are natural, renewable and recyclable products and made from wood grown in well-managed forests and other controlled sources. The logging and manufacturing processes are expected to conform to the environmental regulations of the country of origin.

Orders: please contact Hachette UK Distribution, Hely Hutchinson Centre, Milton Road, Didcot, Oxfordshire, OX11 7HH. Telephone: +44 (0)1235 827827. Email education@hachette.co.uk Lines are open from 9 a.m. to 5 p.m., Monday to Friday. You can also order through our website: www.hoddereducation.com

ISBN: 978 1 3983 6979 5

First published in 2022 by
Hodder Education,
An Hachette UK Company
Carmelite House
50 Victoria Embankment
London EC4Y 0DZ

www.hoddereducation.com

Impression number 10 9 8 7 6 5 4

Year 2026 2025 2024

Cover photo © AndSus - stock.adobe.com

Illustrations by Aptara, Inc.

Typeset in India by Aptara, Inc.

Printed in India

A catalogue record for this title is available from the British Library.

FSC
www.fsc.org
MIX
Paper | Supporting responsible forestry
FSC™ C104740

Contents

Introduction

About this book

Computer science is the study of computers, computing hardware and software, computer networks and the design of computer programs. It also includes the study of the way humans interact with computers and computing technology.

Computer science is linked to all areas of the world you live in today. It helps you to make positive changes to the world you live in, and provides important tools and **applications** to help you solve a wide range of problems. Computer science is continually evolving to provide new and valuable ways of improving your life and your interactions with the world around you.

This Student's Book will help you to understand some of the key areas of computer science, such as:

- cyber security
- **algorithms** and programs
- robotics, **artificial intelligence** and **augmented reality**
- gaming
- **databases** and **spreadsheets**
- software development.

This book also supports the learning objectives within the five strands of the Cambridge Lower Secondary Computing framework:

- **Computational thinking** is built into the tasks in this book. It looks at how computing can be used to explore and analyse data collected from the world around you. It is also about the development of skills to support problem-solving, for example how to describe a problem, and the data needed to solve that problem, in a way that a computer can understand.
- **Programming** explores the steps involved in designing and creating a computer program that can be used to carry out a particular task. In this book, you will study **text-based programming** languages such as Python and explore how to program a physical computing device to solve a problem.
- **Managing data** looks at how computers and computer programs can be used to store, organise and manage different types of data. It also explores how that data can be used to support problem-solving. In this book, you will learn how to use, edit and create databases and spreadsheets to help with managing different types of data.
- **Networks and digital communication** focuses on the methods used to transfer digital data between different computing devices, and how these devices are used to support communication. In this book, you will explore how different computing devices can be linked together to support data transfer.
- **Computer systems** is about how computer hardware devices and computer programs work together to support users in solving problems. It involves considering how the hardware and software and the data input is **processed**, stored and then output, to help a user solve a problem. In this book, you will explore the network and communications devices used to transmit data and information around a computer, and the world, in the process of solving a problem.

KEYWORDS

applications software: the software that users access to carry out tasks

algorithm: step-by-step instructions to solve a particular problem

artificial intelligence (AI): the study of machines and algorithms designed to carry out tasks in a way that is similar to humans

augmented reality (AR): a simulation that superimposes digital images on the user's real-world environment and allows the user to interact with those images

database: an application that is used to organise data that can then be stored, processed and accessed electronically

spreadsheet: an application that uses rows and columns to organise data and carry out calculations using that data

text-based programming: programming that requires the programmer to type text, e.g. Python

process: carrying out an operation on data, e.g. querying a database or doing a calculation using data in a spreadsheet

This Student Book has six units:

8.1 Building networks: Network structure and security builds on skills developed in Stage 7, investigating ways in which devices can communicate over networks. The unit provides an insight into the threats to networks that exist and the ways in which skilled engineers can protect against them. You will explore ways that networks can be structured and built, including the essential hardware and software required for scalability.

8.2 It's all in the planning: Pseudocode and algorithms develops knowledge and skills using MicroPython with the BBC micro:bit, including sending a message from one micro:bit to another. You will plan an algorithm and program with MicroPython to send an image, text and numbers and use ASCII to send a message.

8.3 Let's talk technology: What's going on inside provides an insight into the different types of software that support interaction with digital devices. It also covers the various types of computer memory; how files can be reduced in size; converting between binary and denary numbers; and using truth tables to model logic gates. You will investigate newer areas of computing such as robotics, artificial intelligence and augmented reality.

8.4 Testing conditions: Developing games allows you to develop your Python programming skills, focusing on the use of sequencing and selection. You will decompose a complex problem and develop a game that meets a brief.

8.5 Data input: Data collection and validation builds on knowledge and skills developed in Stage 7 where real-life situations were modelled using MS Access and MS Excel. You will study how to incorporate automatic checks into database and spreadsheet models, how to design data-capture forms and how to link data elements in a spreadsheet using formulae. Finally, you will investigate how to use a spreadsheet data model to ask what-if questions and make predictions.

8.6 Iterating through a solution: Software design and development focuses on the flow of a project and iterative development from start to finish. You will learn about using selection in Python to create a question-based quiz to determine whether or not an item can be recycled. You will develop the solution iteratively, from planning with algorithms through to programming with Python.

How to use this book

In each unit, you will learn new skills by completing a series of tasks.

These features appear in each unit:

Get started!

This box introduces the unit and asks you some questions to discuss in pairs or a small group.

Learning outcomes

This box lists the learning outcomes that you will achieve in the unit.

Warm up

This box provides a task to do in pairs or a small group to get the learning started.

SCENARIO

This box contains a scenario that puts the tasks in the unit into a real-world context.

Do you remember?

This box lists the skills you should already have before starting the unit.

DID YOU KNOW?

This box provides an interesting or important fact about the task or theme.

Learn

This box introduces new concepts and skills.

Practise

This box contains tasks to apply and practise the new skills and knowledge from the 'Learn' box.

Go further

This box contains tasks to enhance and develop the skills you have previously learned in the unit.

Challenge yourself

This box provides challenging tasks with additional instructions to support new skills.

Final project

This box contains a final project that encompasses all the skills you have developed over the unit, in the context of the Scenario. The tasks in this box can be used to support teacher assessment of the learning objectives from the Learning outcomes box.

Evaluation

This box provides guidance on how to evaluate and, if necessary, test the final project tasks.

What can you do?

This box provides a summary of the skills you have learned in the unit and can be used to support self/peer assessment of the learning objectives.

Computational thinking

Most computational thinking skills are embedded into the 'Practise' tasks. However, where you see this box, an individual computational thinking skill is highlighted for your attention.

KEYWORDS

Important words are shown in **emboldened orange font** and are defined in this box. They also appear in the glossary at the back of the book.

Speech bubbles provide hints and tips as you complete the tasks.

Student resource files, used in some of the Practise boxes, are available at www.hoddereducation.com/cambridgeextras

Unit 8.1 Building networks: Network structure and security

Get started!

In this unit, you will take a close look at the ways in which devices can communicate over networks, including the hardware and software components required to make this happen. Safety and security of data transmission are crucial for modern networks and you will investigate methods of keeping them secure.

Discuss the following with your partner:

- What are the different methods of data transmission on a network?
- Which is the fastest wireless data-transmission method?
- How can you ensure that data cannot be intercepted?

In this unit, you will develop your understanding of ways in which network technology can improve transmission and keep you safe while using networks.

Learning outcomes

In this unit, you will learn to:

- identify different types of network, such as PAN, LAN and WAN
- identify the type of network that should be used in different scenarios
- describe the uses and characteristics of copper and fibre-optic cables to transmit data
- describe the advantages and disadvantages of wired and wireless networks
- describe the advantages of security features in different types of networks
- describe how echo checks are used to detect errors in transmission
- explain how firewalls protect a network and why they are important
- explain how antivirus and anti-spyware software provides protection to keep data secure on a network
- explain the security features used by different types of networks
- explain the purpose of operating systems and describe some of the main tasks an operating system carries out
- explain what a network operating system is
- explain why a network operating system is labelled 'utilities software'
- identify and describe how augmented reality is used in education, gaming and robotics
- follow a flowchart that uses conditional statements to illustrate how error checks work.

Warm up

All devices connected to a network have a unique IP address. The devices below, which are yet to be assigned IP addresses, are all part of the same network.

Complete the table to assign valid IP addresses to the devices. The devices that you need to assign addresses to are listed on the left-hand side of the table. Make up the IP addresses, remembering to ensure that they follow the rules of an IP address.

Device	IP address
Router	192.168.1.1
Smart TV	
Laptop	
Tablet computer	
PC	

Remember: IP addresses are made up of four sets of three numbers between 0 and 255.

SCENARIO

A youth group working in the community is setting up technology centres for young people to meet, play games (including augmented-reality games) and socialise in a safe, supervised environment. The technology centres will be based in local community centres.

The youth group's aim is to help educate young people with steps that they can take to keep their digital devices and online activity secure.

It has employed you as its new network security and communications specialist. Your job is to advise the youth group on the types of network, telecommunications links, technology and software that it will require in the community centres to help keep the young people safe while they are using their own devices.

You are also responsible for helping the youth group organisers learn about networks, telecommunications and data security before it opens its first community group in your local area.

DID YOU KNOW?

A cyber-attack happens about once every 39 seconds worldwide.

Do you remember?

Before starting this unit, you should be able to:

- ✔ explain different ways in which devices can transmit data
- ✔ understand how a DNS enables users to access websites on their devices and explain the steps a DNS takes
- ✔ understand how IP addresses and web servers work
- ✔ explain what the structure of a URL looks like and identify the different parts

- ✔ explain what types of encryption can be used on websites
- ✔ find information on the security certificates of a website
- ✔ understand how errors can occur in data transmission and apply ways to check that a message is sent correctly
- ✔ modify a program based on a basic cipher
- ✔ encode and decode messages using a cipher
- ✔ understand how search engines categorise data
- ✔ explain how AI is used to improve search-engine results.

Networking: It's not just about meeting people

Learn

Networking: it's not just about meeting people! **Networks** come in all shapes and sizes, from small networks between just two computers to large networks spanning the globe with thousands of devices connected to them.

There are three types of network that you need to be familiar with: PAN, LAN and WAN. Each type of network has its own advantages and disadvantages and uses. All network types allow devices to communicate, with the main difference being the geographic area that they cover.

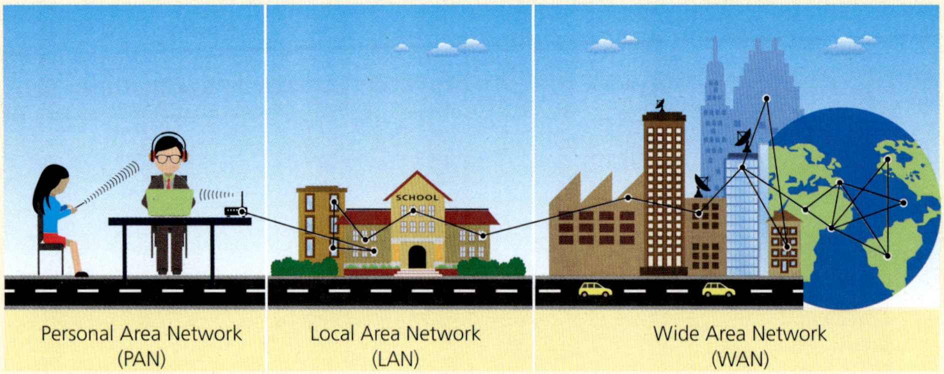

Personal Area Networks (PAN) are the smallest type of network, usually connecting devices that are in close proximity to an individual. These are useful for smart watches, headsets and wireless headphones. PAN networks are usually connected via **Bluetooth**.

Local Area Networks (LAN) allow devices to communicate over a small geographic area, usually a single site, such as a single building, school or college.

Wide Area Networks (WAN) allow devices to communicate in the same way, but over a larger geographical area, and are usually made up of several LANs connected together. Companies often use this method if they have a number of different offices spread across a geographical region. The largest example of a WAN is the internet.

Lots of smart tech has emerged that provides new technologies to users. Robot vacuum cleaners, smart lawnmowers, smart fridges, smart doorbells and many other 'smart' devices provide convenience and extra functionality to users. Most of these devices are usable on a LAN.

It's often quite difficult to tell whether a device uses a PAN or a LAN. Remember that for a device to be on a PAN, it will work only when in close proximity to the device it is connected to; smart watches, wireless headphones and smart medical devices all work on PANs. Technologies such as smart light bulbs and plug sockets would be on a LAN because they can be accessed and switched on and off from anywhere on a local network, not just from one user's phone, for example.

Why network devices?

There are several benefits and drawbacks of networking devices.

Benefits	Drawbacks
• Users can share devices such as printers and scanners. • Users can share **software** licences (which means that software is often cheaper). • Users can communicate with each other over the network. • Users can share an internet connection.	• Networking **hardware** can be very expensive. • Managing a network can be complicated and may need skilled people to manage it. • Viruses can spread to all devices on the network if a single user's device becomes infected.

Smart devices often make use of networks. For example, if a user has a robot vacuum cleaner, the software that comes with the device allows the user to set the time of day that it cleans, which rooms it cleans and how powerful the suction should be. This functionality allows the cleaner to clean **autonomously**, as it has been programmed to adjust to the user's preferences the more they use it. This makes a user's life easier and completes tasks that otherwise the user would have to do.

Servers

A **server** is a computer that is usually very powerful and is connected to a network. Different types of server provide different services for the devices connected to them via the network. In Stage 7, you investigated the way in which web servers function, but a server can provide a number of other useful services.

- **File servers** offer devices on a network a place to store and access files. On large networks, files are often stored on the server, not on the device that the user is working on. This can be beneficial in a business where a number of people need to access the same files.
- **Print servers** enable devices on a network to share printers. If you imagine a large office, it would not be feasible for every device to have its own printer. A print server manages which devices can print to a single printer so that users can share it.

- **Mail servers** store email messages and allow users to **authenticate** themselves so that they can send and receive messages.
- **Web servers** provide internet-accessible files and transmit files to users over the world wide web.

Servers are also very important for maintaining the security of a network. **Antivirus**, **anti-spyware** and **firewall** applications on the server keep all the networked devices safe. You will investigate these security features in more detail in upcoming lessons. Servers co-ordinate the communication of devices on the network.

In the modern world, most devices form part of a network. In the home, even fridges, vacuum cleaners, lawnmowers and light bulbs can often be networked to increase their functionality.

Network operating systems: Just like regular systems, servers require an **operating system**. The type of operating system a network uses is usually more advanced, as it controls how network services are delivered to all the devices on the network.

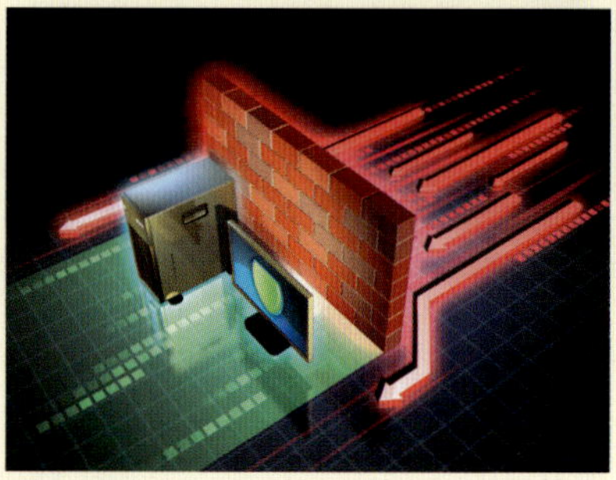

KEYWORDS

network: a collection of computing devices connected to each other, either wired or wirelessly

Personal Area Network (PAN): a type of network that communicates over an area of no more than 10 metres, usually connecting smart devices within the immediate area of a user

Bluetooth: a wireless technology that allows data transmission using radio waves

Local Area Network (LAN): a type of network that communicates over a small geographical area, such as a single building

Wide Area Network (WAN): a type of network that communicates over a large geographical area, such as across a city or country

software: the programs or set of instructions that tell a computer what to do to complete a task; aspects of a device you cannot touch

hardware: the physical parts of a computer that you can touch and see, e.g. the processor, storage devices, input devices, output devices

autonomous programming: computer hardware and complex AI software working together to solve a problem without any human interaction

server: a computer that offers a service to other devices on a network, such as file-sharing services and printer-sharing services

authenticate: allowing a computer or a human to verify that the user is who they say they are

operating system: the systems software that manages hardware and software, giving the user an interface to operate the computer

antivirus: software that detects and removes viruses from a computer

anti-spyware: software that detects and removes spyware from a computer

firewall: software or hardware that prevents unauthorised access to a network

Practise

1 Using your knowledge of different networks, categorise the following scenarios into PAN, LAN or WAN:
   a a home network containing three PCs, two laptops, one tablet, four mobile phones, three smart TVs, one smart vacuum cleaner and one games console
   b a business with 5000 PCs in total across three different office blocks in three separate countries; all the devices are on the same network
   c a smart fitness band that a runner wears, who also carries their mobile phone.

2 a Open the worksheet **PAN_LAN_WAN activity.docx** provided by your teacher. Investigate all the devices you can find that connect to a network. For each of the devices, identify which type of network it connects to. Add some devices to the list that you can find on either your home or school network. Complete the table on the worksheet.
   b Think about the answers to the questions below and be ready to feed back to your classmates.
      i Why does networking devices increase the security risk?
      ii Are there ways in which security risks can be prevented?

3 As a class, discuss the security implications of having so many networked devices in the home and at school.

4 How many of the networked devices people have in their homes automatically change how they operate based on how the people use them? Look at the list below and see whether you can expand it.

Device	How it changes based on how people use it
Smart speaker	Adjusts volume based on the surrounding noise or the time of day

Making connections

Learn

Hardware

For networks to function properly, they need a number of different pieces of network hardware. Each piece of hardware has its own role to play in ensuring that the network functions correctly.

Servers

Servers provide services to a network. You investigated the functions that they can offer devices in the previous Learn box.

Network Interface Controller

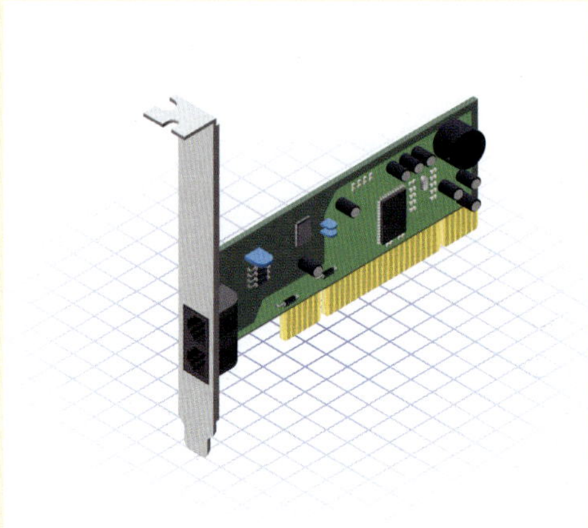

A Network Interface Controller (NIC) must be present in a device to enable it to communicate with other devices over a network. Sometimes these are physical cards that can be plugged into a PC, but often they are built into a device using smaller electronic circuitry. Mobile phone NICs are much smaller than a PC NIC, for example. Every NIC has a MAC address that uniquely identifies the device on a network. The MAC address is assigned when the device is manufactured and cannot be changed.

Switch

A **switch** connects together multiple devices on a network. It stores the MAC address of every device that it is connected to. When one device wants to send **data** to another, it uses the MAC address to send the data only to the device that is meant to receive it. Often switches connect large numbers of devices together using **ethernet cables**.

Wireless Access Point

A **Wireless Access Point (WAP)** allows devices to connect to a network using Wi-Fi.

Router

A router connects different networks together and provides access to the internet. If you want to send data from one place to another, a router finds the fastest route to send the data.

All-in-one devices

Home networks often use an all-in-one device that combines a router with a WAP and switch. The WAP allows devices to connect to the network via Wi-Fi, and a four-port switch allows users to connect up to four devices directly to the network via an ethernet cable.

Wired vs wireless

The devices that make up a network can be connected in a variety of ways, all of which can be categorised into wired or wireless.

Wired connections

Wired connections use copper wire or fibre-optic cable. Fibre-optic cables are usually used to connect LANs together to form WANs across large geographic areas.

Copper wire: Copper wire, also known as **ethernet cable**, transmits data as electrical pulses and can transmit around 10 Gb per second. It is often used to connect devices on a LAN as it transmits data reliably over a distance of about 100 metres. Copper wire is fairly cheap but is prone to **interference**.

Fibre-optic cable: Fibre-optic cables transmit data as pulses of light, which is much faster than electrical signals. This means that they have a high **bandwidth** of up to 100 Tb per second, much faster than the copper alternative. Fibre-optic cables are not as prone to interference, so they are more reliable than copper cables.

Wired connections are often much more reliable and faster than wireless connections; however, they do have some drawbacks:

- Wired connections can be expensive to install. Imagine how much ethernet cable you would need to wire up every device to the network switches in your school!
- Devices connected via cabling are not portable, as they can move only as far as the wires will allow!

Wireless connections

The table shows the most common standards of wireless communication.

Method of wireless transmission	Bandwidth
Wi-Fi	The latest version of Wi-Fi is capable of transmitting data at 9.6 Gbps (9600 Mbps).
Bluetooth	Bluetooth is capable of transmitting data at 2 Mbps.
3G	The average speed of 3G is 3 Mbps.
4G	The average speed of 4G is between 8 and 10 Mbps.
5G	The average speed of 5G is 100 Mbps.

Wireless connections are great for convenience, but they have some drawbacks.

- Wireless networks are often subject to interference, which can prevent data from transmitting accurately.
- The data transmitted over a wireless network can be intercepted easily.
- Wireless networks are often slower than wired networks.

Different types of wireless networks fit into three categories: WPAN, WLAN and WWAN.

WPAN: A **Wireless Personal Area Network** is a type of PAN that can be connected using wireless technology only. This is most often Bluetooth, as a PAN generally does not need to connect to a device further than 10 metres away.

WLAN: Wireless Local Area Networks are often used in homes and in small businesses located in one building over a small geographical area. Here, devices connect to the WLAN using Wi-Fi, as the transmission distance of Wi-Fi is around 9 metres (or more without obstructions such as walls).

WWAN: Wireless Wide Area Networks are types of Wide Area Networks that are often used for telecommunications by mobile devices using 3G, 4G and 5G. Devices connect to a 'mast' or 'tower', which can be done over a distance of up to 15 kilometres.

Modern-day users require wide bandwidths, so that they can transfer large files quickly.

Augmented-reality gaming

Imagine that you are gaming **online**. Which of the technologies above would you use and why? Would a wired or wireless connection be best for gaming? Would you choose copper or fibre connection to the WAN?

Game designers are pushing the boundaries of what is possible in online gaming and they are introducing **augmented-reality** games to the market.

Augmented reality in gaming is an enhanced version of the real world, showing digital elements on top of what humans can already see. This type of game requires a lot of computing power, and involves large amounts of data being transmitted via networks. This means that the existing networks need to be improved and speeded up continually to be able to keep pace with the demands of the modern world.

Practise

Now you are going to build some networks.

1 For each of the scenarios below, draw the network hardware and devices on a large sheet of paper. Use coloured pens to represent the different types of connection methods according to the 'Connections key' below.

Connections key	
Ethernet cable	Red
Bluetooth connection	Blue
Wi-Fi connection	Purple
3G/4G/5G	Yellow
Fibre cable	Green

a **Scenario 1**

A small office (Office 1) has a LAN with five laptops connected via Wi-Fi, two printers connected via ethernet and five PCs connected via ethernet to the network. Two of the workers have smart watches that connect to their smartphones via Bluetooth. The two smartphones in the office do not connect to the Wi-Fi, but use 4G or 5G networks to communicate.

b **Scenario 2**

The main office in Scenario 1 is part of a larger office complex of two offices in total. Office 2 is much smaller than Office 1, and has two workers who both have a smartphone and a laptop. When the company built the offices, it wanted to make sure that they were future proof, so it installed a fibre-optic cable between the two offices.

2 Add the second office to your network diagram.

3 Now highlight which areas of the network are a PAN, LAN or WAN. Also show in the diagram any additional network hardware the offices may require (routers, switches, access points, and so on).

4 Would the network you have drawn be appropriate for the youth group in the Scenario at the start of this unit? Explain your answer to your partner.

KEYWORDS

switch: a network device that forwards data from one device to another

data: raw facts and figures

ethernet cable: a popular type of copper cable used to transmit data between devices

Wireless Access Point (WAP): enables devices to connect to a network using Wi-Fi

interference: what happens when something interrupts the transmission of a signal; this could be a physical obstruction such as a wall, or other radio waves

bandwidth: a measure of the maximum number of bits that can be transmitted over a network or cable in a specified amount of time

online: connected to the internet

augmented reality (AR): a simulation that superimposes digital images on the user's real-world environment and allows the user to interact with those images

You said what?

Learn

Transmitting data

Networked devices transmit **binary** data, which consists of 1s and 0s. Eight bits of 1 or 0 make up a byte.

The devices transmit data using a wired or wireless method, and need to be able to do this extremely quickly, even for large amounts of data.

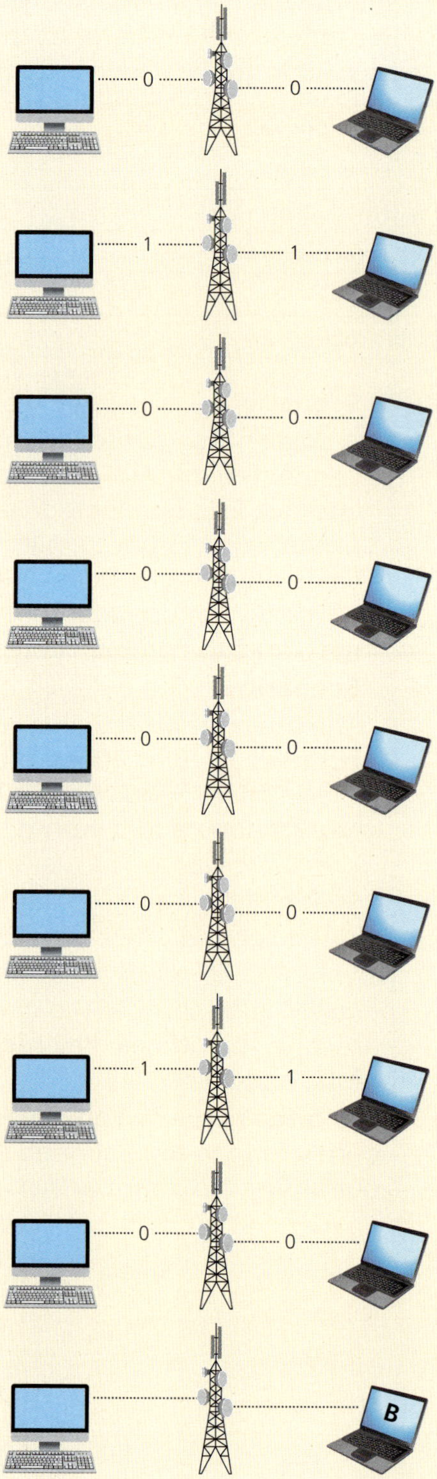

ASCII

ASCII is a set of codes that represent characters (for example, letters, numbers and punctuation marks) in a format a computer system can recognise. ASCII assigns each character a specific binary code. You will learn more about ASCII in Unit 8.3.

Character	Binary
A	01000001
B	01000010
C	01000011

Serial transmission

ASCII binary codes are 8 bits, or a byte. For example, '01000010' is the binary representation in ASCII of 'B'. In **serial transmission**, a device transfers one bit at a time to the receiving device.

Parallel transmission

In **parallel transmission**, 8 bits, or 1 byte, of data can be sent simultaneously.

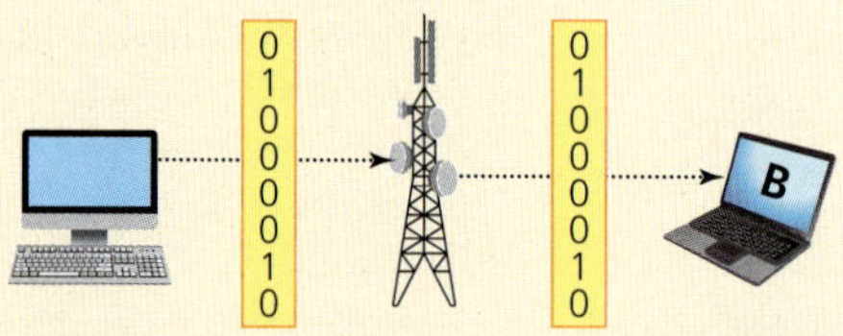

Transmission errors

When computers communicate, it is important that the information sent and received is correct. Take an air traffic control team in an airport, for example.

It is essential that the messages the controllers communicate to pilots are correct, otherwise an aeroplane could be landing on a runway before another plane has taken off, which would be a disaster.

Another example is in hospitals. Most hospitals have complex network structures that rely on data transmission to show how many beds they have available in various departments. If this is not accurate, people could be turned away from a hospital because the network showed that there were no beds available, when in fact there were.

Large skyscrapers often use network-connected carbon-monoxide and heat detectors. What if a computer mistakenly reported that a heat detector was cold, when there was a fire in the room it was monitoring?

People rely on computers to send data accurately across networks. Unfortunately, errors in systems do happen, but computers have some clever ways to find them quickly.

Why do errors occur?

When sending data over a network, there are a number of reasons why the data that is received could be incorrect. Imagine that a laptop wants to transmit the message '00000001' over a large WAN to a PC. Here are some examples of things that could cause an error:

- Interference to the Wi-Fi signal connecting the laptop to the network could cause one of the bits to **flip**.
- A **power surge** on one of the networked devices that the data is travelling through could cause a bit to flip.

How can errors be detected?

Echo checking ... Echo checking ... Echo checking.

When a computer receives data, it immediately returns it to the sending computer for comparison.

The sender then compares the two **sets** of data to check whether they match. If they match, there is no error. However, if they do not match, then the data is sent again.

The following **algorithm** shows a basic echo check.

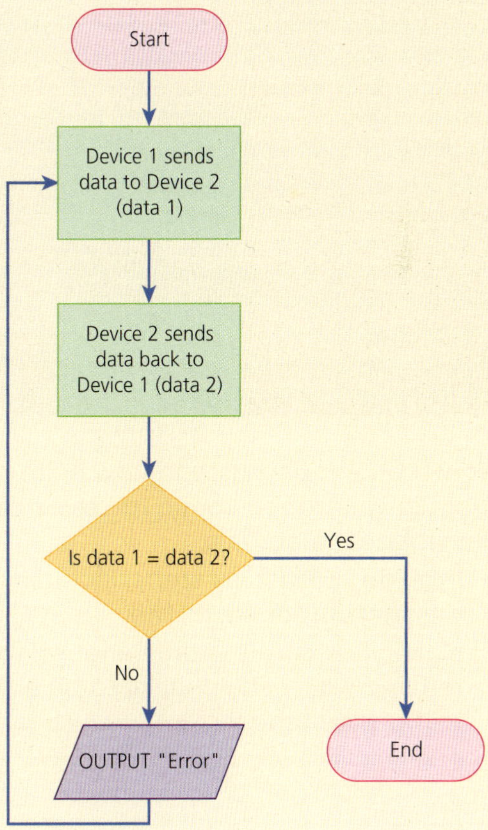

For example, a computer transmits the binary number 00000001 (which represents **denary** 1). An error occurs causing 10000000 (denary 128) to be received. 10000000 is sent back to the first computer and the error is highlighted as the values do not match, so the original data is sent again.

Problems with echo checking

- Echo checking makes it impossible to tell whether the error occurred when the data was originally sent, or when it was returned to the sender.
- Echo checks mean that a lot more data is sent over a network.

KEYWORDS

binary: the number system that uses just two digits: 0 and 1; also known as 'base 2'

ASCII (American Standard Code for Information Interchange): a 7-bit binary code that represents all the keys on a standard keyboard

serial transmission: data is transferred one bit at a time

parallel transmission: 8 bits (or 1 byte) of data are transferred simultaneously

bit flip: when a single bit changes from 0 to 1, or 1 to 0, during transmission

power surge: a temporary increase in power, often caused by lightning, which can damage computer hardware

data set: a collection of data items that are all related

algorithm: step-by-step instructions to solve a particular problem

denary format: a number system that uses the digits 0, 1, 2, 3, 4, 5, 6, 7, 8, 9 to represent every numerical value

Practise

Now that you understand how echo checks function, create a graphic-illustration comic to use as part of your youth group promotional materials.

- Provide at least six steps, including an illustration with a description for each step.
- Make your comic simple enough for somebody who is not familiar with echo checks to be able to follow the guidance and understand it.

Security concerns

Learn

You now know how echo checking can be used to help detect errors, but how do you know that the data that is being transmitted is secure? What are the threats to networks?

Hackers constantly try to gain **unauthorised** access to networks. There are a number of reasons for this, including to earn money illegally, to gather data (which is often also worth money) or to cause criminal damage.

There are four main types of threats: viruses, ransomware, spyware and unauthorised access.

Viruses

A virus is a computer program that is usually hidden within another **program** or file. It can replicate itself into other programs or files, which are then often passed between users/computers, or transmitted over networks. Viruses exist to cause harm, often damaging or deleting data without the owner's consent. Even small changes to a computer's **operating-system** files can be devastating to the system and cause it to malfunction.

One of the best-known viruses was the ILOVEYOU bug. In the year 2000, millions of people received the virus via email, with the subject line 'I love you'. When the recipient clicked and downloaded the file 'LOVE-LETTER-FOR-YOU.TXT.vbs', the virus was run. It overwrote important operating-system files and replicated itself multiple times. It is estimated to have cost users a total of $15 billion in damages.

Ransomware

Ransomware is a type of software designed to block access to the files on a computer system until somebody pays a ransom.

Ransomware called 'WannaCry' targeted users of Windows operating systems and told them that they had to pay a fee, otherwise all their files would be encrypted and deleted, making them impossible to recover. This hit around 230,000 computers globally, including hospitals and doctors' surgeries.

Spyware

Spyware monitors the target computer's actions. For example, details of the keys that the user presses on the keyboard may be sent to the hacker. This means that the hacker could discover the keystrokes of passwords, giving them access to confidential login details.

A hacker often installs spyware on a computer or a network after they have gained unauthorised access. The software that the hacker installs cannot usually be detected and gives the hacker full control of and access to the computer system. They can also carry out this style of attack on mobile phones and tablets.

Unauthorised access

There are a number of ways in which hackers may try to gain access to computers and systems that they should not have access to.

- **Social engineering**

  Hackers have developed ways of trying to find out as much information about somebody as possible in an attempt to guess their passwords. For example, if you met somebody and they asked you who your favourite sports team is, what month your birthday is in or what city you were born in, you would probably not consider this to be sinister. However, the hacker could use this information to try to guess your passwords.

  Hackers may also try to use 'forgotten password' tools to answer secret questions that would give them the opportunity to reset a password.

- **Cracking passwords**

  Brute-force attacks are a technique hackers use to try to gain access to computer systems or network devices. Hackers use very large 'dictionary' files that contain millions of words or known passphrases and they try every combination until they find the correct password. Hackers use computer programs that are able to try millions of different passwords every second to crack passwords automatically.

  The most commonly used known passwords are often at the start of the dictionary files, and can be cracked very quickly.

Dictionary	How long to crack this password?	How many users have this password?
123456	Less than 1 second	Over 106 million
123456789	Less than 1 second	Over 46 million
12345	Less than 1 second	Over 32 million
qwerty	Less than 1 second	Over 22 million
password	Less than 1 second	Over 20 million

- **Using information in an unauthorised way**

  People become hackers when they access networks that they are not allowed to. For example, if a company has sacked a member of staff and forgets to disable their user account, this person could still log into the company's systems and cause a threat to the network.

KEYWORDS

unauthorised: not allowed

program: the instructions that tell a computer system how to complete a task

operating system: the systems software that manages hardware and software, giving the user an interface to operate the computer

brute-force attack: a type of cyber-attack that uses a dictionary to try to discover passwords automatically

Practise

Use the internet to find out about famous **cyber-attacks**. Find an example for each of the following types of attack: **virus**, **spyware**, **unauthorised access** and **ransomware**. Find out the name of the cyber-attack, when it took place and what effect it had on the devices that were infected.

1 Create a mind map explaining what each type of cyber-attack is. This can be completed on paper or using any suitable software you have access to.

2 Find at least one appropriate example of each type of cyber-attack and add these to your mind map.

3 Try to find a cyber-attack that had an impact on a large number of people. Find the best example that you can and make a note of its name, what it did and the number of people it affected. Share your examples with the class to see who can find the cyber-attack that impacted the greatest number of people.

KEYWORD

cyber-attack: the collective name for all types of attacks on a computer or computer network

Operating systems

Learn

With large amounts of data moving around networks each day, people rely on their data being transmitted and received without problems. Hackers can gain access to networks and damage them, and data can be damaged when it is sent across networks, so **network administrators** need to do everything they can to make sure that information travels around their network as efficiently and safely as possible, to allow their users to access their data reliably.

Most **Local Area Networks** contain a **server**, which provides services to the devices (**clients**) that are connected to it on the network. Imagine a large network in an office block. A network typically includes a server and lots of PCs. PCs are connected via wired ethernet connections to **switches**, and then the switches are connected to a router.

Each PC has an operating system installed on it, as does the server. Which one do you think is the most powerful? Operating systems and the utilities software on them play a big part in making sure that a network is reliable, safe and speedy.

Operating systems

Operating systems are responsible for managing all the hardware and software on the computer. They manage the files and folders and enable users to interact with the system and applications installed.

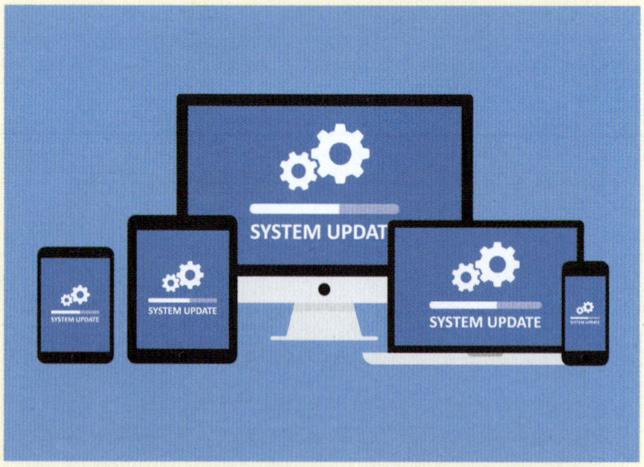

User interfaces

The operating system is responsible for providing the user with a way in which they can interact with the computer. There are four main types of operating-system user **interface**:

Command line: A command-line interface **processes** commands that the user types in. The computer displays a prompt, and the user types in their command and presses Enter. The earliest operating systems allowed users to interact only like this, and users had to know all the commands to be able to use them. Modern operating systems still have a facility for advanced users to input commands in this way.

In the example below, a network administrator first lists the folders available. This finds a folder called 'users'. The administrator then goes to the 'users' folder and lists all the files inside it.

```
network-admin: $ls
users
network-admin: $cd users
network-admin: $ls
list
```

Natural language and speech: Some devices have an interface that allows users to operate it by speaking to the device. Smart speakers are a popular example that uses this type of interface.

Graphical user interface (GUI): A graphical user interface has windows, icons, menus and pointers to enable a user to navigate the functions of the operating system and access their applications, files and folders. It is the most common type of operating system for PCs, laptops, tablets and smartphones.

Network operating systems

Network operating systems (NOS) work in the same way as a standard operating system, but offer some additional features that are useful to network administrators. A NOS is often installed on the server only, with the standard operating system installed on the client's device. This means that network administrators can access the server and manage the devices on the network.

Imagine needing to install a new piece of software on every device of a large network. Thankfully, NOS include utility software that can install or update software on all devices on the network automatically.

Administrators use NOS to create user accounts, to control what each user has access to and to configure the network.

NOS are often highly stable and provide good security against threats, due to the additional utilities that are included to help maintain networks.

Hardware

For your PC to be able to interact with hardware (a keyboard, for example), the operating system manages the drivers to teach the system how to interact with that particular device. Each type of device needs a driver; this includes graphics cards, network interface cards (NIC), keyboards, mice and monitors.

The operating system is also responsible for managing the **RAM (Random Access Memory)** and storing information in the RAM that is currently being used. For example, if a user is browsing the web using a web browser, the files the web browser requires are loaded into the RAM. The operating system works out how much memory each piece of software should use.

Each PC has its own operating system, which receives regular updates. It works similarly to the way in which smartphones receive updates.

KEYWORDS

network administrator: a person responsible for the maintenance and security of a network

Local Area Network (LAN): a type of network that communicates over a small geographical area, such as a single building

server: a computer that offers a service to other devices on a network, such as file-sharing services and printer-sharing services

client: a computer device that requests access to a service that a server provides

switch: a network device that forwards data from one device to another

interface: how a user interacts with a product

process: carrying out an operation on data, e.g. querying a database or doing a calculation using data in a spreadsheet

random access memory (RAM): a form of memory that stores tasks that are currently running, which the operating system controls

Practise

As the communications specialist at the youth group, it is important that you understand the functions of operating systems and utilities software, so that you can plan how the youth centre will use them.

Read the Scenario at the start of this unit.

1 In small groups, complete the file **Systems and Software.docx** provided by your teacher. You will need to use the internet to research which operating systems can be used on which devices.
2 At the bottom of the task document, describe in your own words the purpose of operating systems.

Keeping it all safe

Learn

Having seen some of the risks to data, you will now learn about some ways in which computers on networks can be protected from cyber-attacks. Utility software helps to keep a computer system or network safe and secure and running smoothly. It is a collection of programs, each of which has a specific task, and is usually installed alongside the operating system.

Antivirus software

Antivirus software prevents viruses from opening and infecting files on computers. The most common ways of infecting computers with viruses are via **malicious** email attachments, or files disguised as something else, which users unwittingly download from the internet.

Antivirus software performs real-time scans of chunks of data coming into a device to detect whether they have been infected with a virus. The software also regularly scans the computer, tablet or smartphone for files that could be harmful. Antivirus software uses large **databases** of code that it looks for in files to see whether they match known threats or look harmful. If it detects a file as harmful, the antivirus software will try to **quarantine** the file and let the user know that a virus has been detected. The user can then decide whether to delete the file.

To be effective in preventing viruses, users need to keep antivirus software up to date.

Anti-spyware/ransomware software

Anti-spyware works in a similar way to antivirus software. Anti-spyware regularly scans for files that could be troublesome to the user. Spyware is often more difficult to detect because it installs tools that are not always damaging to a user's computer, but which covertly enable hackers to spy on people using their devices.

Similarly to viruses, users download spyware unwittingly, often from email attachments or free software downloads.

Anti-spyware looks for software such as **adware** and **trojans**. When it detects threats, it removes them from the system and informs the user.

Firewalls

Firewalls are designed to keep networks safe by limiting the access that devices have to networks. They prevent **unauthorised** users from accessing a network.

Firewalls usually sit between the LAN and the WAN and can be either a hardware device or a piece of software. They are often built into routers and also pre-installed into operating systems.

Firewalls examine all the data entering and leaving a network to check that they do not break any rules. For example, a rule could be set so that devices from outside the network are not allowed to access devices within the network. Other rules may include preventing certain types of file from being received or filtering access to specific internet sites. Network administrators spend a lot of time deciding on the rules that should be in place for the network that they are working on.

If something that a user tries to do breaks one of the network rules, then the action will not be completed and the user will be notified.

KEYWORDS

malicious: describing something that intends to cause harm

database: an application that is used to organise data that can then be stored, processed and accessed electronically

quarantine: moving a file to a safe place where it cannot contaminate other files on the computer

adware: a type of spyware that increases the number of adverts a user has on their computer system, often displaying adverts as banners or pop-ups inside software and sometimes enticing users to click on links to insecure or malicious websites or downloads

trojan: software that pretends to be something that it is not; trojans track keystrokes and mouse movements - even sometimes webcams

unauthorised: not allowed

DID YOU KNOW?

Experts estimate that, in 2021, organisations suffered ransomware attacks every 11 seconds. They expect that there will be a new attack every 2 seconds by 2031.

Practise

1 As part of your work with the community youth group, it has asked you to recruit a new network administrator to help it with network security. Whoever is successful in the interview will be in charge of making all of the youth group's networks secure, so you need to be confident that they have enough knowledge about threats to network security and ways to protect the network.
   a Write a list of ten interview questions that you could ask an applicant about network security.
   b For each question, write a model answer: what would be the perfect answer to the question?
   c You must include at least one question on each of the following:
      - operating systems
      - utility software
      - firewalls
      - antivirus software
      - anti-spyware software.

2 When you have written your interview questions, give them to your partner to answer.
   a Make notes beneath each question of the key points that they make.
   b Compare each answer with your model answer and tell your partner if they missed anything to help them to improve their response.
   c At the end of the interview, explain whether or not they are successful and why!

Go further

Network security software is an extremely popular and important part of keeping our devices safe. You are going to investigate the different products that are available in the antivirus and anti-spyware markets for customers to purchase and use on their computers.

1 Copy and complete the table to compare some of the available types of network-security software.
   - **Price:** find the cost of the software; if the cost is yearly, then work out how much the software would cost to use for three years, for comparison.
   - **Compatibility:** find out which operating systems the software is compatible with, for example Microsoft Windows, macOS, Android, iOS, Linux or something else.
   - **Features:** find out the top three features of the software; also state what makes this software unique compared to the other software options.
   - **Protection:** find out what the software protects against (viruses, spyware, ransomware, unauthorised access).

Name	Price (3 years)	Compatibility	Features	Protection
Norton 360				
Bitdefender Internet Security				
Adaware				
Radio Silence				
Avast Mobile Security				

2 When you have completed the table, write a paragraph explaining to the youth group which of the products you think it should use to keep its network secure.

Challenge yourself

Checking that data is correct is an important part of keeping networks safe. You already know how devices can use echo checks to test the information that is transmitted between devices, but this requires a lot of additional data to be sent between the devices, which costs valuable time and bandwidth. You will now investigate another method of checking that data is correct during transmission: **ARQ (Automatic Repeat reQuests)**.

ARQ error detection uses **acknowledgements** and **timeouts** to make sure that data is sent accurately, often over connections that might be unreliable.

When data is sent from the sending device to the receiver, the receiver sends back an acknowledgement to the sender that is either **negative** or **positive**. If the acknowledgement is positive, it means that the data is correct and it has passed an error check. If the acknowledgement is negative, then the data cannot be used as it failed an error check and the sender must send it again.

The acknowledgement needs to be sent back within a certain amount of time, which is the timeout part of the ARQ process. If the acknowledgement is not received by the timeout, the device will keep sending the data until the acknowledgement is received.

Open the file **Flowchart Symbols.docx** provided by your teacher. Cut out the flowchart symbols and descriptors. Match each flowchart symbol to the correct descriptor and use connectors to complete the **flowchart**.

KEYWORD

flowchart: a visual representation of an algorithm

Final project

The skills that you have developed in this unit mean that you are now able to develop your learning into a project.

Refer back to the Scenario at the start of this unit to remind yourself of what the youth group is and how it expects you to help it.

Develop a presentation for the youth group organisers that will inform them of what you have learned in this unit. Your task is to give them security advice so that they can keep their networks safe, but also ensure that they have sensible network structures set up for their organisation.

Use the file **Final Project Presentation .pptx**, provided by your teacher, as a template. You will find some prompts on the template to help you to cover all the information that is required.

- **Slide 1**
  Explain in ten bullet points the key facts that you have learned in this unit.

- **Slides 2–4**
  Explain what is meant by PAN, LAN and WAN and provide one example of a device for each of the network types; also find an appropriate image for each slide.
- **Slide 5**
  Explain the different uses and characteristics of both copper and fibre-optic cables and find an image that illustrates one of the uses or characteristics.
- **Slide 6**
  Explain three advantages and three disadvantages of wired and wireless networks, including performance and security aspects. Which is the most secure and why?
- **Slide 7**
  Explain fully how an echo check tests for accuracy in transmission.
- **Slides 8–9**
  - Complete the table containing a list of threats and how you can protect against them. Include firewalls, antivirus and anti-spyware software, as a minimum.
  - Add a paragraph that explains the function of operating systems.
  - Add a paragraph defining what is meant by utilities software.

Evaluation

1. Swap your presentation with your partner and read/listen to/watch each other's content. Add comments in the speaker notes about the following:
   - Does it cover all the requirements?
   - Is the content easy to understand?
   - How could your partner improve their presentation?
2. Open your presentation and read the comments your partner has left.
3. Make a list of recommendations to improve your presentation.

What can you do?

Read and review what you can do.

- ✔ I can identify different types of network, such as PAN, LAN and WAN.
- ✔ I can identify the type of network that should be used in different scenarios.
- ✔ I can describe the uses and characteristics of copper and fibre-optic cables to transmit data.
- ✔ I can describe the advantages and disadvantages of wired and wireless networks.
- ✔ I can describe the advantages of security features in different types of networks.
- ✔ I can describe how echo checks are used to detect errors in transmission.
- ✔ I can explain how firewalls protect a network and why they are important.
- ✔ I can explain how antivirus and anti-spyware software provides protection to keep data secure on a network.
- ✔ I can explain the purpose of operating systems.
- ✔ I can follow a flowchart that uses conditional statements to illustrate how error checks work.

Unit 8.2 It's all in the planning: Pseudocode and algorithms

Get started!

Have you ever wondered how messages are sent safely from one place to another? Discuss with your partner:

- How are messages sent from one place to another?
- How do you stop someone else reading the message?

Sending messages has evolved over time, and keeping these messages private has changed from keeping a letter unopened to keeping an electronic message unopened.

In this unit, you will look at encryption and how it is used to secure messages sent from one micro:bit to another. You will look at how pseudocode is used as part of the planning stage for the algorithm that can be applied to sending messages from one micro:bit to another.

Learning outcomes

In this unit, you will learn to:

- identify the key characteristics of pseudocode
- follow and understand an algorithm presented as pseudocode
- follow flowcharts and pseudocode algorithms that use conditional statements
- describe linear searches and use them to find a data item
- explain and use the rules AND, OR and NOT to create logic within an algorithm
- predict the outcome of algorithms that use pseudocode
- develop a MicroPython program that uses conditional statements and Boolean operators
- identify and describe the data types in a MicroPython program
- develop a MicroPython program that uses different data types
- develop a MicroPython program that sends an image or text from one micro:bit to another
- develop a MicroPython program that uses rules involving AND, OR and NOT
- develop and apply a test plan when testing and debugging a program
- develop the test data to use when testing an algorithm
- explain why a range of test data is important when developing a test plan.

Warm up

1 In pairs, think about how one person can send a message to someone else today.
   a How do you know the message is kept private?
   b How would you feel if you thought anyone could read the message?

2 Make a list of any ways in which you send and/or receive messages with and without computing devices. Discuss how the messages are kept secure when you send them.

There are many ways of sending and receiving messages. Some of these are through technology and some are not. All methods require the message to be kept private and seen only by the sender and the receiver. Can this be guaranteed?

SCENARIO

You encounter lots of ways to send and receive messages, and technology is rapidly increasing the number of ways. Society has moved from messages being delivered by hand to pressing a button and the message being received on the other side of the world in a fraction of a second.

Each time you press a key on a keyboard to type a message, the computer registers this as a binary code. Every letter, number and symbol has a unique binary code and the computer uses a keyboard map to identify the character and find the correct code. ASCII was invented to standardise the numbers assigned to each character.

Computers are made up of millions of switches. They use binary numbers because each switch can be only ON or OFF, which can be represented by 1 and 0 in binary. All data that is sent between computing devices is sent as binary.

The micro:bit is a physical computing device and can communicate with another micro:bit. You will create a working prototype for sending and receiving encrypted messages.

You will present the algorithm for your program for both micro:bits as pseudocode.

Your program will send a message from one micro:bit to another, where each letter is represented as a binary number.

Your challenge is first to create the pseudocode for your program to send messages between two micro:bits, and then to create the program in MicroPython. You will need to test your algorithm and program with a range of possible inputs and document the outcomes.

KEYWORDS

ASCII (American Standard Code for Information Interchange): a 7-bit binary code that represents all the keys on a standard keyboard

switch: a network device that forwards data from one device to another

data: raw facts and figures

physical computing device: a device that can be programmed using block- or text-based programming languages

program: the instructions that tell a computer system how to complete a task

pseudocode: a textual representation of an algorithm

MicroPython: the programming language used on the micro:bit

Do you remember?

Before starting this unit, you should be able to:

- ✔ create a simple algorithm using flowchart symbols
- ✔ discuss why flowcharts are used to represent an algorithm
- ✔ create a program using MicroPython and the micro:bit, using the different inputs and outputs
- ✔ identify the difference between an input and an output
- ✔ use sensors on the micro:bit to determine the output of the program
- ✔ discuss how more than one input can be used on the micro:bit
- ✔ create a program using MicroPython and download the program to run on the micro:bit.

Before starting this unit, you will need to access MicroPython on a computer through online software. To access MicroPython:

1 Open your chosen web-browser software.
2 Go to **https://python.microbit.org**

You will also need the following physical computing devices:

- two micro:bits
- two USB cables
- optional battery pack for each micro:bit.

Pseudocode

Learn

An **algorithm** is a set of instructions that can be followed step by step to solve a particular problem. An algorithm can be represented in a range of ways: it can be represented visually as a **flowchart**; or it can be represented as text – this is called **pseudocode**.

As a programmer, you develop an algorithm to plan the program that you are going to create. You do this before you start to write the program code. When developing an algorithm, you can begin by writing the instructions as a list. You can then use this to create a flowchart or write the pseudocode.

Pseudocode is the link between our spoken or written word and the programming language, and there are certain rules to follow in the way it is written, which are like the rules of grammar that you follow in English.

Pseudocode must have a start and a stop to show where the program begins and ends. It uses specific keywords that you see in the programming language, such as `INPUT` to represent an input.

KEYWORDS

algorithm: step-by-step instructions to solve a particular problem

flowchart: a visual representation of an algorithm

pseudocode: a textual representation of an algorithm

Here is an example.

The left-hand side shows the pseudocode for an algorithm to take the value 6 and store it against a **variable** called 'number'. The value stored in the variable 'number' is then added to 4 and the new value of 10 is stored in the variable 'number'. Remember that a variable is a temporary storage location and the value stored can be called upon in the program as well as edited throughout the program. The new value of 10 that is stored in the variable is then output.

```
START
number = 6
number = number + 4
OUTPUT number
STOP
```

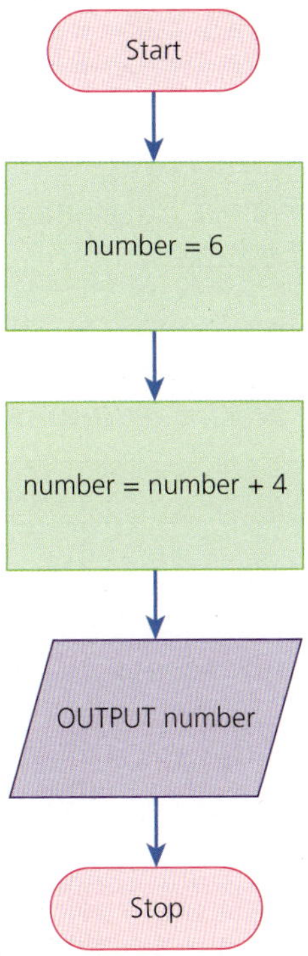

Comparing this pseudocode with the flowchart on the right, you can see that the content of the flowchart symbols is almost identical to the pseudocode.

When you create a program in a programming language, it has a specific **syntax** you must follow; this is the rules of how to write the program. Pseudocode has no fixed syntax; the way it is written is in a list of simple instructions. Each instruction has its own line and you do not need to worry about the use of brackets and colons like you would when writing the program itself.

Look at an example where you have been asked to plan a program to calculate the area of a square. You know that a square has four sides and that to calculate the area you need to know the length of one of the sides and multiply it by the same value.

KEYWORDS

variable: a named temporary storage location in a computer; it can hold one value and this can be changed at any point in a computer program

syntax: the defined rules required for a programming language

1 First, you need to consider how to obtain the length of one side of the square. One way is to get the user to input the value and then store this value in a variable.

```
length = INPUT
```

2 Second, you need to give the calculation using the variable contents, and also store the answer to the equation in a new variable.

```
area = length * length
```

Notice that the symbol to multiply is the same as you would expect to see in the programming language: *. This is used when programming to help distinguish between the letter x and the multiplication symbol.

3 Finally, you need to output the content of the variable 'area', which is the answer to the equation that involves multiplying the length of one side by the same value.

```
OUTPUT area
```

4 These steps can then be combined, using **START** and **STOP** to complete the program by defining where it begins and ends.

Square	Pseudocode	Flowchart

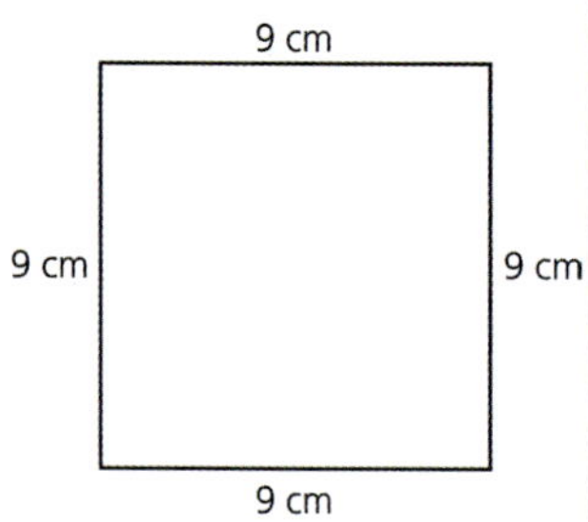	`START`
	`length = INPUT`
	`area = length * length`
	`OUTPUT area`
	`STOP`
		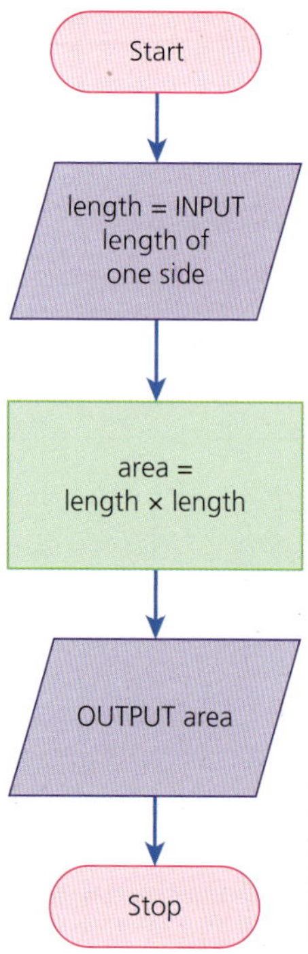

Practise

You have been asked to follow the pseudocode for this problem.

A company needs to calculate the new salary of its employees after a 10% increase. The algorithm needs to allow the user to enter a value as a whole number, multiply it by 1.10 and output the new salary including the 10% increase.

```
START
salary = INPUT "What is your current salary?"
salaryIncrease = salary * 1.10
OUTPUT salaryIncrease
STOP
```

1 **Decompose** the problem into:
   a variables you will need
   b the calculation that needs to take place
   c the individual steps of the program.
2 Create the flowchart.
3 Discuss with your partner the benefits of using pseudocode as part of planning algorithms.
4 Create the program in Python following the pseudocode and your flowchart.

KEYWORD

decompose: break down

Selection and pseudocode

Learn

In programming, the use of **selection** shows a choice that needs to be made to determine the next instruction to **execute** in the program. There is a **condition** that must be met (TRUE) to allow one instruction to run, and if the condition is not met (FALSE), then another instruction is run.

You make a choice that decides what you do next in lots of situations. For example:

- **if** it is raining, **then** take an umbrella with you; **else** leave the umbrella at home.
  The condition is **if it is raining**. If it is raining, then the condition has been met and the output is TRUE and you need to take an umbrella. If the condition is not met, FALSE, then you leave the umbrella at home.
- **if** you have eaten your vegetables, **then** you can have pudding; **else** keep eating.
  The condition is **if you have eaten your vegetables**. If you have eaten all your vegetables, then the condition has been met and the output is TRUE and you can have pudding. If the condition is not met, FALSE, then you need to keep eating.

- **if** you have collected all the coins, **then** you can go to level 2; **else** keep collecting coins. The condition is **if you have collected all the coins**. If you have collected all the coins in the game, then the condition has been met and the output is TRUE and you can move to level 2. If the condition is not met, FALSE, then you need to keep collecting coins.

The condition is the selection question that follows the use of **if**.

You have looked previously at creating flowcharts with selection and followed the flow. Now look at a flowchart for entering a password to gain entry, for example to a website.

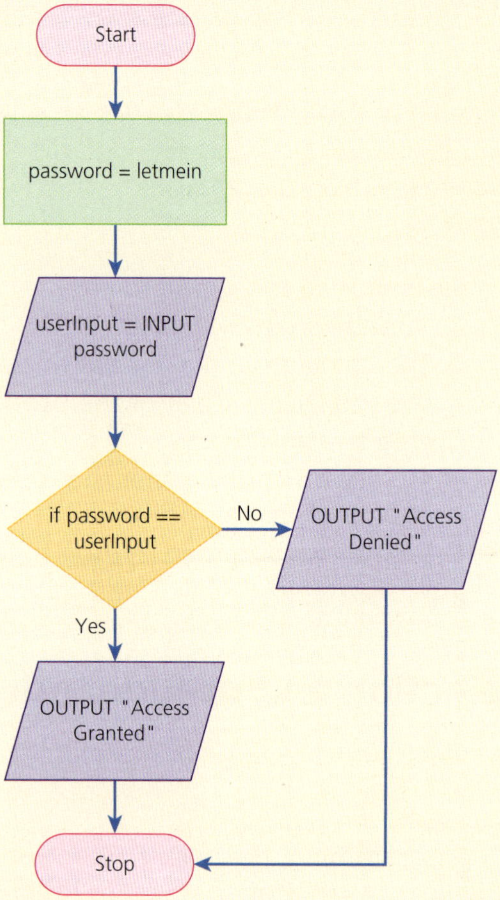

The flowchart shows that the password is set as 'letmein' and stored in a variable 'password'.

The user is asked to enter their password and this is stored in a new variable 'userInput'.

The selection question is **if** the password and userInput match, **then** output 'Access Granted'; **else** output 'Access Denied'.

Notice that in the condition, the **conditional operator** used to carry out the comparison between the two variables is a double equals (**==**). This means 'equal to'.

To create this algorithm using pseudocode, you need to break the algorithm down in the same way as has been done to create the flowchart.

1 The program start is defined.

```
START
```

2 The password is set by storing it in a variable.

```
password = "letmein"
```

3 The user is asked to enter their password and this is stored against a new variable.

```
userInput = INPUT
```

4 The values stored in the variables 'password' and 'userInput' are compared: **if** they are the same, **then** access is granted; **else** access is denied.

```
IF password == userInput THEN
  OUTPUT "Access Granted"
ELSE
  OUTPUT "Access Denied"
ENDIF
```

5 The program ends.

```
STOP
```

Combine this all together to create the final pseudocode.

```
START
password = "letmein"
userInput = INPUT
IF password == userInput THEN
  OUTPUT "Access Granted"
ELSE
  OUTPUT "Access Denied"
ENDIF
STOP
```

There are a few key characteristics that are visible.

The password 'letmein' is stored as a string and is defined with quotation marks around it.

The keywords in the selection are in uppercase – **IF**, **THEN**, **ELSE**, **ENDIF** – and this helps to make them visible.

The outcome of the condition is indented underneath to show it is the next instruction if the output is TRUE. The outcome if the answer is FALSE is indented underneath the **ELSE**.

ENDIF shows the end of the selection in the program.

By comparing the selection that is being used in both the flowchart and the pseudocode, you can see the similarities and differences.

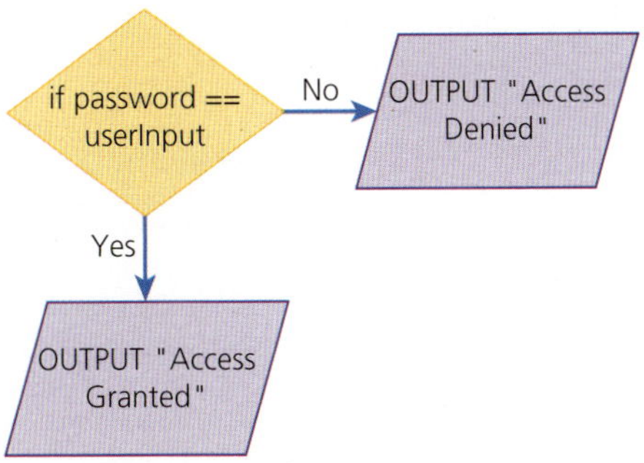


```
IF password == userInput THEN
  OUTPUT "Access Granted"
ELSE
  OUTPUT "Access Denied"
ENDIF
```

Similarities	**Differences**
• Both use `IF` • Both show the comparison as the condition in the selection: `password == userInput` • Both use `==` to show the comparison 'equal to' • Both have an output if the answer to the selection question is **yes** or **no** • Both use quotation marks to show a text output	• The use of `THEN` in the pseudocode instead of `Yes` on the flowchart • The use of `ELSE` in the pseudocode instead of `No` on the flowchart • The use of `ENDIF` in the pseudocode to show the end of the selection • The use of indentation in the pseudocode to show the output if the condition is met or not met

KEYWORDS

selection: a choice in a program that is based on a question; the answer determines the next instruction to be run

execute: to run

condition: the question that is asked to determine the next instruction in a program

conditional operator: symbol such as >, < and =; used to carry out comparisons between two values

string: a sequence of characters that can be text, numbers or symbols; quotation marks around the characters define them as a string

indented: describes a line of code that has been moved away from the left-hand margin to represent the code that will run if a condition is met

Practise

Part 1

1. Look at the flowchart and pseudocode in the file **Quiz Question.docx** provided by your teacher.
2. Decompose the sections of the flowchart to annotate the following:
   a. the variables
   b. the selection.
3. Make a list of the variables and the **data type** each one uses.
4. Compare the flowchart and the pseudocode and discuss with your partner the similarities and differences between them.

Part 2

1. Look at the file **Pseudocode Example.docx** provided by your teacher.
2. Follow the algorithm represented as pseudocode and predict with your partner what the algorithm is showing.
3. Create the flowchart to represent the pseudocode.
4. Discuss with your partner your preferred method for representing selection.

KEYWORD

data type: the set type of data that is being stored, e.g. number, string, date

Searching algorithms

Learn

Algorithms are used to plan a wide range of programs. One type of algorithm is a *searching* algorithm. Searching algorithms are used with large sets of data in order to find a particular **data item**. The **data set** does not need to be in order for a searching algorithm to be carried out.

Look at the images below. If you were asked to find the banana, you would be able to look and identify quickly that the banana is the third image in from the left. A computer cannot make that comparison; it has to be programmed to find a particular item.

One type of searching algorithm is a **linear search**. The aim of a linear search is to look at each item in turn, from left to right, to find the item being looked for.

The aim is to find the banana in the row of fruit.

1 The first step is to compare the first item with the banana.
If they match, then you have found the correct item; **else** move to the next item.

In this comparison they do not match, so the computer moves on to the second item.

2 The second step is to compare the second item with the banana.
If they match, then you have found the correct item; **else** move to the next item.

In this comparison they do not match, so the computer moves on to the third item.

3 The third step is to compare the third item with the banana.
If they match, then you have found the correct item; **else** move to the next item.

In this comparison they match, so the computer knows it has found the correct item and stops its search.

A linear search can look at a set of data of any size to find a set data item. However, this can take a long time as the data item being searched for could be the last item in the list.

Selection is used in each comparison of the searched-for item with a data item. This can be represented in both pseudocode and as a flowchart.

Pseudocode	Flowchart

`IF searched for item == data item THEN`
`  OUTPUT "Item found"`
`  STOP`
`ELSE`
`  Move to next item`
	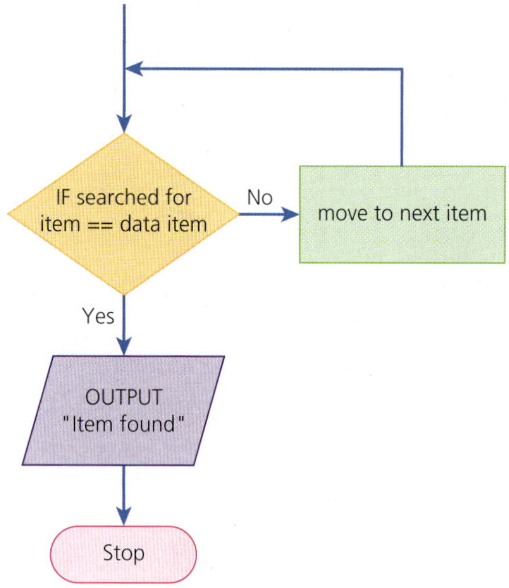

This pseudocode for selection can be applied to any instance where a linear search is being completed.

Practise

Part 1

This is a data set for different types of fruit.

apple	banana	pear	grape	melon	lemon	orange	mango	papaya	raspberry

1 Follow the pseudocode in the Learn box above to answer the following question.
What would the order of comparisons be to find the data item:
a pear b melon c papaya d orange?

2 Discuss with your partner the advantages and disadvantages of a linear search.

Part 2

1 Using the worksheet **Numbers.docx** provided by your teacher, place the numbers face down in a line in front of you.
- With your partner, take it in turns to complete the linear search while the other chooses the data item to search for.
- Act out the steps of a linear search, turning over each number in sequence to locate the data item being searched for.

2 Consider how you could use a linear search to find a hidden letter.

KEYWORDS

data set: a collection of data items that are all related

linear search: searching for an item in a list by comparing each item in turn with the searched-for item

data item: a single piece of data

Pseudocode, selection and the micro:bit

Learn

The micro:bit is a **microprocessor** that has multiple inputs, and can be used with block-based programming or **text-based programming**. You may recall using the micro:bit in previous stages and experimenting with the different inputs and outputs.

Inputs and outputs

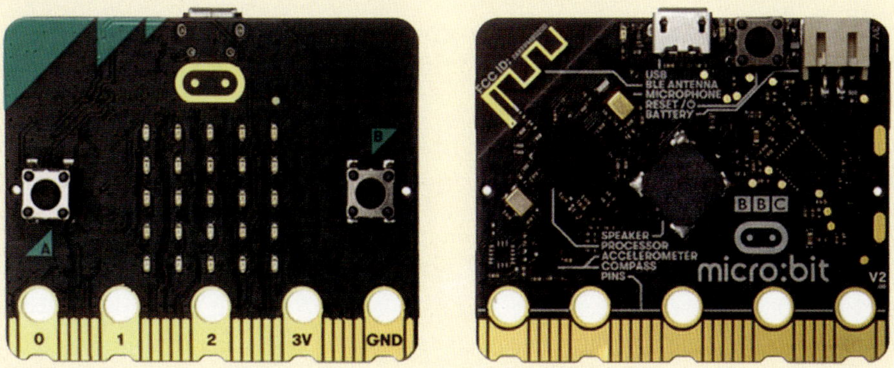

Here are the inputs and outputs on a micro:bit.

Input	Output
A button	display
B button	buzzer
light sensor	
temperature sensor	
compass	
accelerometer	
touch sensor	
microphone	

The inputs can be used as part of a condition in selection. You will now see how to plan, using pseudocode, an algorithm that uses the light sensor.

Light sensor

The aim of this algorithm is to use light level to activate the output. A value can be set as part of the condition, and for this example it will be set at 50. The condition for the selection will be: **if** the light level is greater than 50, **then** the output is activated and a heart is displayed on the micro:bit.

Using this plan, you can write the pseudocode:

```
IF light level > 50 THEN
  OUTPUT heart
ENDIF
```

The pseudocode shows the selection and the condition that has been set. The output is to run if the light level that the sensor detects is greater than 50.

You can use this pseudocode as the plan for the program you will create for the micro:bit using MicroPython.

The micro:bit uses MicroPython as the Python programming language. MicroPython is a smaller version of Python and is specific to the micro:bit. MicroPython cannot be used outside of its use with the micro:bit.

The rules of a programming language are called the syntax. Like any programming language, the syntax of MicroPython is specific. The code must be written correctly for it to run as expected.

The MicroPython code required to use the light sensor is `display.read_light_level()`.

This is the code you need to add as part of the condition to ensure that it uses the light level detected through the light sensor. The light sensor is part of the LED display of the micro:bit and can detect a range of 0 to 255. The value that the sensor detects is stored as an **integer** data type. An integer is a whole number.

To use selection in MicroPython, you need to use **if** before the condition, followed by the code to read the light level through the sensor. To use the value detected as part of the condition, you need to use a **conditional operator** followed by a pre-set value. The conditional operator can be:

- < less than
- > greater than
- == equal to
- != not equal to
- <= less than or equal to
- >= greater than or equal to.

There can be only two outcomes to a condition. The output of the condition is either TRUE or FALSE: if the condition is met (TRUE) or not met (FALSE).

You can use the pseudocode `IF light level > 50 THEN` to create the MicroPython condition by following these steps.

1 First, break down the pseudocode condition into its individual elements and match this to the MicroPython code used for each part.

Pseudocode	MicroPython
`IF`	`if`
`light level`	`display.read_light_level()`
`>`	`>`
`50`	`50`
`THEN`	`:`

You can see from the comparison above that **if** is written in lowercase in MicroPython. This is followed by the code to read the light level; the conditional operator for *greater than*; the set value of 50; and finally a colon (:) to represent the end of the condition.

The colon is an important element of the syntax as it tells the program that the condition stops here. In pseudocode, the use of **THEN** has the same meaning.

Combined together, the MicroPython for the condition is:

```
if display.read_light_level() > 50:
```

2 The next step is to add the code for the output if the condition is TRUE.

It is important to note that the indentation you used in the pseudocode is essential in the programming language. In the same way that the colon defines the end of the condition, the indentation underneath the condition defines the output if the condition is TRUE.

```
if display.read_light_level() > 50:
    display.show(Image.HEART)
```

It is important to test that any program works as expected. Using a **test plan** can help to check that the output is run at the correct time.

In this program, the condition is 'greater than 50'. Therefore, you need to check a selection of values less than 50, the value 50 itself and values greater than 50. That way, you will test that the program runs only when the value detected is greater than 50.

It is important to complete the 'Expected outcome' column before you test the program. This is what you expect to happen when you test the program. You can then test the program and see whether the outcome matches what you expected to happen.

Test number	Data entered	Expected outcome	Pass/fail
1	10	Nothing displayed	
2	49	Nothing displayed	
3	50	Nothing displayed	
4	51	Display a heart	
5	55	Display a heart	

By testing a program, you can identify any errors and fix them. This is called **debugging**.

KEYWORDS

microprocessor: a mini-computer able to execute and store one program

text-based programming: programming that requires the programmer to type text, e.g. Python

integer: a whole number

conditional operator: symbol such as >, < and =; used to carry out comparisons between two values

test plan: a document that details the tests to be carried out when a program is complete and whether or not they are successful

debugging: finding and fixing errors

Practise

Part 1

1 Open the files **MicrobitSelection.py** and **Pseudocode Challenges.docx** provided by your teacher.

Edit the MicroPython code to represent each pseudocode challenge in turn.

2 Download the MicroPython by sending the program to the micro:bit.
   - Connect the micro:bit to the online MicroPython software using the USB cable.
   - Click the 'Send to micro:bit' button and follow the steps to connect and send the program to the micro:bit.

3 After each challenge, discuss with your partner:
   - what the **conditional statement** is
   - what values would be good test values to check that the program works as expected.

Part 2

1 Open the file **MicrobitDebug.py** provided by your teacher. Look at the pseudocode below:

```
IF light level < 90 THEN
  OUTPUT sad face
ENDIF
```

Compare the pseudocode and the MicroPython to find and fix the errors in the MicroPython.

2 Download the MicroPython by sending the program to the micro:bit:
   - Connect the micro:bit to the online MicroPython software using the USB cable.
   - Click the 'Send to micro:bit' button and follow the steps to connect and send the program to the micro:bit.

3 Discuss with your partner what you should include in a checklist to identify and fix errors in MicroPython.

4 Complete the 'Expected outcome' column on the test plan below for the micro:bit.

Test number	Data entered	Expected outcome	Pass/fail
1	light level = 0		
2	light level < 90		
3	light level > 90		

5 Once you have completed what you expect to happen, test your program on the micro:bit and complete the final column.

KEYWORD

conditional statement: a statement or expression that uses conditional operators and produces results that are either TRUE or FALSE

Extending selection with the micro:bit and pseudocode

Learn

In the previous section, you looked at the use of selection and how it is laid out in both pseudocode and MicroPython. You can extend the use of one input as part of a condition to two inputs by using **Boolean operators**. A Boolean operator can be **AND**, **OR** or **NOT**. Each can change the meaning of the condition.

Look at the difference each can make to a condition.

In pseudocode, a single condition contains one input that returns a value of TRUE or FALSE and this output is used to select the next instruction to run in the program. The use of the AND and OR Boolean operators increases this to two conditions.

AND

To set a condition that uses **both** the A and B buttons being pressed on the micro:bit, you can use the **AND** Boolean operator.

Look at the example below, which is the pseudocode for using the **AND** Boolean operator in a condition with two inputs. The inputs used are the A and B buttons. By using the Boolean operator, the micro:bit will display the happy face only if the A and the B buttons are pressed together.

```
IF the A AND B buttons are pressed THEN
  OUTPUT happy face
ENDIF
```

To take this pseudocode and create the MicroPython code, you first need to know the individual code for each of the inputs.

A button	`button_a.is_pressed()`
B button	`button_b.is_pressed()`

1 To use two inputs in a condition, write the code with **AND** between each input.

```
button_a.is_pressed() and button_b.is_pressed()
```

2 You now have the condition, but need to structure it to form the selection section of the MicroPython. Start the sentence with **if** and end the sentence with a colon.

```
if button_a.is_pressed() and button_b.is_pressed():
```

3 Now define the output by indenting it underneath the condition.

```
if button_a.is_pressed() and button_b.is_pressed():
    display.show(Image.HAPPY)
```

It is important to test all programs using a test plan. For this program, the tests need to be representative of whether or not the buttons are pressed. You should consider how the test will need to be different in this case, when compared to a value being the input. You would need to test that the micro:bit displays the happy face only when both the A and B buttons are pressed.

OR

To set a condition that uses **either or both** the A and/or B buttons being pressed on the micro:bit, you can use the **OR** Boolean operator.

Look at the example below, which is the pseudocode for using the **OR** Boolean operator in a condition using the same two inputs as in the previous example. By using the **OR** Boolean operator, the micro:bit will display the happy face if either or both the A and/or B buttons are pressed.

```
IF the A OR B buttons are pressed THEN
  OUTPUT happy face
ENDIF
```

1 To take this pseudocode and create the MicroPython code, follow the same steps as before. Place the code for the two inputs together, with **OR** between them.

```
button_a.is_pressed() or button_b.is_pressed()
```

2 You now have the condition, but need to structure it to form the selection section of the MicroPython. Start the sentence with **if** and end the sentence with a colon.

```
if button_a.is_pressed() or button_b.is_pressed():
```

3 Now define the output by indenting it underneath the condition.

```
if button_a.is_pressed() or button_b.is_pressed():
    display.show(Image.HAPPY)
```

Notice that the **OR** Boolean operator allows either of the two inputs to activate the output.

When testing this program, you would need to test that the happy face is displayed when either the A or B button is pressed and when both buttons are pressed.

NOT

The **NOT** Boolean operator is different from AND and OR. The **NOT** Boolean operator uses only one input but reverses the condition that has been set. If you want an output to be activated when the A button is **not** pressed, then you can use this Boolean operator.

Look at the example below, which is the pseudocode for using the **NOT** Boolean operator to have the micro:bit display the happy face when the A button is not pressed.

```
IF the A button is NOT pressed THEN
  OUTPUT happy face
ENDIF
```

1 To use the **NOT** Boolean operator, place **not** before the input to be used in the condition.

```
not button_a.is_pressed()
```

2 You now have the condition, but need to structure this to form the selection section of the MicroPython. Start the sentence with **if** and end the sentence with a colon.

```
if not button_a.is_pressed():
```

3 Now define the output by indenting it underneath the condition.

```
if not button_a.is_pressed():
    display.show(Image.HAPPY)
```

When testing this program, you would need to test whether the happy face is displayed when the A button is not pressed.

Testing

With Boolean operators, like all other programs, it is important to test the program using a test plan. When the condition is buttons being pressed, the tests need to be representative of whether or not the buttons are pressed.

> **KEYWORD**
>
> **Boolean operator:** the three main Boolean operators are AND, OR and NOT

Practise

Look at the pseudocode below for a program using a Boolean operator.

```
IF the A OR B buttons are pressed THEN
  OUTPUT "Access Granted"
ENDIF
```

1 Predict what the conditional statement is for the program to run.
2 Discuss with your partner what you would need to change to ensure that the program output runs only when both buttons are pressed.
3 Open the file **MicrobitBooleanOperator.py** provided by your teacher.
4 Edit the program code to reflect the change in Boolean operator.
5 Discuss with your partner what the data type generated by the conditional statement would be.
6 Download the MicroPython by sending the program to the micro:bit.
   - Connect the micro:bit to the online MicroPython software using the USB cable.
   - Click the 'Send to micro:bit' button and follow the steps to connect and send the program to the micro:bit.
7 Test your program to ensure that the output runs only when both buttons are pressed.
8 Discuss with your partner whether you will need to use AND, OR or NOT in your Final project.

Using two micro:bits

Learn

The programs you have seen in this unit so far have used one micro:bit and the inputs and outputs on that micro:bit. Now think about sending an image from one micro:bit to another.

The micro:bit has the ability to communicate wirelessly with other micro:bits, creating a simple network. A **network** is a collection of computing devices that are connected to each other, either with or without cables. When two or more micro:bits are connected to each other through the use of the *radio* function, they form a network.

Look at a program for sending an image from one micro:bit to another when the A button is pressed. The network is going to contain two micro:bits. The plan for the program has two parts.

- The input is the A button.
- An image is sent.

The characteristics of the program are that an image is sent, and the A button (the input) is used to activate the program.

You can create pseudocode to represent the main program, with the A button as the input and the message being sent using the radio function. This program will give the illusion of a giraffe travelling from one micro:bit to the other.

```
START
set radio channel to 40
IF micro:bit 1 A button pressed THEN
  OUTPUT giraffe on micro:bit 2
ENDIF
IF micro:bit 2 A button pressed THEN
  OUTPUT giraffe on micro:bit 1
ENDIF
STOP
```

The radio function sends and receives messages across the network of devices.

Look at the program created in MicroPython.

```
from microbit import *
import radio
radio.config(group=40)
radio.on()
```

The radio **library** is imported at the start. The radio group is set to a value between 0 and 255. It can be any number in this range.

```
while True:
    message = radio.receive()
    if message:
        display.show(Image.GIRAFFE)

    if button_a.is_pressed():
        display.clear()
        radio.send('giraffe')
```

The variable 'message' will temporarily store the image received. If any radio message is received, the giraffe image is displayed.

If the A button is pressed, the radio message is sent and the display is cleared.

You must send the program to both micro:bits you are using. To do this, connect each micro:bit to the computer in turn using the USB cable and send the program, then connect a battery pack to each micro:bit to allow the program to run. You cannot send to both micro:bits at the same time.

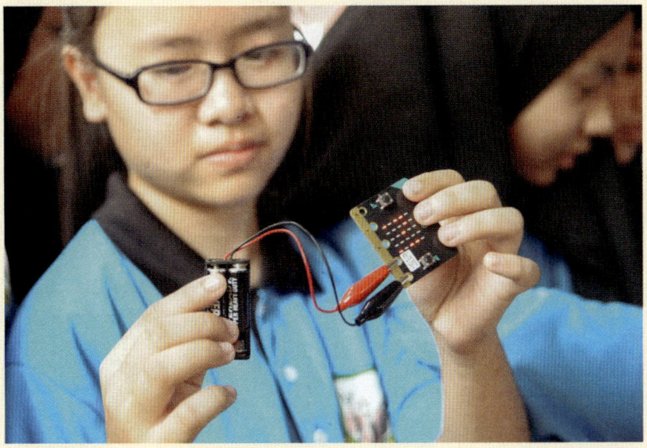

The micro:bit program is downloaded (sent) to the micro:bit. The program is stored on the micro:bit. The battery pack gives the micro:bit the power to run the program.

It is important to test the program to check that the giraffe is sent from one micro:bit to the other. A test plan can help to structure what you expect to see from a specific test, and what happens when you carry out the test.

There are only two tests required for this program: testing that the giraffe displays on micro:bit 2 when the A button on micro:bit 1 is pressed, and that the giraffe displays on micro:bit 1 when the A button on micro:bit 2 is pressed. To test this program, the micro:bits are identified as 1 and 2. This is for the purpose of the test to help identify which is being tested.

Test number	Input	Expected outcome	Pass/fail
1	A button pressed on micro:bit 1	Giraffe displayed on micro:bit 2	
2	A button pressed on micro:bit 2	Giraffe displayed on micro:bit 1	

KEYWORDS

network: a collection of computing devices connected to each other, either wired or wirelessly

library: an additional set of functions that can be imported into a Python program

Practise

As well as an image, you can also send a message from one micro:bit to another. You can do this secretly by using numbers to represent the letters of the alphabet.

A	B	C	D	E	F	G	H	I	J	K	L	M	N	O	P	Q	R	S	T	U	V	W	X	Y	Z
1	2	3	4	5	6	7	8	9	10	11	12	13	14	15	16	17	18	19	20	21	22	23	24	25	26

You have been given the following program to allow a series of numbers to be sent from one micro:bit to another.

```
from microbit import *
import radio
radio.config(group=42)
radio.on()

while True:
    message = radio.receive()
    if message:
        display.scroll("8, 5, 12, 12, 15")
    if button_a.is_pressed():
        display.clear()
        radio.send('message')
```

The micro:bit will display the numbers '8, 5, 12, 12, 15' and this represents the letters 'HELLO'.

1 Predict what this program will do.
2 Open the file **RadioActivity.py** provided by your teacher.
3 Run the program using two micro:bits and test your prediction.
4 Test that your program outputs the correct number to represent the alphabet position.

Test number	Input	Expected outcome	Pass/fail
1	A button pressed	micro:bit screen cleared and message sent to other micro:bit	
2	Message received on second micro:bit	8, 5, 12, 12, 15 displayed on the micro:bit in turn	

5 What is the number assigned to this network of micro:bits?
6 Change the numbers sent, to change the message sent. Send the program to both micro:bits to test.
7 Discuss with your partner how you would edit the test plan to test a range of data.
8 Discuss with your partner how you might use two micro:bits to send and receive a message in your Final project.

Sending a string between micro:bits

Learn

In the previous section, you looked at how to send an image of a giraffe from one micro:bit to another. You then looked at sending numbers representing the positions of specific letters in the alphabet to the other micro:bit. The micro:bit can also send a string.

Computers use their own language: machine code. The computer translates into machine code everything a user does and everything programmed on the computer. Machine code is **binary**: a series of 0s and 1s. All computers are made up of millions of switches. A switch can only be ON or OFF. ON is represented as a 1 and OFF is represented as a 0. A switch controls the flow of electricity around the computer.

A binary number can be used to represent a letter in the alphabet. An ASCII (American Standard Code for Information Interchange) table can help to identify the letter that the binary number represents. An ASCII table contains numbers, symbols and upper and lowercase letters. The example below shows just the lowercase letters and the binary code used to represent each one.

a	01100001	n	01101110
b	01100010	o	01101111
c	01100011	p	01110000
d	01100100	q	01110001
e	01100101	r	01110010
f	01100110	s	01110011
g	01100111	t	01110100
h	01101000	u	01110101
i	01101001	v	01110110
j	01101010	w	01110111
k	01101011	x	01111000
l	01101100	y	01111001
m	01101101	z	01111010

A computer has received the following two binary numbers: 01101000 and 01101001. Looking for these in the ASCII table, you can see that 01101000 = h and 01101001 = i.

You can send a binary number from one micro:bit to another by putting quotation marks around the number and sending it as a string, so that it will appear on the screen as a series of 1s and 0s. You can use this method to transmit a word or message from one micro:bit to another as a series of binary codes rather than as letters.

KEYWORD

binary: the number system that uses just two digits: 0 and 1; also known as 'base 2'

1 Import the radio function and set the channel to be used by both micro:bits.

```
from microbit import *
import radio
import music

radio.on()
radio.config(group=40)
```

2 Set the message variable to receive the radio message.

```
from microbit import *
import radio
import music

radio.on()
radio.config(group=40)

while True:
    message = radio.receive()
```

3 Set the message to be transmitted when the A button is pressed.

```
from microbit import *
import radio
import music

radio.on()
radio.config(group=40)

while True:
    message = radio.receive()
    if button_a.was_pressed():
        radio.send('message')
```

4 Set the message to be transmitted, including a short delay after each string. The example below shows the binary codes for 'h' and then 'i' being sent, with a 1-second delay after the code for each letter.

```
from microbit import *
import radio
import music

radio.on()
radio.config(group=40)

while True:
    message = radio.receive()
    if button_a.is_pressed():
        radio.send('message')
    if message:
        display.scroll('01101000')
        sleep(1000)
        display.scroll('01101001')
        sleep(1000)
```

5 The person receiving the message needs to know when they have received one binary number and a new one is starting. You can add a sound to the sequence: 'c' represents the musical note 'C'.

```
from microbit import *
import radio
import music

radio.on()
radio.config(group=40)

while True:
    message = radio.receive()
    if button_a.is_pressed():
        radio.send('message')
    if message:
        display.scroll('01101000')
        sleep(1000)
        music.play('c')
        display.scroll('01101001')
        sleep(1000)
```

6 You can also send a sound to represent the end of the sequence you are sending.

```
from microbit import *
import radio
import music

radio.on()
radio.config(group=40)

while True:
    message = radio.receive()
    if button_a.is_pressed():
        radio.send('message')
    if message:
        display.scroll('01101000')
        sleep(1000)
        music.play('c')
        display.scroll('01101001')
        sleep(1000)
        music.play(music.POWER_DOWN)
```

You can now send a message hidden as a sequence of binary numbers for each letter, from one micro:bit to another.

Practise

Part 1

1 Open the file **HiddenWord.py** provided by your teacher.
2 Connect and send the program to micro:bit 1 and then connect the battery pack.
3 Connect and send the program to micro:bit 2.
4 Send the hidden message and decipher the hidden word.

Part 2

1 Use the ASCII table in the Learn box above to write out the binary numbers to represent your name.
2 Use the program from Part 1 to edit and extend the program to send your name in binary from one micro:bit to the other.
3 Add an image of a tick for 1 second on the micro:bit that is sending the message, to represent that the image has been sent.

Go further

An iterative process

Creating a program is a process that starts with planning, by creating an algorithm. The algorithm is presented as either a flowchart or as pseudocode.

Once the algorithm has been created, the process of testing and improving starts. A test may show an error or an area for improvement that the programmer could work on. By means of a basic process of plan - design - develop - test - review/evaluate, you can follow a continuous cycle.

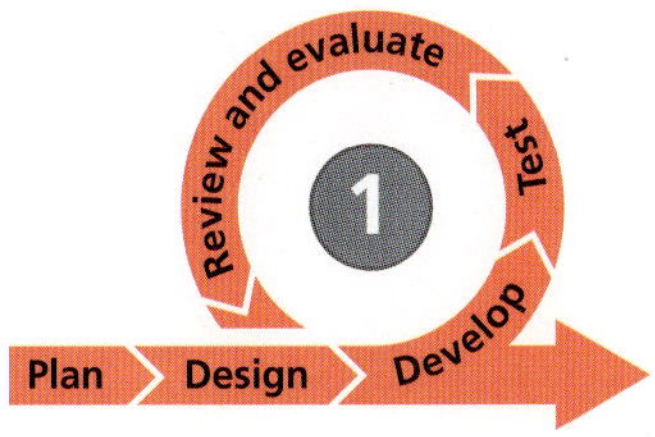

A cycle like this is repeating the steps continuously to improve the program. This is called an **iterative process**. **Iteration** means 'repetition'.

As part of this process, debugging is critical as you test, evaluate and improve.

Errors made in the programming code are the same as making spelling and grammatical errors when writing. This can include spelling words incorrectly and missing punctuation such as brackets, quotation marks or commas.

A program with an error may not run. If you sent the program to the micro:bit, you would get a sad face and the micro:bit would display the line that contains the error. In the software, an error is highlighted with a red line underlining the code and a red circle at the start of the line that contains the error.

You can then use this information to read through your code and find and fix the error.

```
dislay_scroll(hi)
```

There are four errors in this line of code:

- 'Display' is spelled incorrectly.
- An underscore (_) is used instead of a full stop (.).
- The word 'hi' should have quotation marks around it to define it as a string.
- There is a missing bracket at the end of the line.

The correct line of code should be:

```
display.scroll("hi")
```

Having a checklist like this can help you to find errors.

- Spelling is correct.
- Brackets appear in the correct places.

- Brackets are opened and closed.
- A colon is placed at the end of a conditional statement.
- **If** appears at the start of a conditional statement.
- Quotation marks are placed around any strings.

It is important to test, evaluate and debug at different stages of a program's development. It is better to write a small amount of code and to test, evaluate and debug it, before completing the whole program. Finding and correcting an error in a small amount of code is easier than in a large program.

Debugging, testing and evaluating are essential parts of creating a program. They all work together and are linked throughout any project development.

1 Open the file **GoFurtherDebug.py** provided by your teacher.
2 The program should do the following:
   - If the A button is pressed, then display the text 'Hello, World'.
   - If the B button is pressed, then display a happy face.
   - If the A and B buttons are pressed, then play the music 'Power up'.
3 Discuss with your partner the checks you could use to look for errors.
4 Create a test plan to use when checking your program.
5 Through testing, locate and fix the errors to create a working program.

Test number	Input	Expected outcome	Pass/fail
1			
2			
3			

Challenge yourself

You have looked at how to use the *radio* function on the micro:bit to send an image or text from one micro:bit to another.

You used the button on the micro:bit as the input. There are a range of inputs that you could use on the micro:bit.

You could develop the program to use the movement of the micro:bit as the condition to send the message from one micro:bit to another.

You could use:

- face up
- face down
- left
- right
- up
- down
- freefall
- shake.

The MicroPython for using the movement of the micro:bit is

```
if accelerometer.was_gesture('shake'):
```

You would replace 'shake' with the new movement.

1 Open the file **ChallengeYourself.py** provided by your teacher.

KEYWORDS

iterative process: how a project develops throughout stages

iteration/iterate: repetition/to repeat

2 Create the program to use the new input as part of the conditional statement.
3 Discuss with your partner how you can test whether the program works as expected.
4 Discuss with your partner how you are using the **Boolean** output from the conditional statement.
5 Consider the possible errors that could occur and create your own checklist to use when creating a program.
6 Discuss with your partner how testing is important throughout the process, from an algorithm through to the program code.

KEYWORD

Boolean: can store only one of two values: TRUE or FALSE

Final project

The skills you have learned in this unit are all about following algorithms that are written as pseudocode. You have learned about the use of the Boolean operators AND, OR and NOT to help control the inputs into a program. You have explored how to use the *radio* function on the micro:bit to send messages displayed as an image, integer or string from one micro:bit to another.

You are now going to create your own program for sending a message from one micro:bit to another. You will need to use two micro:bits and create a program that sends your message to the other micro:bit.

Before you start writing the code:

1 Plan the program algorithm and consider the inputs that you will use as part of the conditions set in the program.
2 Explain how your solution will incorporate one of the Boolean operators and what the possible outputs will be.
3 Create the flowchart to represent your algorithm.
4 Using ASCII, plan the word you are going to send.
5 Test, evaluate and improve your algorithm before moving to programming.

When you are sure that your plan fully covers the requirements of your program, write the program in MicroPython.

Once you have written your program, you need to test it.

6 Consider how you can test the program and at what stages.
7 Create a test plan to use. Write down what you expect to happen before you test the program and document the actual outcome.
8 Discuss how you will continuously test and improve your program.
9 Highlight how you checked for errors throughout the program development.
10 Explain how a linear search works. Consider how a computer would locate the letter that the binary number represents when these are written in a list.

Evaluation

1 Swap programs with your partner and test their micro:bit program. Comment on the following:
   a Does it cover all the requirements?
   b Is the solution easy to use?
   c Did the inputs work as expected?
   d Did the program work correctly, sending the ASCII for the letters?
2 Now open your own program and look at the code. Reflect on what you could improve in your program.
3 Based on the evaluations, make a list of recommendations to improve your final program.

What can you do?

Read and review what you can do.

- ✔ I can identify the key characteristics of pseudocode.
- ✔ I can follow and understand an algorithm presented as pseudocode.
- ✔ I can follow flowcharts and pseudocode algorithms that use conditional statements.
- ✔ I can describe linear searches and use them to find a data item.
- ✔ I can explain and use the rules AND, OR and NOT to create logic within an algorithm.
- ✔ I can predict the outcome of algorithms that use pseudocode.
- ✔ I can develop a MicroPython program that uses conditional statements and Boolean operators.
- ✔ I can identify and describe the data types in a MicroPython program.
- ✔ I can develop a MicroPython program that uses different data types.
- ✔ I can develop a MicroPython program that sends an image or text from one micro:bit to another.
- ✔ I can develop a MicroPython program that uses rules involving AND, OR and NOT.
- ✔ I can develop and apply a test plan when testing and debugging a program.
- ✔ I can develop the test data to use when testing an algorithm.
- ✔ I can explain why a range of test data is important when developing a test plan.

Unit 8.3 Let's talk technology: What's going on inside

Get started!

Throughout this unit, you will learn all about the different types of software that allow users to interact with digital devices. You will learn how digital devices represent and store text, images, sound and numbers and how they carry out basic calculations. You will also investigate how to reduce the size of image files to support their transfer across the internet. In studying how a digital device stores numerical data, you will learn how to convert numbers from denary to binary format, and gain an understanding of how digital data can be generated to support digital applications in the areas of robotics, **artificial intelligence (AI)** and **augmented reality (AR)**.

Discuss the following questions with your partner.

- Do you have a digital device in your home that uses AI?
- Can you name an AR application you have used?

KEYWORDS

artificial intelligence (AI): the study of machines and algorithms designed to carry out tasks in a way that is similar to humans

augmented reality (AR): a simulation that superimposes digital images on the user's real-world environment and allows the user to interact with those images

Learning outcomes

In this unit, you will learn to:

- explain the purpose of operating systems and describe some of the main tasks that an operating system carries out
- describe the purpose of utility programs and give examples of some utility programs and the tasks they complete
- explain how characters entered into a computer system are stored in ASCII format
- explain the term compression and describe why compression techniques are used to support the reduction of file sizes
- explain what denary means and know how to convert binary to denary and denary to binary
- create truth tables for AND, OR and NOT gates
- describe how primary memory such as RAM and ROM is used in a digital device
- explain the term machine learning
- identify and describe how augmented reality is used in education, gaming and robotics
- describe how autonomous programming and artificial intelligence is used to support robotics in some industry areas.

Warm up

Complete this activity in pairs. Think of a simple task you would like your partner to complete (for example, pushing their chair underneath their desk; packing a book away at the end of a lesson; switching on the lights in the classroom; or opening a textbook at a particular page, such as page 24). Provide instructions telling them what to do to complete your task (but you cannot tell them what the task is meant to be so, for example, if you wanted your partner to open a textbook at page 24, you might issue instructions such as: open your school bag, search for your mathematics textbook, place the textbook on your desk, open the front cover, turn each page, read the page numbers, keep turning the pages until the page number reads 24).

Write your instructions in a step-by-step format for your partner to use to complete the task you have created for them.

Read out your instructions one a time and get your partner to follow them.

> Think carefully:
> How much detail do you need to give your partner to help them to understand how to open their school bag? If they were being programmed to complete this task, would they know what 'open your school bag' means?

1 How difficult was it to help your partner to complete the task successfully?
2 How difficult would it be to provide these instructions if you were communicating in another language and had to translate them line by line?

Computers operate like this all the time. Computer programs provide instructions. Programmers write the programs in one language but computers understand a completely different language.

3 Now tell your partner what the simple task was and let them work out for themselves how to complete it.
4 Was it easier for your partner to complete the task using your step-by-step instructions or was it easier for them to complete the task when you told them what you wanted them to do and then they worked out the instructions for themselves? Why do you think that was?
5 What programming languages can you name that programmers use to give instructions to computers?
6 What is the name of the language computers understand?

Computer programs are saved in different types of computer memory depending on whether the program is being run at that moment or whether it is being saved to be run at another time. The paper you used to record your instructions is like long-term computer memory and your instructions are like a computer program.

Think how easy it was when you told your partner what the task was; they could think for themselves and work out how to do the task. In this unit, you will explore some computer systems that can operate in this way. However, before you do that you need to look at how digital devices save instructions and how they process some data.

SCENARIO

A local telecommunication company is asking for input from young people to help it to design a futuristic method of communicating online. The company owners want you to help them to develop a communication system that uses augmented-reality glasses or a similar technology to beam your friends from your computer screen into your living room so that you can chat to them as though they are there with you. Before you get started on your project with the telecommunication company, you need to brush up on your knowledge of AI, AR and the underlying computing concepts. Get moving though, before another company develops the technology first!

KEYWORD

telecommunication: the transfer of information in the form of video and/or sound using cables, radio or satellite

augmented-reality (AR) glasses: glasses or goggles that add information, normally in the form of 3D images or videos, to the user's real-world environment by placing a computer-generated image over the user's real-world image viewed through the glasses

DID YOU KNOW?

AR devices are no longer limited to displays using specialised goggles or glasses. For example, AR apps that allow you to test paint colours or furniture items in a room are now available on some mobile phones.

Do you remember?

Before starting this unit, you should be able to:

- ✔ explain the difference between computer hardware and software and be able to name a range of software applications that people commonly use on a daily basis
- ✔ explain the role of systems software and understand that an operating system is part of systems software
- ✔ explain how to convert data, for example sound and text, into binary format before a digital computer can store or process it
- ✔ explain how AND, OR and NOT logic gates operate
- ✔ explain how some digital applications work without human intervention and that some devices can also learn from experience
- ✔ identify a range of applications that use complex image processing or transmit complex images during their operation (for example, video conferencing/online gaming)
- ✔ explain the role of artificial intelligence in some applications
- ✔ explain the term *automation* and describe how digital devices can complete some tasks without human intervention.

Before starting this unit, you will need to make sure that you can access Microsoft Excel (or a similar spreadsheet software application) on your own personal device.

All about software

Learn

Systems software refers to computer **programs** that are designed to manage or control the computer's **hardware** while the user completes tasks using other programs known as **applications software**. There are two main categories of systems software:

- **operating systems**
- **utility programs**.

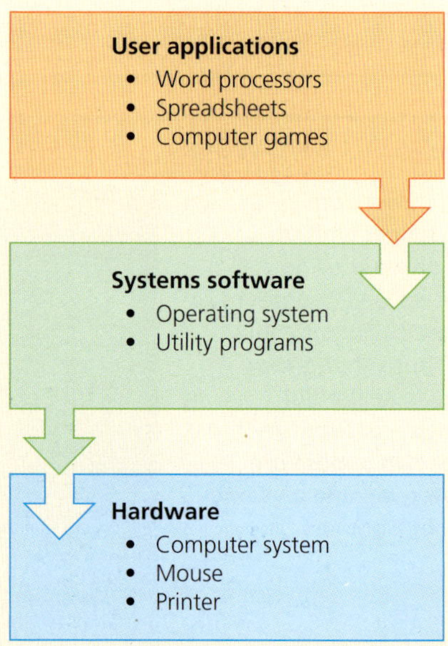

If you think of a computer as being put together in layers, it is easy to see where these two types of systems software are used.

Systems software provides an important layer between the user and the digital device. It acts as an **interface** between the hardware and the user applications. When using digital devices such as computers, mobile phones, tablets and gaming consoles, it is the operating system part of the systems software that users mainly interact with. However, they can also use an additional group of systems software programs called *utility programs* to help to ensure that digital devices function smoothly.

Even though the operating system and utility programs are both part of systems software, they have very different roles to play in the operation of a digital device.

The key roles of the operating system are shown below.

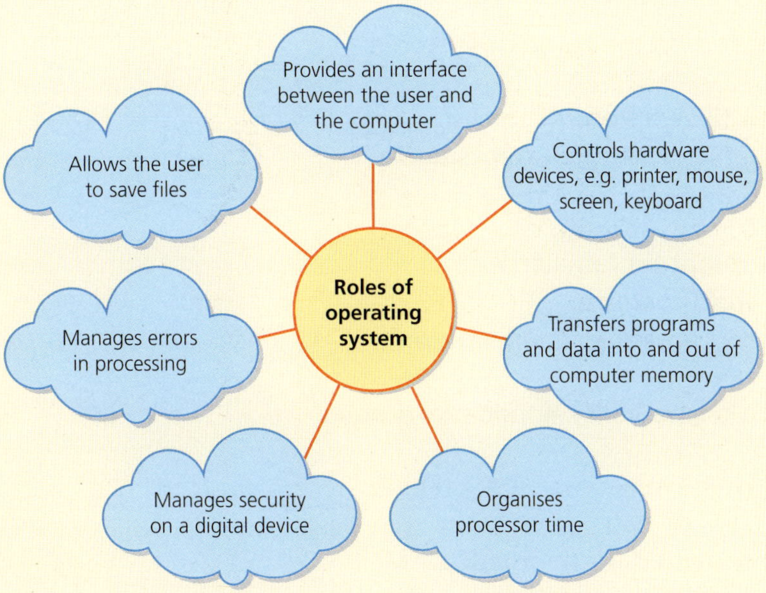

Most of the work the operating system carries out is in the background, and often the user is not even aware of these tasks. Utility programs, however, are programs that the user must select if they want to complete a specific task. Some examples of utility programs are shown on the right.

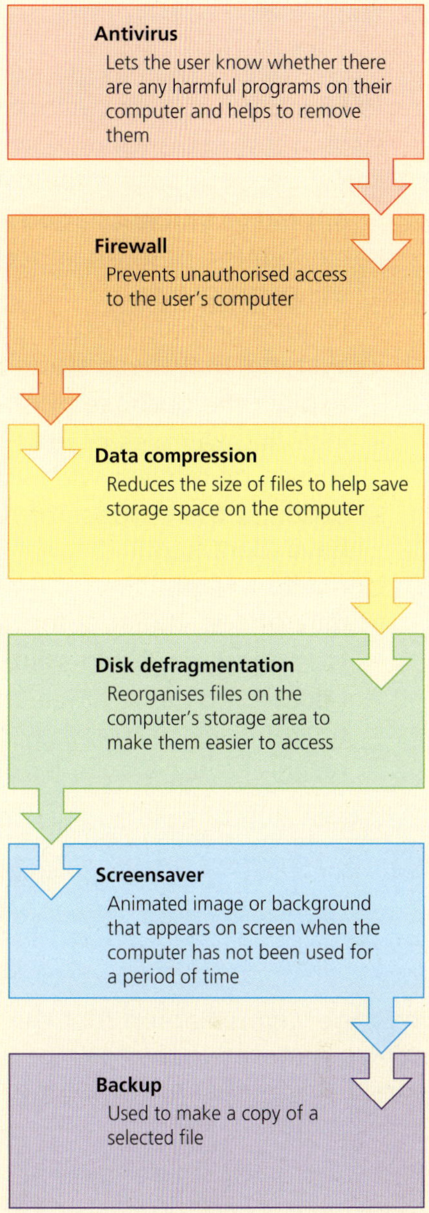

KEYWORDS

systems software: the software that helps a user run the computer

program: the instructions that tell a computer system how to complete a task

hardware: the physical parts of a computer that you can touch and see, e.g. the processor, storage devices, input devices, output devices

applications software: the software that users access to carry out tasks

operating system: the systems software that manages hardware and software, giving the user an interface to operate the computer

utility program: a program used to help maintain a digital device

interface: how a user interacts with a product

Practise

You have been asked to create an information page for a new child-friendly **online** encyclopaedia.

1 Design a student-friendly info page on the topic of systems software. Your page should:
   - appeal to students aged 11 to 12 years old
   - explain the difference between operating systems and utility programs
   - include graphic illustrations to show examples of operating systems that these students might be familiar with
   - explain the purpose of operating systems
   - include examples of utility programs that these students should be familiar with
   - describe the purpose of each of the utility applications you have identified.

2 Consider a digital device that you have access to, such as a mobile phone, tablet computer, PC or gaming console.
   a Name the operating system provided on the device.
   b Locate and name at least two utility applications available on your device. You may need to do some additional research online to help you to locate the utility applications.

KEYWORD

online: connected to the internet

Using binary to store text

Learn

In Stage 7, you learned that the text a user enters into a digital device is stored in the form of 1s and 0s, and you practised converting some messages into 1s and 0s in the way that a digital device does.

Each digital device generates a special combination of 1s and 0s to represent each character available to the user on the device. When you enter text into a digital device, you often want to share this text with another person. Imagine that you want to send a text message to your friend but they use a different mobile-phone device from you, or that you want to submit work to your teacher and have completed that work on a PC but they want to view it on a digital tablet.

Because users share **data** in the form of text using so many different **platforms**, it is important to have a standard set of 1s and 0s to show which character they have typed on the keyboard, otherwise a message or a piece of homework will not make sense when the other person receives it!

KEYWORDS

data: raw facts and figures

platform: the combination of hardware and software used to complete a digital task

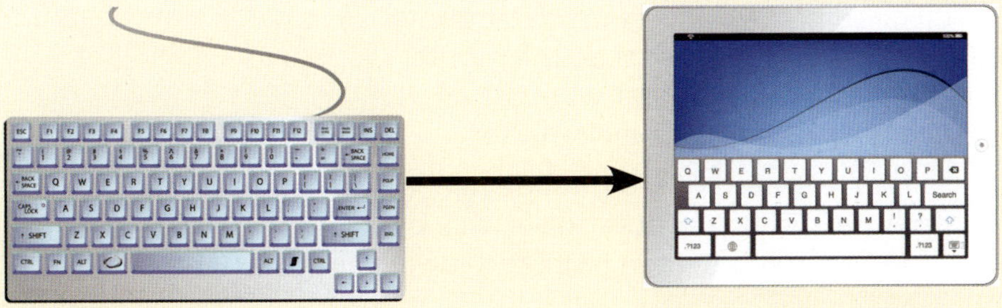

Homework completed on a PC

Teacher would like to view homework on a digital tablet

The characters available on a digital device are referred to as the *set of characters* that can be represented on that device, or the device's **character set**. The character set is made up of all the letters, numbers, punctuation symbols and special characters represented on a device. Each character is represented by a distinct set of 1s and 0s.

Most devices use a common code so that a user can easily transfer the characters they type from one computer to another. One of the most commonly used codes is called the American Standard Code for Information Interchange or **ASCII** (pronounced as-kee).

ASCII is a 7-bit code that represents all the keys on a standard keyboard. Each byte contains a unique combination of 0s and 1s to represent a character. Part of the ASCII character set is shown here.

ASCII Code - Character to Binary

Char	Binary	Char	Binary	Char	Binary	Char	Binary
0	0011 0000	I	0100 1001	b	0110 0010	v	0111 0110
1	0011 0001	J	0100 1010	c	0110 0011	w	0111 0111
2	0011 0010	K	0100 1011	d	0110 0100	x	0111 1000
3	0011 0011	L	0100 1100	e	0110 0101	y	0111 1001
4	0011 0100	M	0100 1101	f	0110 0110	z	0111 1010
5	0011 0101	N	0100 1110	g	0110 0111		
6	0011 0110	O	0100 1111	h	0110 1000	:	0011 1010
7	0011 0110	P	0101 0000	i	0110 1001	;	0011 1011
8	0011 1000	Q	0101 0001	j	0110 1010	?	0011 1111
9	0011 1001	R	0101 0010	k	0110 1011	.	0010 1110
		S	0101 0011	l	0110 1100	'	0010 1111
		T	0101 0100	m	0110 1101	!	0010 0001
A	0100 0001	U	0101 0101	n	0110 1110	,	0010 1100
B	0100 0010	V	0101 0110	o	0110 1111	"	0010 0010
C	0100 0011	W	0101 0111	p	0111 0000	(	0010 1000
D	0100 0100	X	0101 1000	q	0111 0001	)	0010 1001
E	0100 0101	Y	0101 1001	r	0111 0010	space	0010 0000
F	0100 0110	Z	0101 1010	s	0111 0011		
G	0100 0111			t	0111 0100		
H	0100 1000	a	0110 0001	u	0111 0101		

KEYWORDS

character set: all the letters, numbers, punctuation symbols and special symbols that can be represented on a device

ASCII (American Standard Code for Information Interchange): a 7-bit binary code that represents all the keys on a standard keyboard

binary: the number system that uses just two digits: 0 and 1; also known as 'base 2'

DID YOU KNOW?

The way in which a computer represents a numerical value using ASCII is different from the way that the number is represented if the device needs to use it to carry out a calculation. Look carefully at the ASCII code for the keyboard character 0 (zero); it is 00110000. This will become important later in this unit.

You will notice that each ASCII code in the conversion chart above uses 8 bits, while ASCII is a 7-bit code. This is because the eighth bit was originally used to help the computer detect whether an error had occurred when it received the code for a character.

When a user presses a key on the keyboard of a digital device, a group of 8 **binary** digits is generated. The computer does this by varying the electrical pulses it generates between high and low, to represent 1s and 0s.

For example 'H' = 01001000 and 'i' = 01101001, so 'Hi' is represented as the following pattern of 1s and 0s: 01001000 01101001.

Practise

1 Use the ASCII conversion chart in the Learn box to show how the following words are represented in binary:
   a school
   b computer.

2 Convert your name to binary using the ASCII conversion chart.

Computational thinking – pattern recognition

The combinations of binary values listed below all represent phrases.

1 Use the ASCII conversion chart from the Learn box to translate the binary values into English.
   a 01001000 01100101 01101100 01101100 01101111 00100000 01100110 01110010 01101001 01100101 01101110 01100100
   b 01001101 01111001 00100000 01100001 01100111 01100101 00100000 01101001 01110011 00100000 00110001 00110011

Remember: ASCII codes are 8 bits long (with the special error-checking bit included).

2 Write a short message to your partner in binary using the ASCII conversion chart.

3 a Ask your partner to work out what your message says.
   b With your partner, discuss the ASCII codes you have used in this exercise. What patterns do you notice? Think about:
   - how the codes for lowercase and uppercase letters are represented
   - how the codes change from one alphabet character to the next
   - how the codes for lower and uppercase letters differ from codes for special characters such as '?' or '('
   - the codes used to represent the numerical digits 0–9.

Using binary to store numbers

Learn

Representing binary numbers

You have already seen that the binary code generated when you press the key for the number '0' on a computer keyboard is 00110000.

When a user enters numbers into a digital device, they may sometimes want to perform calculations using those values, for example using a **spreadsheet** application to add two numbers together.

When numerical values are to be used in calculations, computers do not use the ASCII code to carry out these calculations. Instead, they store the value in a **binary number format**. The binary number system got its name because it uses two symbols: 1 and 0.

Before you think further about how binary numbers are represented, revise the **denary** number system. Every number in the denary number system is made up from these digits: 0, 1, 2, 3, 4, 5, 6, 7, 8, 9.

When you were younger, you used ones, tens, hundreds and thousands to help you to understand the value of numbers greater than 9. For example, the number 7623 is shown in this place-value table.

Work out each column heading by multiplying the previous heading by 10. The next heading in this table would be Ten thousands (1000 × 10).

Thousands	Hundreds	Tens	Ones
1000	**100**	**10**	**1**
7	6	2	3
= 7 × 1000	= 6 × 100	= 2 × 10	= 3 × 1
7000	600	20	3

Each column can contain only one of the digits 0–9. Depending on which column a digit is placed in, a 3 could represent 3 or 30 or 300 or 3000. The column and heading used to work out the value of each digit in your number is known as a **place value**.

So the number 7623 is actually calculated as 7000 + 600 + 20 + 3.

DID YOU KNOW?

The prefix *bi* means 'two'; just as a bicycle is called a *bicycle* because it has two wheels.

Denary is also known as **base 10** due to it containing 10 digits and all the numbers being based on powers of 10.

Since binary has only two digits, 0 and 1, the place-value headings in binary must increase in multiples of 2 and each column can contain only a 0 or 1.

For example, look at this binary number: 10010110_2.

The subscript $_2$ indicates that the number is a binary number. Here is what this actually means.

When working with more than one number system, remember to use a subscript to distinguish one from the other. For example, if this number were written with a subscript $_{10}$ (10010110_{10}) the number would be ten million, ten thousand, one hundred and ten.

Each column heading value is worked out by multiplying the previous heading by 2.

64 × 2 | 32 × 2 | 16 × 2 | 8 × 2 | 4 × 2 | 2 × 2 | 1 × 2

128	64	32	16	8	4	2	1
1	0	0	1	0	1	1	0
= 128 × 1	= 64 × 0	= 32 × 0	= 16 × 1	= 8 × 0	= 4 × 1	= 2 × 1	= 1 × 0
128	0	0	16	0	4	2	0

The digit or bit to the left-hand side of the number is known as the **most significant bit (MSB)** as it has the largest place value.

The digit or bit to the right-hand side of the number is known as the **least significant bit (LSB)** as it has the smallest place value.

So the number 10010110_2 actually represents 128 + 0 + 0 + 16 + 0 + 4 + 2 + 0, which is 150_{10}.

Use a subscript $_{10}$ to indicate that this is a denary value.

Now that you understand how the place values work, you can easily convert any binary number into denary. Binary is often referred to as *base 2* (think about denary as *base 10* to help you to understand why).

You still use 1 byte (8 bits) to represent binary numbers even when the number can easily be written using a smaller number of bits.

For example, here is how to convert 00001111_2 into denary.

128	64	32	16	8	4	2	1
0	0	0	0	1	1	1	1
= 128 × 0	= 64 × 0	= 32 × 0	= 16 × 0	= 8 × 1	= 4 × 1	= 2 × 1	= 1 × 1
0	0	0	0	8	4	2	1

So, $00001111_2 = 8 + 4 + 2 + 1 = 15_{10}$

Computers normally store data in groups of 8 bits. So, even though only 4 bits are needed to store the number 15_{10}, all the 8 bits are used to represent the number.

KEYWORDS

spreadsheet: an application that uses rows and columns to organise data and carry out calculations using that data

binary number format: using 1s and 0s to represent numbers

denary format: a number system that uses the digits 0, 1, 2, 3, 4, 5, 6, 7, 8, 9 to represent every numerical value

place value: the numerical value a digit has as a result of its position in a number, e.g. the number 24_{10} represents (2 × 10) + (4 × 1)

base 10: another term for the 'denary number system' as it is based on 10 digits

most significant bit (MSB): the digit at the left-hand side of the number; the bit with the largest place value

least significant bit (LSB): the digit at the right-hand side of a number; the bit with the smallest place value

Practise

Place values

1 Copy and complete the following place-value headings for the denary number system.

		Thousands 1000	Hundreds 100	Tens 10	Units 1

2 Using the denary number place-value system explained in the Learn box, show how the following numbers are represented and calculated in the denary number system:

a seventy-nine

b one hundred and forty-six

c one thousand two hundred and twenty-four

d one hundred thousand and thirty-seven.

3 Show what each of the numbers below represents in the denary number system.

- For example, 10000000_2
  This example has a $_2$ subscript so the number is in binary format. You need to convert this number into denary format, so the answer for this example is 128.
- For example, 00000001_{10}
  This example has a $_{10}$ subscript, which shows that this number is already in denary format so no conversion is needed. The answer for this example is 1 (as the denary number system doesn't show leading 0s).

a 01011110_2

b 00111111_2

c 00001011_{10}

d 00001101_2

e 10000011_2

f 00000111_{10}

Pay close attention to the number base as you complete the tasks in this Practise panel.

Converting denary into binary

Learn

In the previous Learn box, you looked at how to calculate the denary equivalent of an 8-bit binary number. You also need to know how to convert denary numbers into binary format. There are two approaches to this task. Explore both methods by converting the number 176_{10} into binary format.

Method 1: Divide by 2

176 / 2	=	88	Remainder	0	Divide the original denary number by 2 and write down the remainder (the remainder is always either 0 or 1).
88 / 2	=	44	Remainder	0	Divide the result by 2 and record the remainder.
44 / 2	=	22	Remainder	0	Repeat the previous step until the result of the division by 2 is 0.
22 / 2	=	11	Remainder	0	Write out the binary result from left to right, starting with the last remainder produced.
11 / 2	=	5	Remainder	1	
5 / 2	=	2	Remainder	1	
2 / 2	=	1	Remainder	0	
1 / 2	=	0	Remainder	1	

176 in binary = 10110000_2

Method 2: Use place values to create a binary pattern

- First, write down the place values for a binary number.
- Examine the highest place value and check to see whether you can subtract this value from the original denary number, without creating a negative number.
- If you can, place a 1 underneath the place value and keep a note of the result left from your calculation.
- If you cannot, place a 0 underneath the place value.
- Go to the next place holder, and repeat the process to see whether you can subtract that value from the result, without creating a negative number in the answer.
- If you can, place a 1 underneath the place value and keep a note of the result left from your calculation.
- If you cannot, place a 0 underneath the place value.
- Repeat this process until you have examined all the place holders.

128	64	32	16	8	4	2	1
Can 128 be subtracted from 176? Yes, result = 48	Can 64 be subtracted from 48? No	Can 32 be subtracted from 48? Yes, result = 16	Can 16 be subtracted from 16? Yes, result = 0	Can 8 be subtracted from 0? No	Can 4 be subtracted from 0? No	Can 2 be subtracted from 0? No	Can 1 be subtracted from 0? No
1	0	1	1	0	0	0	0

176 in binary = 10110000_2

Practise

Converting denary numbers into binary format can be a complicated process.

1 Copy and complete the **flowchart** to design an **algorithm** to convert a denary number to binary using the divide-by-2 method.

2 Write a set of step-by-step instructions in your own words to help your partner to convert a denary number to binary using the place-value method.

3 Use the divide-by-2 method to convert the following denary numbers into binary format:

a 129_{10}

b 45_{10}

c 98_{10}

4 Check that your answers to question 3 are correct by repeating the conversion but this time using the place-value method.

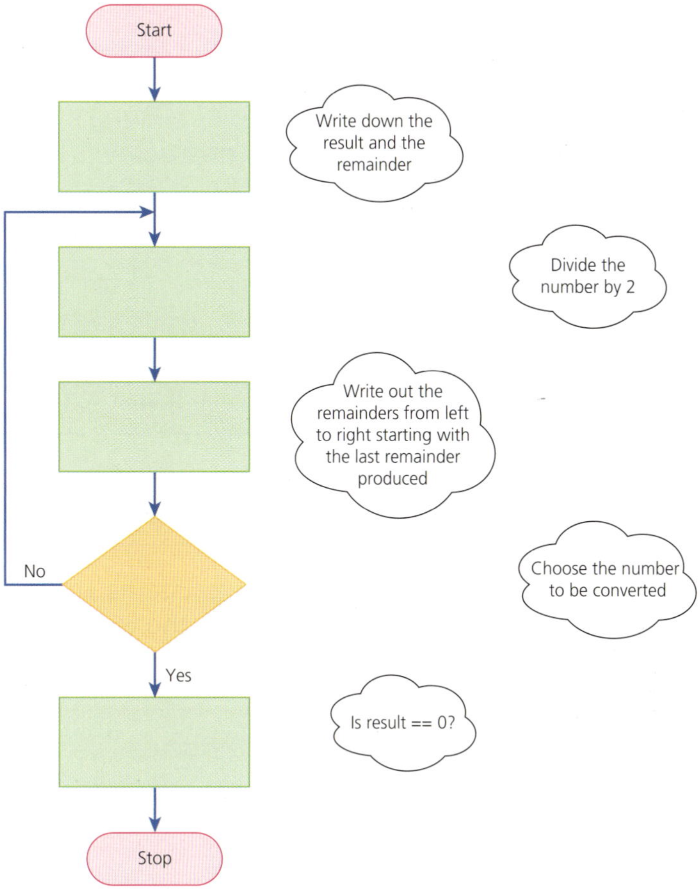

Binary inside

Learn

You have learned that computers do not represent letters and numbers in the same way people do; instead, they represent them using a combination of 1s and 0s. You have also learned that even images and sound are stored in binary format. This is possible because of the way in which digital devices use electrical signals to represent binary digits. Each digital device is made from millions of tiny binary switches called **transistors**. Each of these switches can only ever be ON (1) or OFF (0).

KEYWORDS

flowchart: a visual representation of an algorithm

algorithm: step-by-step instructions to solve a particular problem

transistor: a tiny switch that can be activated by electrical signals – if the transistor is ON, it represents 1; when it is OFF, it represents 0

Practise

You will now create a spreadsheet model to help you to understand how binary numbers are represented inside a digital device.

1 Open a blank spreadsheet and save it as **Binary Conversion.xlsx**.

2 Set up a spreadsheet similar to the one below.

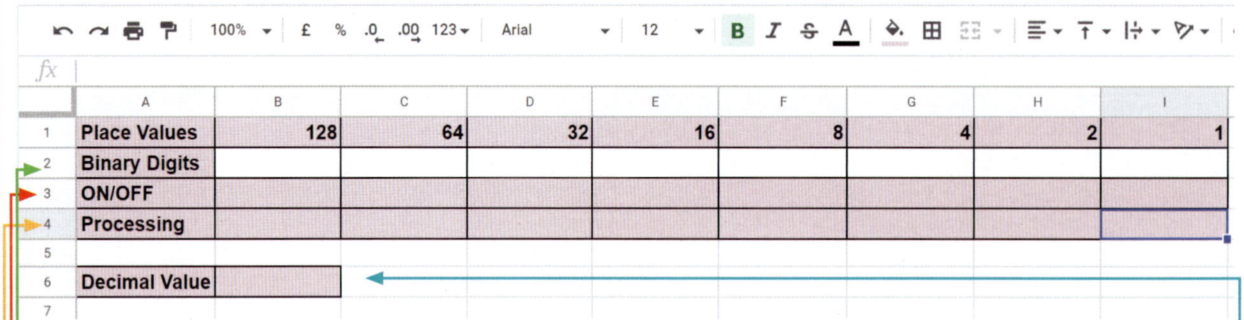

Binary Digits: Each cell in this row contains 1 bit; the 8 bits together represent a binary number that is to be stored in the computer memory.

ON/OFF: This row shows the ON/OFF pattern for each transistor used to store the binary number shown in the row above.

Processing: This row calculates the denary value of each bit entered into row 2 by multiplying the bit stored (1 or 0) by its place value in the number.

Decimal Value: This calculates the number stored by adding together the values calculated in row 4 of the spreadsheet.

3 Click on cell I4 and enter a formula that will correctly convert the binary digit in cell I2 into its denary equivalent.

4 Copy this formula into cells H4 to B4 so that you can also convert any binary values in each of these cells into their denary equivalents.

5 Test your model by entering a set of binary digits into cells B2 to I2.

Remember: All formulae in a spreadsheet start with equals (=). Don't forget that I2 can contain only 1 or 0. What must you do with that value to work out its denary equivalent?

	A	B	C	D	E	F	G	H	I
1	Place Values	128	64	32	16	8	4	2	1
2	Binary Digits	0	0	0	0	1	1	1	1
3	ON/OFF								
4	Processing	0	0	0	0	8	4	2	1
5									
6	Decimal Value								

6 Now add a formula to cell B6 to calculate the final denary value.
For example, you know that 00001111_2 should generate the value 15_{10}:

	A	B	C	D	E	F	G	H	I
1	Place Values	128	64	32	16	8	4	2	1
2	Binary Digits	0	0	0	0	1	1	1	1
3	ON/OFF								
4	Processing	0	0	0	0	8	4	2	1
5									
6	Decimal Value	15							

You have now successfully created a spreadsheet model that shows how to convert binary numbers into their denary format.

BUT

How does the computer represent the binary-number format using transistors?

You can use the ON/OFF row in the spreadsheet model to show how this happens.

7 Click on cell B3 and enter the following formula: = IF(B2 = 0, "OFF", "ON")

B3 =IF(B2=0,"OFF","ON")

	A	B	C	D
1	Place Values	128	64	
2	Binary Digits	0	0	
3	ON/OFF	OFF		
4	Processing	0	0	
5				
6	Decimal Value	15		
7				

If the value entered in B2 is 0, the transistor is OFF.

8 Copy this formula across your spreadsheet from B3 to I3 to work out whether the other transistors are switched ON or OFF.

9 Test your spreadsheet with the binary code for 27_{10} (00011011_2).

	A	B	C	D	E	F	G	H	I
1	Place Values	128	64	32	16	8	4	2	1
2	Binary Digits	0	0	0	1	1	0	1	1
3	ON/OFF	OFF	OFF	OFF	ON	ON	OFF	ON	ON
4	Processing	0	0	0	16	8	0	2	1
5									
6	Decimal Value	27							

Computational thinking – logic and evaluation

Ask your partner to test your spreadsheet with some binary-number representations they have calculated themselves.

Ask them to create a table similar to the one below to show the outcome of their testing.

Binary number entered	ON/OFF transistor pattern	Denary value generated

KEYWORDS

logic gate: an electronic switch used in digital devices, which produces an output of 1 or 0 (TRUE or FALSE)

circuit board: a small board with electrical circuits attached

truth table: a table used to evaluate the outcome of a logical expression

How it all happens

Learn

Processing inside a digital device is carried out using millions of tiny circuits. These circuits are known as **logic gates**. Logic gates are found on **circuit boards** inside any digital device.

A logic gate is an example of an electronic circuit that can have one or more inputs. Logic gates are designed to make decisions. These decisions are based on the values input into the logic gate. The output that the gate generates always depends on the input and the type of logic gate being used. Logic gates are said to carry out 'logical operations'. Using the input(s) received, they produce a single output.

You should already be familiar with the operations that the following logic gates carry out.

Logic gate	Symbol	Rules of operation
AND gate	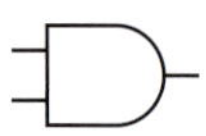 AND	Output from this gate is 1 if BOTH inputs are 1
OR gate	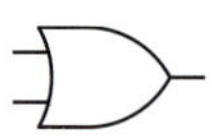 OR	Output from this gate is 1 if EITHER input is 1
NOT gate	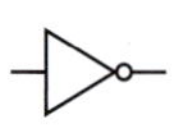 NOT	The output from this gate is always the opposite of the input

The input to any logic gate is always digital in format, which means that it is always either 1 or 0 (TRUE/FALSE or ON/OFF).

You can represent the processing that a logic gate carries out in a **truth table**. A truth table shows all the possible inputs to a logic gate and models the output from the logic gate for each combination of inputs.

You are going to use what you know about AND gates to create a truth table to show the combination of inputs and outputs for an AND gate.

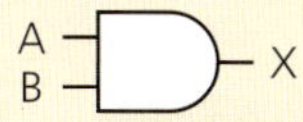

AND

Input A	Input B
0	0
0	1
1	0
1	1

Remember: Most logic gates have only two inputs. This is the case with an AND gate.

When creating a truth table for an AND gate, you first need to create a list of all possible input combinations into the gate.

Remember: Input A and Input B must both be 1 (ON) if the output is to be 1; otherwise, the output is 0.

You can then expand your truth table to include an output column for Output X:

Input A	Input B	Output X
0	0	0
0	1	0
1	0	0
1	1	1

Practise

Copy and complete the truth tables for an OR gate and a NOT gate using the process described in the Learn box.

1 OR gate

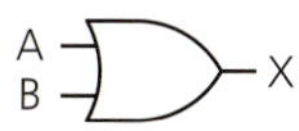

OR

- Step 1: Write out all possible combinations of inputs.
- Step 2: Complete the output column using the rules of operation for the logic gate.

Input A	Input B	Output X

Remember: With an OR gate, the output is 1 if either input is 1.

2 NOT gate

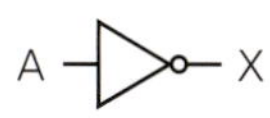

NOT

- Step 1: Write out all possible combinations of inputs.
- Step 2: Complete the output column using the rules of operation for the logic gate.

Input A	Output X

Remember: A NOT gate has only one input; with a NOT gate, if the input is 1 the output is 0 and vice versa.

Where is it all stored?

Learn

Most users of digital devices are aware that they need some kind of storage device to allow them to use their data at a later time. For example, it would be pointless having digital cameras on mobile phones if users were unable to save the photographs they have taken and view them later. If a user wants to store data so that they can access it later, they use a storage device. Storage devices that are used to store data for long periods of time are called **secondary storage devices**.

Digital devices also need to be able to store computer programs and data when the devices are currently in use. Memory used in this way is called **primary memory**.

Primary memory is built into the main internal components of a digital device. Since primary memory is very close to the main processor of the computer, it can provide very fast access to the programs and data currently being used.

There are two main types of primary memory.

Random access memory (RAM): Memory that is used to store the programs and data currently in use; when you load a word-processing application and open a file containing some homework you have worked on previously, you are loading the word-processing application and the file from secondary storage into RAM.

The more RAM available to the computer's processor, the more data and program instructions it has fast access to. This helps the processor to work quickly.

Read-only memory (ROM): Memory used to store the data and instructions needed to start up a digital device.

ROM often holds an important program called the **boot-up program**. This is the program that locates the computer's operating system in secondary storage and loads it into RAM so that the processor can provide the user with a way of using the digital device.

KEYWORDS

secondary storage device: any storage device used to store programs or data for a long period of time to allow the user to access them at a later stage

primary memory: storage to hold programs and data currently in use on a digital device

random access memory (RAM): a form of memory that stores tasks that are currently running, which the operating system controls

read-only memory (ROM): stores the data and instructions needed to start up a digital device

boot-up program: the program that locates the computer's operating system in secondary storage and loads it into RAM so that the processor can provide the user with a way of using the digital device; another name for this program is the 'BIOS' (Basic Input/Output System)

Main features of RAM and ROM

RAM	ROM
• **Volatile**; this means the data is lost when the computer is switched off • Can be read from and written to • Holds the computer programs and data when the computer is running • If many programs are running on a computer at the same time, this can slow the computer down because too many **data items** and instructions are being moved into and out of RAM	• **Non-volatile**; this means the data is not lost when the computer is switched off • Can be read from but cannot be written to (the user is unable to change the contents of ROM) • Holds programs and instructions that the computer needs to be able to start up • The contents of ROM are programmed by the computer manufacturer

Primary memory is expensive to produce so it is small in size, which means that there is a limit to how much data it can hold. When purchasing a new digital device, it is important to check the **hardware specification**.

Remember: More RAM means faster processing.

KEYWORDS

volatile: describes a type of memory (RAM) that loses the data in it when the computer is switched off

data item: a single piece of data

non-volatile: describes a type of memory (ROM) that does not lose the data in it when the computer is switched off

hardware specification: a document that details the main components of a digital device

Practise

1. Use the internet to carry out some research into the amount of RAM available on a number of different digital devices you use at school or at home, for example a laptop, portable tablet, PC or mobile phone. (Investigate a minimum of two devices.)
2. With your partner, compare the RAM specifications of the devices you have investigated.
   a. List the devices in order of available RAM (from lowest to highest).
   b. Based on the RAM available to each of the devices, which do you think would be fastest and why?
3. Produce a mind map to summarise the key differences between RAM and ROM. Include in your mind map details about how each memory type is used on a digital device.

Compression facts

Learn

Many of the computer programs in use today include high-quality graphic images and sound. Users interacting online often do so using **live video streams** or high-quality **interactive graphics**, for example when making a video call or when gaming online. High-quality images require a lot of data. When these images are stored on a digital device, they require a lot of storage space. Likewise, when they are broadcast across the internet, they need more **data-transmission time** and communication **bandwidth** than lower-quality images. The more transmission time and the higher the bandwidth needed, the more expensive it can be to transmit high-quality graphics. Think about the increased cost of making a video call on your digital device compared with making a voice call. Making a video call requires much more of your data allowance on a mobile device. This is why voice calls are often made available for little or no cost to the user, but video calls are much more expensive.

Compression methods can be used to reduce file sizes. This is achieved by reducing the number of 1s and 0s used to store the data in the file. Compressed files require much less storage space than uncompressed files, which means that shorter data-transmission times and smaller bandwidths are needed to transmit the files.

Data compression also has some disadvantages. Before the user can view a compressed file, it needs to be uncompressed again. If a reduced number of 1s and 0s is used to store the data in the file, then there is a chance that some data in the original file may be lost when the file is uncompressed. Specially designed computer programs are needed to compress files. One example of a program that allows users to compress files is the **WinZip** program.

Data compression can be divided into two types:

Lossy compression describes when some data is lost when a file is compressed, so when the file is uncompressed there is some loss of quality. For example, an image may have a reduced range of colour or a sound file may be of lower quality.

Lossless compression describes when no data is lost when a file is compressed, so that when the file is restored it retains its original quality.

KEYWORDS

live video stream: continual images and sound that are broadcast via the internet as they are being filmed

interactive graphics: graphic images (often animated) that a user can interact with using a device such as a mouse, keyboard or joystick

data-transmission time: the amount of time from the beginning to the end of a message being sent

bandwidth: a measure of the maximum number of bits that can be transmitted over a network or cable in a specified amount of time

compression: reducing the size of a file by removing some data items

WinZip: compression software designed for use with Windows, macOS, iOS and Android operating systems

Images, sound and text files can all be compressed. Different algorithms are used to compress different file types.

You will now look at one of the algorithms used to support the compression of image files. This compression algorithm is called **run-length encoding** or **RLE**.

Run-length encoding works by replacing repeated values in a file with a character and a number. The character is used to describe the value being replaced. The number describes the length of each run. The more similarities there are in the characters being recorded, the smaller the compressed file will be.

KEYWORDS

run-length encoding (RLE): a specialised algorithm used to support the compression of image files

web server: a computer that stores web pages that can be accessed by other devices using the internet

DID YOU KNOW?

When you pay a company to host a website, you are buying space on their web server where they store your website. Web pages that make use of lots of images often use compressed image file types. This means that web space does not run out too quickly and it also means that your web page loads faster.

Practise

Look at the bitmap image below.

1 Copy and complete the RLE code to encode the rest of this image.

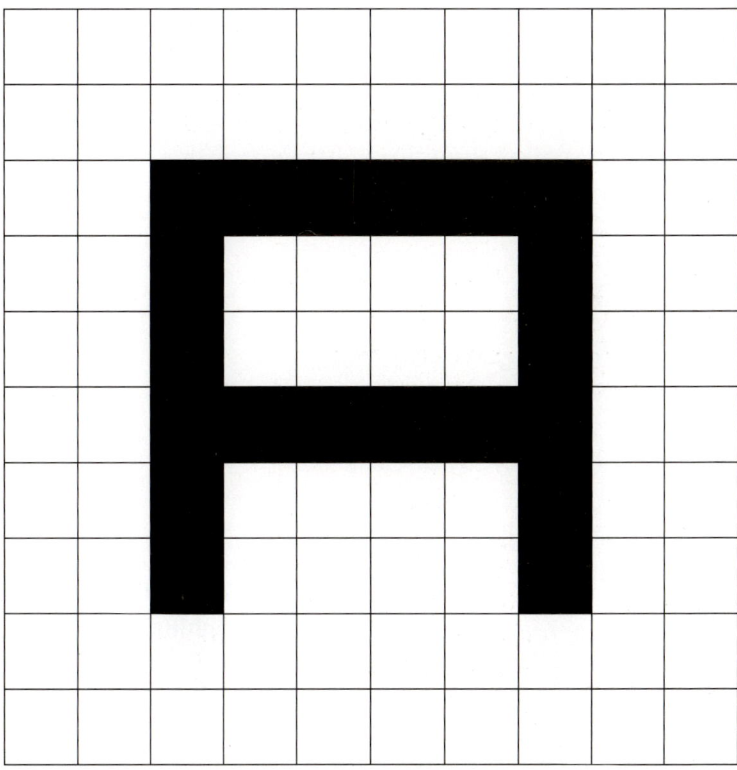

The following RLE code could be used to represent this simple black-and-white image:
10W
2W1B4W1B2W

2 Design your own black-and-white bitmap image on a 10 × 10 grid.
3 Create the RLE code that could be used to represent your image.
4 Give your code to your partner and ask them to recreate your image on their own 10 × 10 grid.
5 Explain to your partner what *compression* means and why you may need compression when sending images.

Developing device learning

Learn

Many of the digital systems in use today make effective use of images, sound and other forms of input to allow users to interact with them in a natural way. Think about the way you interact with some digital devices at home, for example giving spoken instructions to digital assistants such as 'Alexa' or 'Siri'. Think also about how, when you are sending a text to a friend, your mobile phone is able to predict what you are trying to say and will suggest possible words for you to use next in your message.

All these devices are able to understand what you are saying and carry out your instructions quite easily, especially after you have used them for a period of time. Was it just as easy when you first started to use your mobile phone? For most people, it will have taken time for their digital device to 'learn' what they are trying to say.

Machine learning

Many modern devices use artificial intelligence (AI) and **machine learning** to help them to understand the tasks that users want them to complete. Machine learning is about teaching computers to do what comes naturally to humans. It allows computer systems to carry out complex tasks by learning from data and past experience rather than by simply relying on carrying out the tasks that they were programmed to carry out. Machine learning helps with many of the tasks you carry out today. Think of digital home assistants that automatically suggest alarms or wakeup calls for school days, based on previous alarm settings, or TV subscription channels recommending viewing based on TV shows that you have watched previously. Many navigation devices are able to work out your home and work/school address based on the time of day that you visit a location and the duration of your stay at that address. Google Maps, for example, uses AI and

KEYWORD

machine learning: when AI systems are able to use data to make a decision without the help of a human

machine learning to verify store opening times on internet search results; using daily traffic at the address at particular times of the day, they are able to correct opening times online, if necessary.

Machine learning occurs when digital systems are able to learn from past experience and act upon that learning.

Autonomous programming

Much research has been done into how machine learning and AI can be combined to create programs that allow computer hardware devices to solve problems by carrying out actions without human interaction. This is called **autonomous programming**.

AI and autonomous programming are combined with robots in many industries to help make them safer or more efficient. An autonomous robot acts on its own, without any human interaction. When an autonomous robot is developed, it can, for example, be programmed to respond to certain outside obstacles that the developer expects the robot will encounter in its normal day-to-day operations. The robot will follow a set routine or pathway, but will also use sensors to detect obstacles. If a sensor detects an obstacle, the robot changes direction to move around that obstacle.

Think about how a robotic vacuum cleaner or lawnmower moves around a chair or table when it is following a pathway around the room or space.

Some autonomous devices work in very restricted environments and use sensors to help them to move around without much planning; other more complex devices use maps and more complex data to help them to complete the tasks assigned to them.

Here are some examples of where robotic technology is combined with AI and autonomous programming.

- Assembly lines: Previously, robots completed only pre-programmed tasks in assembly production lines. Now robot technology is being combined with imaging systems to allow them to evaluate the task they are trying to complete so that they can work out the most efficient steps to complete it.
- Customer service: Robots are being used in some industries to interact with customers. The robots are programmed with AI software to allow them to complete the tasks assigned to them, for example taking a booking for an evening meal. The more they interact with human customers, the more they learn.
- Rover robots: A type of robot used to collect data from hazardous environments for further scientific investigation, for example space rovers.

KEYWORD

autonomous programming: computer hardware and complex AI software working together to solve a problem without any human interaction

Practise

Search the internet for examples of autonomous programming and AI being combined with robotics to allow a task to be completed. For example, some robots in manufacturing applications use AI with image recognition to help them to cut out product shapes or to move around an obstacle. The medical profession sometimes uses autonomous robots to aid room cleaning, to help to ensure high-quality, consistent cleaning of hospital rooms or operating theatres.

Produce a short report of your findings:

- Describe the task that the autonomous robot is designed to complete.
- Include a short description of how the autonomous device is able to move around its environment and avoid obstacles.
- Outline the advantages and disadvantages of using the autonomous robot in this application.

Augmented reality

Learn

AI technology is developing rapidly and is used effectively in many types of industry. However, an alternative technology has now captured users' interest: **augmented reality (AR)**.

Most users consider AR to be very much a fun application. Many people are familiar with AR as an entertainment tool, with some of the most common applications being in the area of gaming.

If you have used the social-media app Snapchat or the Pokémon GO game, you will already be familiar with AR. Both of these applications provide users with filters that superimpose images over the image currently captured by the camera on the user's portable device.

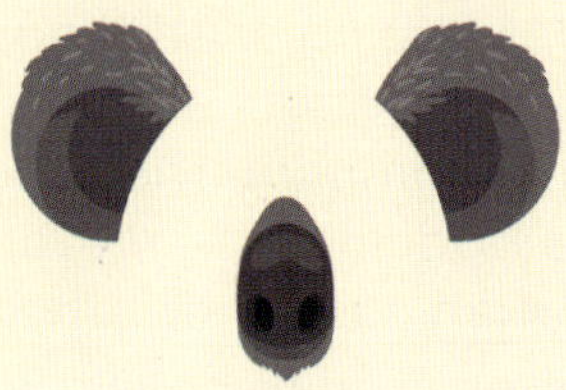

KEYWORD

augmented reality (AR): a simulation that superimposes digital images on the user's real-world environment and allows the user to interact with those images

However, AR has many other real-world uses.

- Medical training: Students can learn about human anatomy using AR devices that allow them to investigate the human body in 3D format.
- Shopping: With many consumers shopping online, they can use AR technology to see how a new item would look in their home or to view a new car with additional sports kit added to it.
- Travel: Potential travellers are able to view new locations without having to visit them; AR even allows travellers to access previously inaccessible locations such as space or inside a volcano
- Education: AR can have a very positive impact on student learning - its interactive nature means that it is more interesting for students and it allows them to learn in a less expensive and safe environment; students are able to interact with the AR representation, which helps to increase their understanding of difficult concepts.
- Gaming: With AR available on devices such as mobile phones, many gamers enhance their gaming experience with AR interactions; doing so can make the gaming experience more real and more enjoyable for the game player.

Practise

1 Carry out some internet research to identify examples where AI and AR are used together to help society today. For example, AI and AR glasses could be used to identify the location of someone injured in a remote location: AI could be used to work out a safe path for the support services and AR glasses could be used to guide them along that pathway.

Make a list of the examples you find.

2 Identify and research ways in which both education and entertainment use AR, such as in gaming. Write a short report on your findings, including the advantages and disadvantages.

Go further

In the 'Compression facts' section earlier in this unit, you learned how digital images can be compressed to save storage space or to increase the transfer speed of an image across a **network** link. Large text files can also be compressed. In fact, most young people already compress information that is in a text-file format, and they do not even realise that they are doing it.

Think about how you communicate with your friends using text messages.

HRU

Gd thnx HRU

Gd thnx hows ur sis?

Sis gd

Thats gr8. Getting l8. GTG b4 its dark

kk c u l8r

In this example, the sender shortens the text by looking for common sequences in the message and then replacing these with shorter sequences, for example 'gr8', 'l8r'.

Computers compress text in a similar way. They look for repeating patterns in a piece of text and they replace these repeating patterns with another symbol or character that was not originally part of the text.

Let's try doing this with a Dr Seuss quotation:

'Today you are You, that is truer than true. There is no one alive who is Youer than You.'

From 'Happy Birthday to You!' by Dr Seuss (1959)

There are some obvious repetitions here: 'You' and the letters 'true'. Imagine how the message would look if these letter combinations were replaced with alternative symbols:

Today you are β, that is |r than |. There is no one alive who is βer than β.

Can you find another set of repeated letters that you can replace with a symbol in this short piece of text?

This type of compression algorithm is called the Lempel–Ziv–Welch (LZW) algorithm.

The good thing about a computer abbreviating a message is that it does not have to worry about the message being easy to read. The computer simply holds a table that records all the

KEYWORD

network: a collection of computing devices connected to each other, either wired or wirelessly

replacement symbols and what they represent. When the text file is recreated, the symbols are replaced by the correct letter combinations.

For example, the following table could be used to recreate the text above.

Symbol	Original text
β	You
|	true

1 Find a short poem online.
2 Use symbols to compress the poem.
3 Create a symbol table for your poem.
4 Give the compressed text and the symbol table to your partner and ask them to reconstruct your poem.

Look for repeating patterns in the text of your poem, circle them and decide on a symbol for each pattern of text before you add them to your table.

Challenge yourself

In the 'How it all happens' section earlier in this unit, you looked closely at how truth tables can describe the operation of logic gates. The processing that logic gates carry out is so complex that electronic circuits often need more than one logic gate.

For example, a student can log in to a school computer as long as the following conditions are TRUE:

- they enter the correct login details OR they use facial recognition to log in

AND

- they are logging in during authorised school hours.

A logic circuit can represent these conditions:

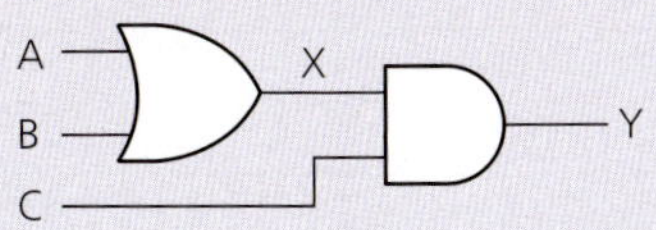

A = login details
B = facial recognition pattern
C = school hours

As there are three inputs, the truth table needs eight rows to account for all the possible inputs.

Using the inputs A and B, the output for the OR gate can be added to the truth table.

Input A	Input B	Input C	Output X = A OR B
0	0	0	0
0	0	1	0
1	0	0	1
1	0	1	1
0	1	0	1
0	1	1	1
1	1	0	1
1	1	1	1

This tells us that the user can log in if they have the correct login details OR if the computer recognises their face pattern.

Using the output from the OR gate as an input value into another gate ensures that even if the student has a login or facial-recognition access to the computer system, they can log in only if this is TRUE AND they are also trying to log in during authorised school hours. A new column added to the truth table helps to evaluate this new logic gate.

Input A	Input B	Input C	Output X = A OR B	Output Y = C AND X
0	0	0	0	0
0	0	1	0	0
1	0	0	1	0
1	0	1	1	1
0	1	0	1	0
0	1	1	1	1
1	1	0	1	0
1	1	1	1	1

Now complete the truth table for the logic circuit below:

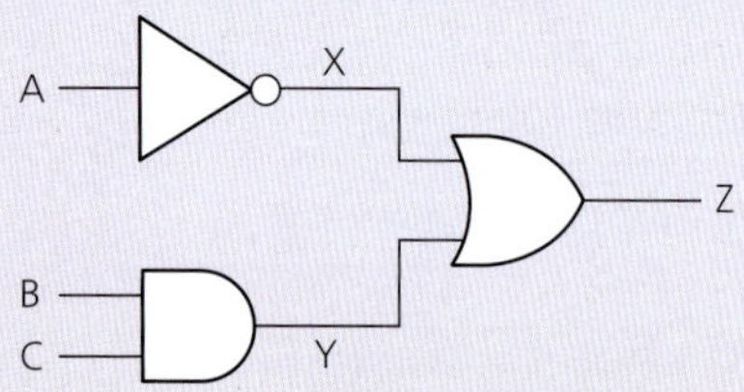

Input A	Input B	Input C	Output X = NOT A	Output Y = B AND C	Output Z = X OR Y

DID YOU KNOW?

Logic circuits that include more than one logic gate are called combinational logic systems.

KEYWORD

combinational logic: logic circuits made up of more than one logic gate

Final project

The telecommunications company you are working with have asked you to plan for the development of a futuristic method of communicating online.

They see augmented-reality glasses as the future of communications, where **3D images** of the person you are communicating with are projected on to your current surroundings, allowing you to chat to the other person as though they are there with you.

As part of the project, they have asked you to help with the following tasks.

Part 1

1 The telecommunication company's design team need advice on some of the hardware and software requirements of their new device. Create a presentation to explain to the team:
   - a what the term systems software means and the roles of operating systems and utility programs
     Include examples of each to illustrate your explanations.
   - b why the hardware specification for the augmented reality glasses will need to include both RAM and ROM memory
     As you are explaining the main features of each type of primary memory, explain how they would be used when the augmented reality glasses are in operation.
   - c the key differences between AI and AR
   - d the term *machine learning*, and provide an example of an application that uses machine learning to support decision-making in:
     - i an AI application
     - ii an AR application.

2 Write a short report to explain to the company's technical team how a username and password must be saved in binary format to allow a user to log in to the actual device. In your report:
   - a show how ASCII is used to store text entered via a keyboard into a digital device
   - b show how your username for your computer at school would be stored in ASCII format
   - c show the difference between how numbers are stored in binary format and how the number would be represented if a user entered it via a computer keyboard, using the number 128 as an example.

KEYWORD

3D image: an image that appears to have depth, as opposed to a flat printout; may be generated digitally and can sometimes be animated

Part 2

Help the company's design team by completing the following truth tables, which will be used as part of the AR communication system.

1

A	B	V = A OR B

2

A	B	V = A AND B

3

A	V = NOT A

Part 3

The new AR communication system needs to be able to transmit high-quality moving images from one location to another. The company's designers are worried about how long an image might take to transmit.

1 Produce a simple image on a 10 × 10 grid (similar to the bitmap image you used in the Compression facts Practise task).

2 Explain why compression may be needed in this instance and then use this image to explain to the designers how they could use run-length encoding to compress this image.

Keep the bits in your image black and white for simplicity.

Part 4

The design team have decided to introduce a 3D interactive gaming element to their new hardware device, but they are unsure about how to record scores for the game. They would like to create a leader board for all players, so some number processing will be needed.

Complete tasks 1–3 below (and show your working out) to explain to the design team how denary numbers can be converted into binary and how binary numbers can be converted back into denary.

1 Use the divide-by-2 method to show how the following denary numbers could be converted into binary:
   a 198
   b 68
2 Use the place-value method to show how the following denary numbers could be converted into binary:
   a 77
   b 154
3 Convert the following binary number into denary:
   00110110
   Explain the steps you followed to help you with this task.

Part 5

The telecommunications company are interested in developing new products that make use of AR and robotics. They have asked you to investigate how other industries use these technologies.

1 Produce a short presentation to:
   - show how AR may be used in education and entertainment
   - describe how robotics uses autonomous programming and AI.
2 Carry out some additional internet research into the use of AR and robotics in industry, education and entertainment. Expand your presentation to include the advantages and disadvantages of using AR in each of these areas.

Evaluation

1 Swap your presentation for Part 1 of the Final project with your partner. Ask your partner to review your content to see whether you have:
   - clearly explained the differences between operating systems and utility programs – make amendments to your presentation, if necessary
   - clearly explained how ASCII is used to store text on a computer system.
2 Compare with your partner your truth tables for the circuit in Part 2.
   - Do your truth tables look the same as each other's?
   - Discuss any differences and try to work out where you may need to make corrections.
3 Provide your partner with the run-length encoding code you generated for your image in Part 3. Ask them to use the code to recreate your image on a 10 × 10 grid.

4 Ask your partner to check the binary and denary conversions you completed in Part 4. Make corrections to your conversions, if necessary.

5 With your partner, discuss your findings for Part 5.
- Did they include any interesting examples that you did not?
- If you have time, update your presentation to include these examples.

What can you do?

Read and review what you can do.

- ✔ I can explain the purpose of operating systems and describe some of the main tasks that an operating system carries out.
- ✔ I can describe the purpose of utility programs and give examples of some utility programs and the tasks that they complete.
- ✔ I can explain how characters entered into a computer system are stored in ASCII format.
- ✔ I can explain the term compression and describe why compression techniques are used to support the reduction of file sizes.
- ✔ I can explain what denary means and know how to convert binary to denary and denary to binary.
- ✔ I can create truth tables for AND, OR and NOT gates.
- ✔ I can describe how primary memory such as RAM and ROM is used in a digital device.
- ✔ I can explain the term machine learning.
- ✔ I can identify and describe how augmented reality is used in education, gaming and robotics.
- ✔ I can describe how autonomous programming and artificial intelligence are used to support robotics in some industry areas.

Unit 8.4 Testing conditions: Developing games

Get started!

There are many different parts that make up a computer game, most of which are taken for granted. A finished game consists of different components that are usually coded by a large team of developers.

Look at the image on the right or consider a game that you play. Discuss the following with your partner.

- Does the player have to control a character? If so, how?
- Are there other icons on the screen? If so, what is their purpose/how does the player interact with them?
- Does the game have levels? If so, what does the player have to do to move up to the next level?

Writing a computer game is a complex task. However, you can break it down into a number of smaller sub-tasks, which makes it easier to plan and code.

In this unit, you will learn how to break down more complex programming problems into smaller problems and use **text-based programming** to write solutions. You will continue to develop your knowledge and skills of coding in Python to create programs that use selection and libraries to solve a variety of problems.

KEYWORD

text-based programming: programming that requires the programmer to type text, e.g. Python

Learning outcomes

In this unit, you will learn to:

- follow and understand an algorithm presented as pseudocode
- predict the outcome of algorithms to check that they meet the expected outcomes
- decompose a problem into smaller sub-problems to make it easier to solve
- explain why programming languages use libraries
- identify and use library functions in Python programs
- identify and describe the data types in a Python program
- create a Python program that uses the conditional statement IF-ELSE
- create a program in Python that uses a range of different data types
- explain and use the rules AND, OR and NOT to create logic within an algorithm
- develop a Python program that uses rules involving AND, OR and NOT
- develop a Python program using an iterative process
- develop and apply a test plan to ensure that a Python program works correctly
- explain why a range of test data is important when developing a test plan.

Warm up

In pairs, consider this arcade game and answer the questions below.

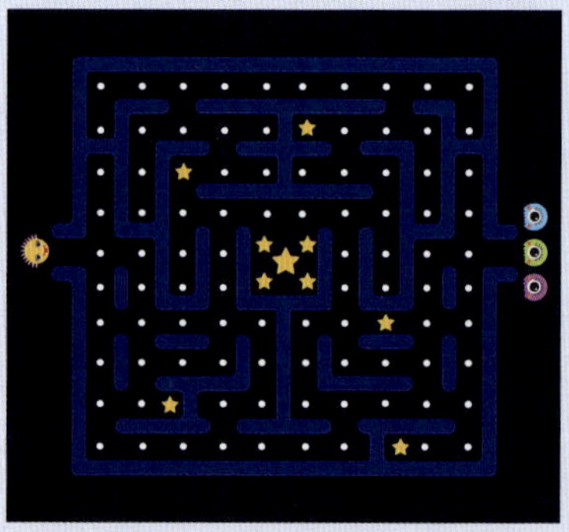

1 What is the aim of the game?
2 What might prevent the player from completing the game?
3 How could you make this game easier/harder?
4 What methods of scoring could the game use?

By completing this exercise, you have already begun to break down the task of writing a program for this game into smaller elements. In this unit, you will learn how to develop programs that make decisions and to test programs to ensure that they work as intended.

SCENARIO

Your school has asked you to develop a new interactive quiz game for students aged 8 years and older. Players will need to complete a series of puzzles to generate a code that will unlock a digital treasure chest and win the game.

The game is a **text-based quiz game** that should include questions on three different areas:

- solving anagrams
- capital cities of the world
- mental-arithmetic mathematics.

The program must collect the user's name and age at the start of the game as they are allowed to play it only if they are at least 8 years old.

Once the program has verified a player's age, it will ask them to choose a puzzle room to enter. Depending on their choice, the player will answer questions based on one of the three areas above. For each correct answer, they will score points and receive letters to form a code. At the end of the game, if their final score is high enough, the player will gain access to the treasure chest.

The team writing the game are already behind schedule and have agreed to release the game in stages. You will help the team to develop different parts of the game, using the plans provided throughout this unit.

As you work through this unit, you will be given sample code to help you to complete some of the tasks.

You will also create new code, edit code and test any changes you have made to the code to ensure that it works correctly.

KEYWORD

text-based quiz game: a game in which the player types in answers to questions or puzzles

DID YOU KNOW?

Some of the first adventure games for computers were text adventure games. This was because the computers were not powerful enough to display good graphics. A famous example is the game Zork, which you can still play online today. Search online for one of the early Zork games to see the quality of the graphics that computers during the 1980s (when this game was created) could display.

Do you remember?

Before starting this unit, you should be able to:

- ✔ identify different types of data that are used in Python
- ✔ create programs in Python that use different data types
- ✔ create programs in Python that use input and output
- ✔ use variables in Python to perform calculations
- ✔ apply a test plan to ensure that a program works correctly
- ✔ identify errors in a program and debug them
- ✔ create flowcharts that use selection statements
- ✔ use different arithmetic operators in programs created in Python
- ✔ identify the constructs sequence and selection when solving problems
- ✔ follow, understand, edit and correct algorithms that use sub-routines.

In this unit, you will use the Python programming language.

Python's Integrated Development and Learning Environment (IDLE) provides features for creating, editing and running programs. Before using Python, you will need to install IDLE on your own personal device:

1. Go to www.python.org/downloads
2. Select `Download Python`.
3. Once downloaded, double-click on the file to open it and then choose `Install Now`.
4. Once IDLE has installed, it should appear in your Start menu.

For more information about IDLE, see the 'Making choices' section later in this unit.

Breaking things down

Learn

Throughout everyday life, you are always solving problems by breaking them down into smaller, simpler steps. Consider the problem of getting to school in the morning. You don't just get to school; there are a number of smaller tasks that you complete before you get there.

Examples of the sub-tasks include:

- getting out of bed
- getting washed/showered
- getting dressed
- making breakfast
- travelling to school.

Completing this series of sub-tasks enables you to complete the main task of getting to school.

You can also break the sub-tasks down further. For example, the process of making egg on toast can be broken down into the following steps.

- Get a slice of bread.
- Put the bread in the toaster.
- Turn the toaster on.
- Get a frying pan.
- Add oil to the frying pan.
- Turn on the stovetop.
- Get an egg.
- Crack open the egg and pour it into the frying pan.
- Cook the egg.
- Butter the toast.
- Place the egg on top of the toast.

There are hundreds of other real-life examples where people break down problems or activities into smaller tasks to make them easier to solve. Other examples include:

- doing the laundry – you have to separate out the different-colour clothes before placing them in the washing machine
- decorating a room – you have to decide what preparation you need to do, for example removing pictures from the walls, what colour paint to use, and so on
- baking a cake – you need to decide what cake you want to make, find the recipe and the ingredients, decide what topping to use, and so on.

The process of breaking down a larger problem or activity into smaller easier-to-solve parts is known as **decomposition**.

Programmers use this approach with computer-based problems. Creating a computer game is a big task, so decomposition needs to take place to break it down into smaller tasks that are easier to solve.

KEYWORD

decomposition: the process of breaking a problem down into smaller sub-problems to make it easier to solve

Consider a football game for a computer and how a programmer could break it down into smaller elements:

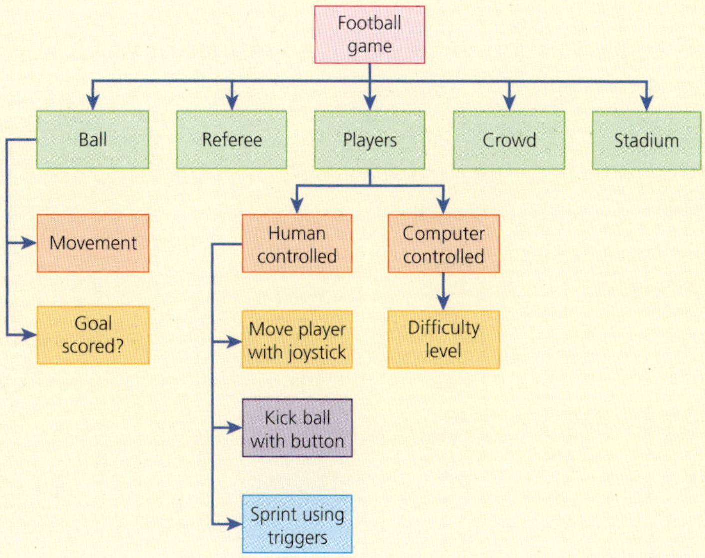

Practise

1 Complete this fill-in-the-gaps activity about decomposition.

Decomposition is the process of ________ a computing problem down into ________ sub-problems. Decomposition makes problems ________ to solve and allows ________ people to work on ________ parts of the same problem. As each sub-problem is solved, it can be tested ________ before being ________ with other code to solve the full problem.

combined	easier	independently	breaking
multiple	smaller	different	

2 Make a list of the different things that a police officer needs to consider when solving a crime.

3 Consider a fantasy adventure game where the character has to complete different levels. The character has a number of movements, actions and special powers that players can use to move through the levels.

The diagram on the right shows a partially completed decomposition diagram. Complete the diagram with the other movement directions, types of action and special powers that you think the character might use.

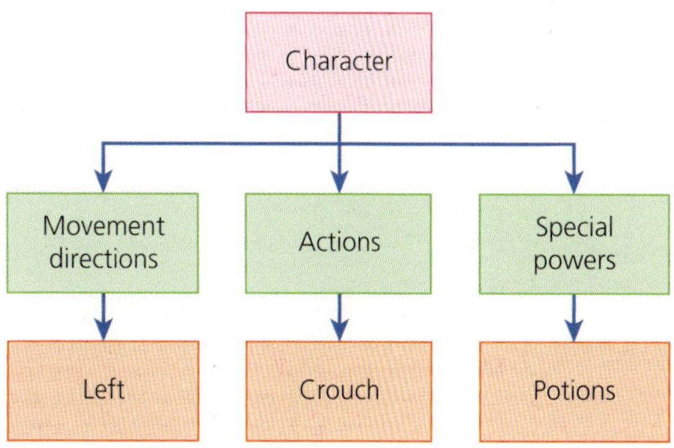

4 Create a decomposition diagram for a car-racing game. Consider:

- race tracks
- cars
- how to win.

Introducing iterative-development processes

Learn

It is possible to develop a solution to a problem in a number of ways. A popular way of doing this in computing is through **iterative development**.

Iterative development involves using decomposition to break a problem down into smaller sub-problems, which are then developed and tested in repeated cycles, slowly adding more features each time.

An iterative-development process can be broken down into several stages. These are:

- Plan
- Design
- Develop
- Test
- Review and evaluate

You will explore the concept of iterative development in more detail in the final unit.

Look at how the football game you explored in the last section could be created using an iterative-development process.

Plan

Before starting any project, it is important to plan what you need to do and to identify what determines success. You should always have a set of requirements to measure against, which you can use in the final review and evaluation stage.

When developing a game, this might include deciding on the different characters and icons you want to include, what movements and actions are needed and what a player must do to complete the game. You then need to decide the order in which you are going to complete the sub-tasks.

If you were creating a football game, this might include deciding the order in which to develop the different parts of the game. Would you design the backdrop and stadium first, or start with the football players and make sure that the player can move them around the screen?

Design

The design stage is when you begin to map out a solution to a problem, often by using **algorithms** to show how you may complete the different sub-tasks.

There would be different requirements for each character and icon in a football game, and you would also need to decide how a player scores goals and how a team can win the game.

The **flowchart** below shows a plan for the player movement controls.

Develop

This stage involves producing the solution to the task that you are trying to complete. When developing **software**, this would involve writing the code for a particular part of the **program**. In this example, that would be the code to control a football player's movement around the screen.

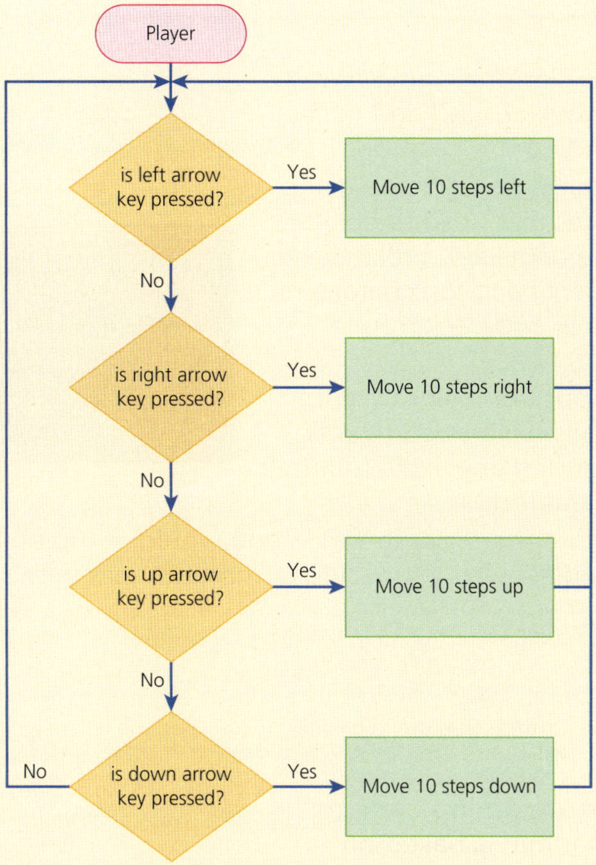

Test

You should test the solution to ensure that it works as it should. Some of this testing may take place during the development phase, but you also need to check functionality thoroughly once you have completed the development.

In the football game, testing would involve checking that the football players can be moved in each direction using the keys you defined in the design.

Review and evaluate

The review stage is completed at the end of the cycle. It checks that the original requirements have been met and evaluates how successfully this has been achieved, before moving on to the next **iteration** of the process.

In the review stage, you may need to reprioritise what you do next based on new information gained or problems encountered during this iteration of the development.

In the football game, this might mean reviewing the actions that a player can make and prioritising which additional ones are required, such as being able to jump or kick the ball.

KEYWORDS

iterative development/process: how a project develops throughout stages

algorithm: step-by-step instructions to solve a particular problem

flowchart: a visual representation of an algorithm

software: the programs or set of instructions that tell a computer what to do to complete a task; aspects of a device you cannot touch

program: the instructions that tell a computer system how to complete a task

iteration: repetition

Practise

This image shows a basic platform game that requires a character to move around and collect different items while avoiding the hazards.

1 Create a decomposition diagram for this game. Identify the main features that need to be developed to create the game and break these down into sub-tasks, identifying the characters, collectable items, hazards and background objects needed.
2 Compare your decomposition diagram with the one your partner has developed to see whether they have included any extra features that you have not considered.
3 Discuss with your partner the order in which you would complete the sub-tasks that you have identified. Explain why you would complete them in this order.

Making choices

Learn

In computer games, there are often situations where the next thing to happen is based on the outcome of a decision. This is known as **selection**. Selection involves asking a question to which the answer is TRUE (YES) or FALSE (NO).

You have looked previously at creating flowcharts with selection, for example to check a password to gain access to a program.

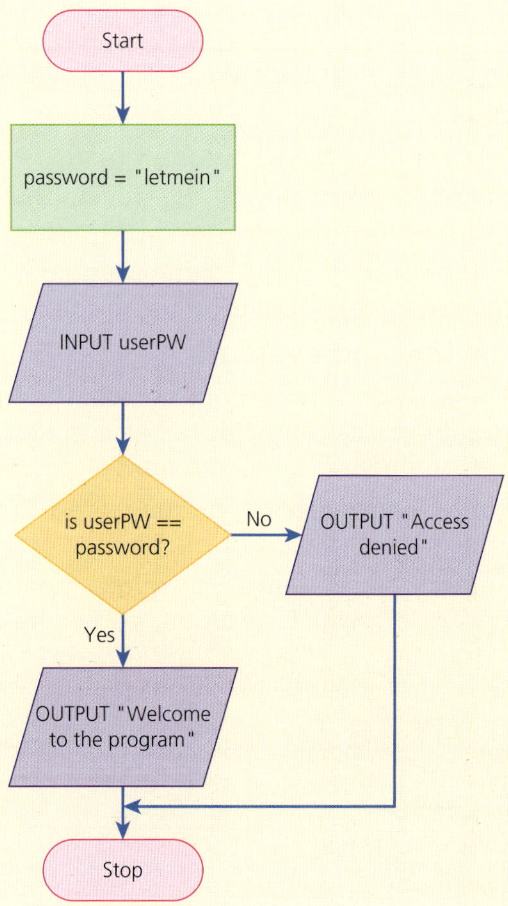

You have also used selection in **MicroPython** programs on the micro:bit to change the display depending on a **condition**, such as which button the user presses.

```
while True:
    if button_a.is_pressed():
        display.show(Image.HAPPY)
    if button_b.is_pressed():
        display.show(Image.SAD)
```

In standard Python code, the first line of an **if statement** consists of the word **if** followed by the condition (the question that can be answered with TRUE or FALSE) and then a colon (:).

To create the condition, you need to use a **conditional operator**:

- < less than
- > greater than
- == equal to
- != not equal to
- <= less than or equal to
- >= greater than or equal to.

Look at this program:

```
points = 75
if points > 100:
    print("An excellent score")
```

The first line of this program creates a **variable** called 'points' with a value of 75.

The second line of the program is the **if statement**, which checks to see whether 'points' is greater than 100; this is the condition.

The final line of code outputs the message if the answer is TRUE: that is, if 'points' is greater than 100. Notice that this code, which is telling the computer what to do if the condition is TRUE, is **indented**.

If you ran this program, nothing would be output as the condition is FALSE ('points' is not greater than 100). However, you can develop the code into an **if-else statement** to run some alternative code when the condition is not met.

When you want to stop the **if** part of the program, you stop indenting the code. You can then add an **else** statement, which is simply the word **else** followed by a colon, and below this indent the code that needs to be run when the **if** condition above is FALSE. For example,

```
points = 75
if points > 100:
    print("An excellent score!")
else:
    print("Not enough to be excellent.")
```

If you ran this program, it would output 'Not enough to be excellent' as the answer to the question 'if points greater than 100' is FALSE (NO).

KEYWORDS

selection: a choice in a program that is based on a question; the answer determines the next instruction to be run

MicroPython: the programming language used on the micro:bit

condition: the question that is asked to determine the next instruction in a program

conditional operator: symbol such as >, < and =; used to carry out comparisons between two values

variable: a named temporary storage location within a program; it can hold one value and this value can be changed or used at any point in the program

indented: describes a line of code that has been moved away from the left-hand margin to represent the code that will run if a condition is met

Practise

1 Look at the **pseudocode** below for a program that tells a user whether they are tall enough to go on a ride.

```
INPUT userHeight
IF userHeight < 130 THEN
    OUTPUT "Sorry, you are too short for this ride."
ELSE
    OUTPUT "Welcome aboard!"
    OUTPUT "Enjoy the ride."
ENDIF
```

2 Predict what will happen if the user enters a height of 140.

3 Open a new file in Python IDLE.
- Open Python IDLE.
- From the Python Shell, select 'File'.
- Then select 'New File'.
- Follow the pseudocode to write the program in Python. Save your program as **RideHeight.py**.

4 Test your program to check that the correct output is shown if a user enters a height of 140.

5 Test your program again to check that the correct output is shown if a height of 120 is entered.

KEYWORD

pseudocode: a textual representation of an algorithm

If ... if ... else if

Learn

You now know how to check whether a condition has been met, and can write a program that does one thing if the condition is TRUE and something else if the condition is FALSE.

However, you can make your programs even more interesting by checking several different conditions in a row. To do this, you use an **elif statement**. *elif* is short for 'else if'.

The program below asks the user to enter two numbers, compares them and then says which is bigger.

```
number1 = int(input("Enter a number: "))
number2 = int(input("Enter another number: "))
if number1 > number2:
    print("The first number is bigger.")
elif number2 > number1:
    print("The second number is bigger.")
else:
    print("Both numbers are the same.")
```

Note that the program tells the computer that each number the user enters is an **integer** – a whole number. If the program did not do this, then Python would assume that the **data** entered is a **string** and so would not be able to compare the values.

The program first checks to see whether number1 is bigger than number2. If it is, then the output is 'The first number is bigger'.

If not, then the program checks to see whether number2 is bigger than number1. If it is, then the output is 'The second number is bigger'.

If neither the first condition nor the second condition is TRUE, then the program moves to the **else** section and outputs 'Both numbers are the same'.

Practise

1 Look at the flowchart below for a program that asks the user to enter the temperature and then tells them what to wear.

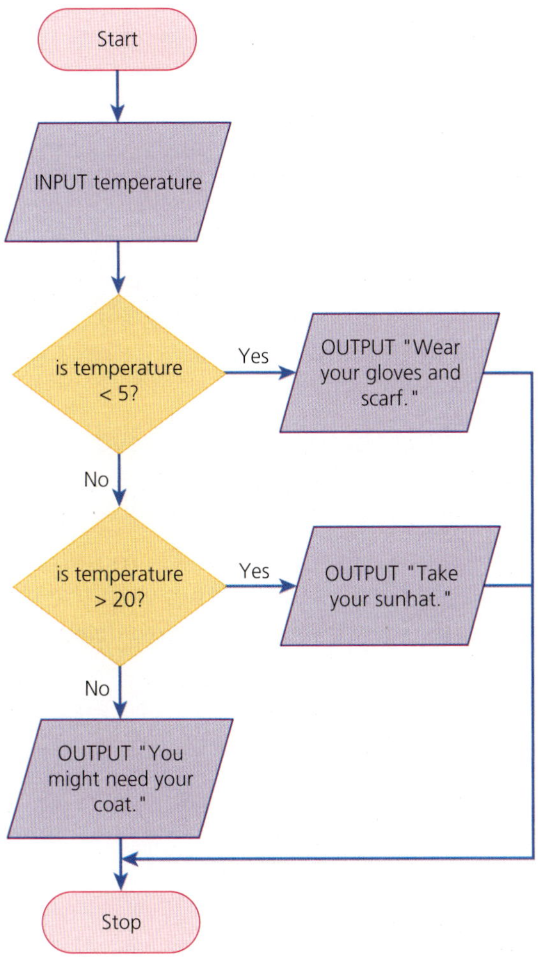

KEYWORDS

integer: a whole number

data: raw facts and figures

string: a sequence of characters that can be text, numbers or symbols; quotation marks around the characters define them as a string

2 Discuss with your partner what temperature you would need to enter for the program to output 'You might need your coat'.
3 Open a new file in Python IDLE and follow the flowchart to write the program in Python. Save your program as **WhatToWear.py**.
4 Test your program to check that the correct outputs are shown for a temperature less than 5, a temperature greater than 20 and a temperature of 10.

Quiz time: It's all in the variables

Learn

In the quiz game you will code for the Scenario at the start of the unit, there will be a number of variables used to store different data. You will need the following variables at the start of the game.

Variable name	Data type	Use/reason
username	String	To store the username that the player chooses This could include letters and/or numbers
userAge	Integer	To store the age that the player enters to check that they are old enough to play This will be an integer as age is a whole number

In addition to string and integer, there are other **data types** that you will use later in the quiz program. These are **real** and **Boolean**.

- Real: a data type consisting of numbers with decimal points.
- Boolean: a data type used to store TRUE or FALSE.

The contents of a variable can change when a program is run. However, it is also possible to use a **constant**. Once it has been **assigned**, the value of a constant does not change during the running of a program.

In the quiz game, you can use a constant to store the minimum age required to play the game. This can be used to compare the age that the player enters with the minimum age using an **if ... else statement**. The pseudocode example below shows how you can do this.

```
minAge = 8
INPUT userAge
IF userAge < minAge THEN
      OUTPUT "Sorry, you are too young to play this game."
ELSE
      OUTPUT "Let the game begin."
ENDIF
```

Using a constant to store the minimum age value means that you can use it elsewhere in the program, and if the minimum age changes, then you need only update it in one place. To indicate a constant in Python it is usual to use uppercase letters.

In the quiz program, you do not want the user to be able to continue with the game if they are too young, so you need to be able to force the program to stop running. To do this, you can use the function `exit()` at the point in the program where you want it to finish. For example,

```
age = 5
if age < 8:
    print("Sorry, you are too young.")
    exit()
```

The program will run normally up to this point and will then ask the user to confirm that they want to exit.

KEYWORDS

data type: the set type of data that is being stored, e.g. number, string, date

real: a data type consisting of numbers containing decimal points, e.g. 7.68

Boolean: can store only one of two values: TRUE or FALSE

constant: a named place in memory that stores a value that does not change while the program is running

assigned: giving a variable a value when it is created

Practise

Now begin coding your quiz game using an iterative-development process, following the steps below.

1 The first part of the program needs to ask for the player's username and age, and check whether they are old enough to play the game. The pseudocode below shows the design for this part of the program.

You can develop the quiz game in small chunks using iterative development and piece it together later to create the full working game.

```
OUTPUT "Welcome to the quiz game."
INPUT username
INPUT userAGE
CONST minAge = 8
IF userAge < minAge THEN
    OUTPUT "Sorry, you are too young to play this game."
    EXIT
ELSE
    OUTPUT "Let the game begin."
ENDIF
```

2 Open a new file in IDLE and use the pseudocode to help you to write this part of the program in Python.

3 Make sure that your program uses appropriate data types for the different variables.

4 Save the completed program as **QuizGameV1.py**.

5 Test your code to make sure that it accepts a user who is aged 8 or over and also rejects a user who is too young and then exits the program.

6 Review your program with your partner to confirm that it meets the requirements set out in step 1. This is the first iteration of your program.

Quiz time: Different pathways

Learn

Reread the Scenario at the start of this unit.

The game can be **decomposed** into the following sub-tasks.

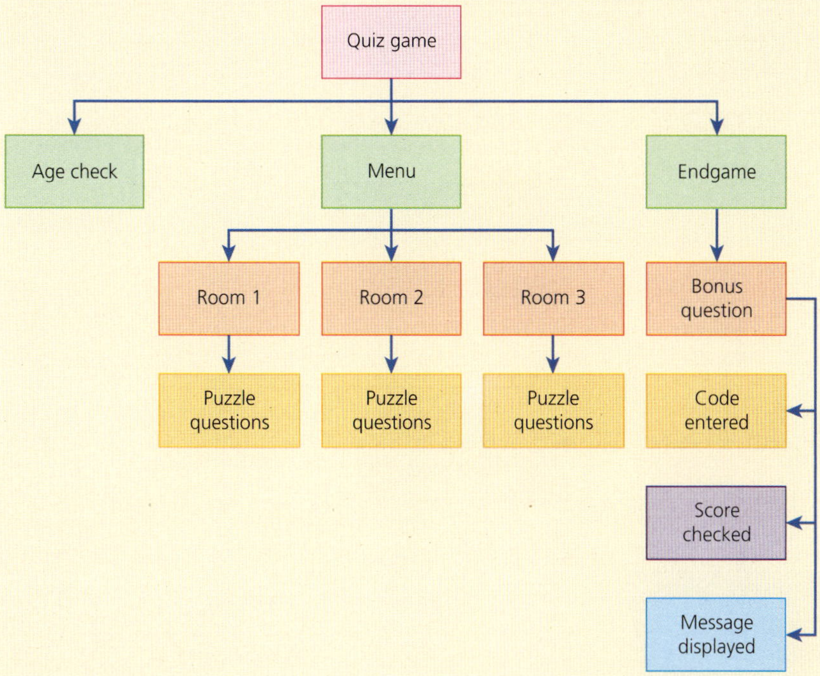

In the first iteration of the program, you wrote and tested the code to check that the player is old enough to play the quiz game. As you can see in the diagram above, the next sub-task is to develop the menu that asks the player which puzzle room they would like to visit.

KEYWORD

decompose: break down

Practise

You are now ready to begin the second iteration of your program.

1 Use the flowchart below to help you to develop your program to include a menu system.

The program should display the list of puzzle rooms and ask the user to enter their choice: 1, 2 or 3. It should then output a suitable message that welcomes them to the room they have chosen.

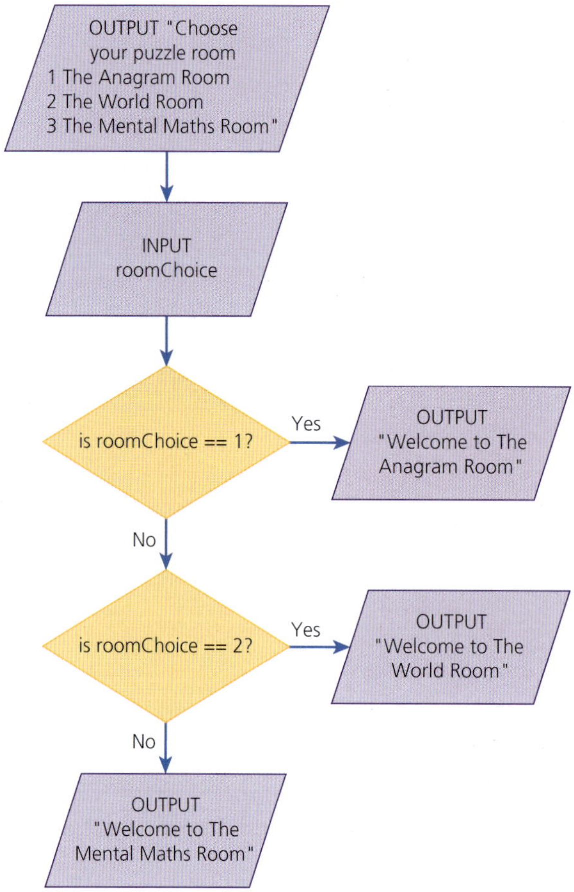

2 Open **QuizGameV1.py** and add your new program code below your existing code.
3 Save the program that you have now developed as **QuizGameV2.py**.
4 Run your program to check that it is functional. An example of what the program could look like when running is shown below.

```
Welcome to the quiz game.
Enter your chosen username: Wh1zK1d
Enter your age: 10
Let the game begin.

Wh1zK1d please choose a puzzle room to enter.
1. The Anagram Room
2. The World Room
3. The Mental Maths Room

Enter your choice 1/2/3 now: 2
Welcome to the World Room.
```

5 Using the template below, create a **test plan** to test all the different pathways through your program. For each test, briefly explain what you are checking. An example test has been included to get you started.

Test number	Data entered	Expected outcome	Pass/fail
1 User who is too young is not allowed to play	username = Wh1zK1d age = 4	'Sorry, you are too young to play this game' and program exits	
2			
3			
4			
5			
6			

Using sub-programs

Learn

You have looked at how decomposition is used to break down a problem into a series of sub-problems. When coding a solution to a problem, each of these sub-problems can be written as a mini program called a *sub-program*. The sub-programs can then be combined to make the finished program.

In Python, a sub-program is created, or defined, by writing the keyword **def** followed by the name you want to call the sub-program, followed by brackets and a colon. All sub-programs are written before the main program.

```
#Sub-program
def welcome():
    print("Welcome to my program.")

#Main program
welcome()
```

In the program above, the sub-program is called 'welcome'. The code to be **executed** when the sub-program is run is indented underneath. In this example, it prints 'Welcome to my program'. To run the sub-program, it is **called** by writing its name followed by brackets in the main program, which is written below all the sub-programs.

Sub-programs can also **return** data as a result to the **main program**. In the example below, the sub-program asks the user to enter two numbers, adds them together and then returns the result of the calculation to the main program. The value that is returned is stored in a variable called 'result' and this value is then used in the final output.

```
#Sub-program
def addition():
    number1 = int(input("Enter a number: "))
    number2 = int(input("Enter another number: "))
    answer = number1 + number2
    return answer

#Main program
result = addition()
print("The numbers added together total",result)
```

When the program is run it will look like this:

```
Enter a number: 6
Enter another number: 8
The numbers added together total 14
```

KEYWORDS

test plan: a document that details the tests to be carried out when a program is complete and whether or not they are successful
execute: to run

Practise

1 Open **QuizGameV2.py**.
2 Define a sub-program called 'puzzleRoom' at the start of your program.
3 Move the program code that allows the user to choose their puzzle room so that it is indented below 'puzzleRoom'. Make sure that all these lines of code have been indented an extra level.
4 Add a line of code at the end of your sub-program to return the number of the room the player has chosen back to the main program.
5 Add a new line of code at the bottom of your main program to call 'puzzleRoom' once the user's age has been verified and store the room number that is returned in a variable called 'room'.
6 Save your program as **QuizGameV3.py** and test it to check that it still works correctly.

The Anagram Room

Learn

You will now develop the first pathway through the quiz game: the Anagram Room.

In this room, the player will be asked to solve three anagrams to gain points and letters to a secret code. An anagram is a word or number of words with the letters rearranged.

An example of the pseudocode for this section of the game is shown below.

```
points = 0
OUTPUT "I am going to give you three anagrams to solve"
OUTPUT "Enter your answers in uppercase letters"
OUTPUT Question1 "What kind of fruit is PPELA?"
INPUT answer1
IF answer1 == "APPLE" THEN
    OUTPUT "Well done. You have gained 20 points and the letters ON from the
    secret code."
    points = points + 20
ELSE
    OUTPUT "Sorry. That's not correct. Lose 5 points."
    points = points - 5
ENDIF
OUTPUT Question2...
OUTPUT Question3...
OUTPUT points
```

You need a variable called 'points' at the start of the code to store the player's score. It has an initial value of 0.

The first anagram that this example asks is 'What kind of fruit is PPELA?' and the correct answer is 'APPLE'. Python treats uppercase and lowercase letters as being different, so if the user enters the answer as 'apple' it will be marked as incorrect. Therefore, the program asks the player to use uppercase letters when typing in their answers.

If the player answers correctly, 20 points should be added to their score and they should be given two letters from the secret code. You need to choose your own secret code and use it in each pathway through the game.

If the player answers incorrectly, then they should have 5 points deducted from their score.

The pseudocode has not been completed in full for the second and third anagrams, but the program needs to follow exactly the same structure.

An example of what this part of the program might look like when run, once it has been developed, is shown below.

```
Welcome to the Anagram Room.

I am going to give you three anagrams to solve.
Enter your answers in uppercase letters.

What kind of fruit is PPELA ? APPLE
Well done. You have gained 20 points and the letters ON from the secret code.

What kind of bird is ORWRAPS ? Sparrow
Sorry. That's not correct. Lose 5 points.

What colour is LURPEP ? PURPLE
Well done. You have gained 20 points and the letters PY from the secret code.

Your final score is 35
```

Practise

Now it is your turn to develop the Anagram Room pathway in your quiz game.

1 Remind yourself of the requirements of this section of the program and decide on the three anagrams that the player will need to solve.

2 Copy and complete the table below to create a test plan to predict what the score and the code for the treasure chest would be, based on different inputs to answer the anagram questions. Each test should check one aspect of the game, for example whether the program gives the correct feedback and score if the first question is answered incorrectly.

Test number	Test data	Expected outcome	Pass/fail
1			
2			
3			
4			
5			
6			

3 Open the latest version of your game; this should be named **QuizGameV3.py**.

4 Define a new sub-program called 'anagram' and code the Anagram Room section of your program. Write this sub-program underneath the 'puzzleRoom' sub-program and before the main program.

5 Add the following code to the end of your main program to call the anagram sub-program if the player selects room1.

```
if room == 1:
    score = anagram()
```

Save the latest version of your adventure game as **QuizGameV4.py**.

6 Run your program and test it using the data from the test plan that you created earlier. Correct any errors that you find when testing your program.

7 Ask your partner to review your program to check that it meets all the requirements for the Anagram Room.

Combining conditions

Learn

People sometimes need to make decisions based on two or more conditions. These conditions can be combined in different ways.

There are three main **Boolean operators**: AND, OR and NOT. Consider how they could be used to decide whether a treasure chest in an adventure game can be opened.

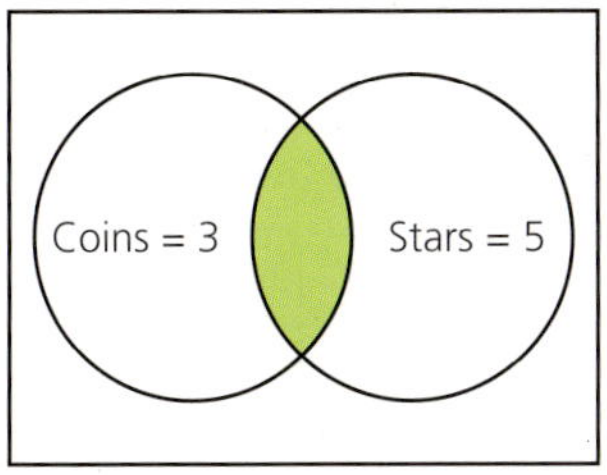

Condition1 **AND** Condition2

AND needs both the conditions to be TRUE to execute the statement that follows. For example, if the player has 3 coins AND 5 stars, then they can open the treasure chest.

```
if coins == 3 and stars == 5:
    print("You can open the treasure chest")
```

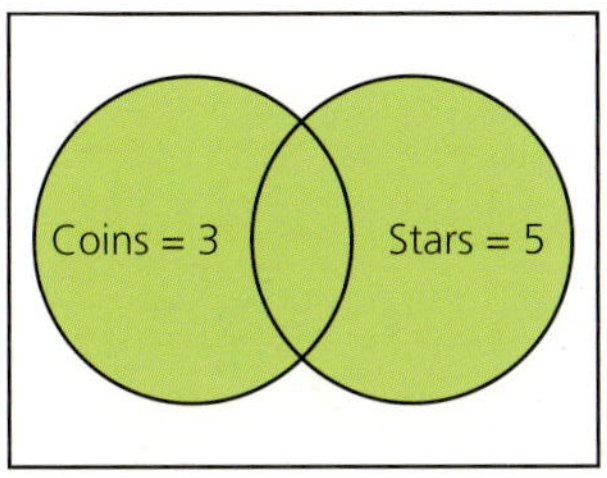

Condition1 **OR** Condition2

OR needs at least one of the conditions to be TRUE to execute the statement that follows. For example, if the player has 3 coins OR 5 stars, then they can open the treasure chest.

```
if coins == 3 or stars == 5:
    print("You can open the treasure chest")
```

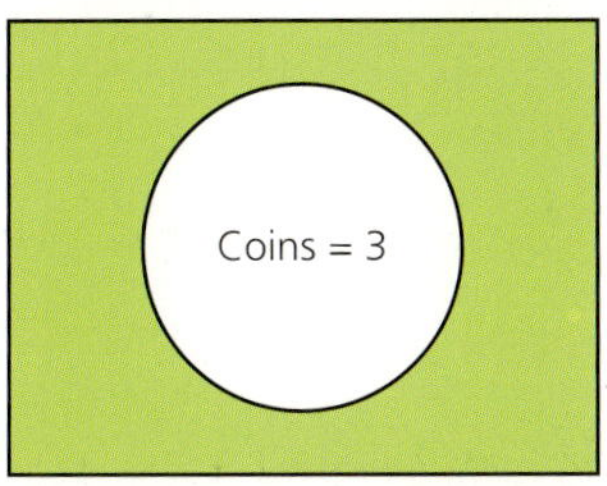

NOT Condition 1

NOT uses just one condition and inverts it to produce the output. For example, if the player does NOT have fewer than 3 coins, then they can open the treasure chest.

```
if not coins < 3:
    print("You can open the treasure chest")
```

In the second pathway through the quiz game, the player goes to the World Room where they visit different countries. They are asked two questions about each country they visit. If they answer both questions correctly, then they gain 30 points and three letters from the secret code. If they get only one answer correct, then they gain 15 points, but no letters from the secret code. If both answers are incorrect, then they lose 5 points.

The pseudocode below shows how you might go about solving part of this task.
This pseudocode is not for the entire room, but gives an indication of how the program should operate.

```
points = 0
OUTPUT "You have been transported to Portugal"
OUTPUT Question1 "What is the capital city of Portugal?"
INPUT answer1
OUTPUT Question2 "What is the currency used in Portugal?"
INPUT answer2
IF answer1 == "LISBON" AND answer2 == "EURO" THEN
    OUTPUT "Well done. You have gained 30 points and the letters ONT from
    the secret code."
    points = points + 30
ELSEIF answer1 == "LISBON" OR answer2 == "EURO" THEN
    OUTPUT "One answer is correct. You have gained 15 points."
    points = points + 15
ELSE
    OUTPUT "Sorry. That's not correct. Lose 5 points."
    points = points - 5
ENDIF
OUTPUT "You have been transported to..."
OUTPUT points
RETURN points
```

The image below shows a version of the World Room sub-program when it is run.

```
I am going to ask you questions about different countries.
Enter your answers in uppercase letters.

You have been transported to Portugal
1. What is the capital city of Portugal? MADRID
2. What is the currency used in Portugal? EURO
One answer is correct.  You have gained 15 points.

You have been transported to the USA
1. What is the capital city of the USA? WASHINGTON
2. What is the currency used in the USA? DOLLAR
Well done. You have gained 30 points and the letters HPY from the secret code.

Your final score is 45
```

KEYWORD

Boolean operator: the three main Boolean operators are AND, OR and NOT

Practise

Now it is your turn to develop the World Room pathway in your quiz game.

When your quiz game transports the player to a country, it must ask them two questions. In the Learn box above, the questions are based on the capital city and currency of that country. You can choose the countries the player visits and the questions they are asked, but it is best if your questions have one-word answers.

1. Remind yourself of the requirements of this section of the program and decide which two countries the player will visit and what questions they will be asked about each country.
2. Complete the first three columns of the table below to create a test plan to predict what the score and the code for the treasure chest would be, based on different inputs. Each test should check one aspect of the game, for example whether the program gives the correct feedback and score if one of the questions about the first country is answered incorrectly.
   Remember to apply the following scoring:
   - both answers correct = 30 points added to the score and 3 letters given from the secret code
   - 1 answer correct = 15 points added to the score, but no letters from the secret code given
   - 0 answers correct = 5 points taken away from the score

   You need to use letters from the same secret code that you chose for the Anagram Room.

Test number	Test data	Expected outcome	Pass/fail
1			
2			
3			
4			
5			
6			

3. Open the latest version of your game; this should be named **QuizGameV4.py**.
4. Define a new sub-program called 'world' and code the World Room section of your program. Write this sub-program underneath the 'anagram' sub-program and before the main program.
5. Add to the code at the end of your main program to call the 'world' sub-program if the player selects room2.

```
if room == 1:
    score = anagram()
elif room == 2:
    score = world()
```

6 Save the latest version of your adventure game as **QuizGameV5.py**.

7 Run your program and test it using the data from the test plan that you created earlier, filling in the final column of the table above. Correct any errors that you find when testing your program.

8 Ask your partner to review your program to check that it meets all the requirements for the World Room.

Python libraries

Learn

If you want to develop your knowledge, you may go to the library and read up on a particular topic. The information contained in a library can help you to learn about and do new things.

In Python, **libraries** are very similar. You can import a library into your program to give you access to extra functions that you can use to do more things in your program. Better still, some of the functions that you import mean that you can complete a task using less program code.

Python has a standard library that you have been using throughout this unit. There are a number of functions that you have used, and in IDLE they are displayed in a purple font. Examples include:

- `input()`
- `print()`
- `int()`
- `str()`
- `float()`
- `exit()`

Programmers can develop their own library of functions that they can share with other programmers, to make it quicker and easier for them to complete different tasks.

Importing a library

Programmers have to import libraries into Python to be able to use them. They do this at the start of the program code by typing `import` followed by the name of the library they require. For example,

```
import random
```

The 'random' library is used to generate random elements in a program.

The following program code generates a random number between 1 and 100 and then outputs the number.

```
import random
number = random.randint(1,100)
print(number)
```

`random.randint(x,y)` generates a random integer between two boundaries. The first value in the brackets (in the code above: 1) is the lowest possible value that could be generated. The second value in the brackets is the highest value that could be generated. If you wanted to generate a random number between 10 and 30, the code would be `random.randint(10,30)`.

KEYWORD

library: an additional set of functions that can be imported into a Python program

Practise

To give players an extra chance to receive more points, once they have answered the questions in their chosen puzzle room, the program will ask them to guess a number between 1 and 30. The program will need to generate a number between 1 and 30 automatically to compare their guess with.

The following should then happen:

- If the guess matches the generated number, then the program should multiply their score by 10.
- If the guess is within 10 of the generated number, then the program should double their score.

1. Open the latest version of your game; this should be named **QuizGameV5.py**.
2. Import the **random library** at the very top of your program.
3. Define a new sub-program called 'bonus' and pass the score into it as a parameter by adding the variable name inside the brackets.

```
def bonus(score):
```

4 Use the flowchart below to help you to create the new program code so that it meets the requirements outlined above.

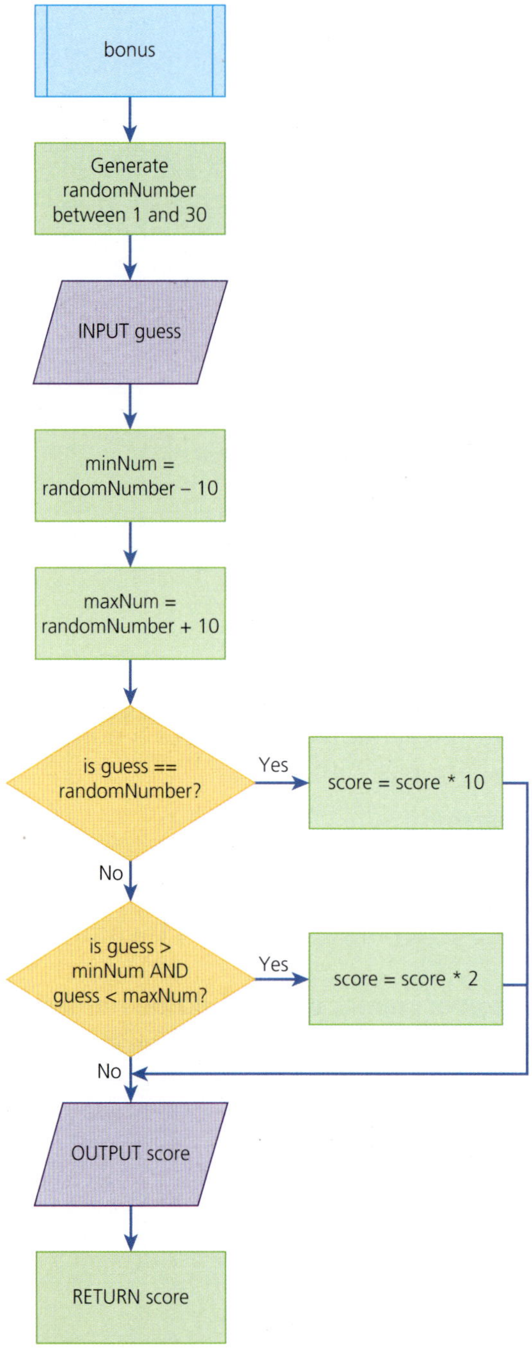

5 Add the following code to the very end of your main program to call the bonus sub-program, passing the value of 'score' into the sub-program as a parameter and storing the final score that is returned from the sub-program in a new variable called 'finalScore':

```
finalScore = bonus(score)
```

6 Save the program that you have now developed as **QuizGameV6.py**.

7 Test your program to see whether it works as intended. If you are not sure whether your program is calculating the final score correctly, you can add three `print()` commands to the end of your sub-program to output the values of 'guess', 'randomNumber' and 'score'. Use these to check the values and work out whether the score has updated correctly. An example of how the output may look with the extra print lines added is shown below.

```
Your final score is 35

Enter a number between 1 and 30 for the chance to add a bonus to your score: 15
Your final score is now 70
Random Number is 18
Guess is 15
Final score is 70
```

8 Explain to your partner why you needed to use a program library to complete this task.

Computational thinking – algorithms

<table>
<tr>
<td>1 Look at the code to the right. Discuss with your partner what the output would be if you entered the following values:
a <code>x = 4, y = 7</code>
b <code>x = 8, y = 8</code>
c <code>x = 11, y = 21</code></td>
<td>

```
x = int(input("Enter the value for x: "))
y = int(input("Enter the value for y: "))
if x < y:
    message = "x is less than y"
elif x == y:
    message = "x is the same as y"
else:
    message = "x is greater than y"
print(message)
```

</td>
</tr>
<tr>
<td>2 Look at the code to the right. Which message would be output if you entered the following values:
a <code>x = 5, y = 4, z = 11</code>
b <code>x = 7, y = 7, z = 99</code>
c <code>x = 12, y = 21, z = 0</code>
d Create a set of values for <code>x</code>, <code>y</code> and <code>z</code> so that the program outputs the message 'Hello world'.</td>
<td>

```
x = int(input("Enter the value for x: "))
y = int(input("Enter the value for y: "))
z = int(input("Enter the value for z: "))
if x < y and x < z:
    message = "Hello world"
elif x == y or x == z:
    message = "Good afternoon"
else:
    message = "Good morning"
print(message)
```

</td>
</tr>
</table>

Go further

Previously, you used the random library to extend the range of functions available in a Python program. In this section, you are going to look at another library you can use to create graphical drawings. This library is called **turtle**.

The following commands may be useful when programming using the turtle library.

Command	Example	What it does
`turtle.pensize(x)`	`turtle.pensize(10)`	Sets the thickness of the line that the turtle draws, where x is the thickness of the line
`turtle.pencolor(x)`	`turtle.pencolor("blue")`	Sets the colour of the line that the turtle draws, where x is either the name of the colour, e.g. blue, or a hexadecimal colour code, e.g. #1F51FF
`turtle.speed(x)`	`turtle.speed(1)`	Sets the speed of the turtle, where x is a number between 1 and 10, with 1 being slow
`turtle.penup()`	`turtle.penup()`	Lifts the pen up from the turtle, so that when it moves it doesn't draw a line
`turtle.pendown()`	`turtle.pendown()`	Puts the pen down on the turtle, so that when it moves it draws a line
`turtle.forward(x)`	`turtle.forward(100)`	Moves the turtle x steps forward, in the direction it is facing
`turtle.right(x)`	`turtle.right(90)`	Turns the turtle x degrees to the right
`turtle.left(x)`	`turtle.left(90)`	Turns the turtle x degrees to the left

The code below would begin to draw a square.

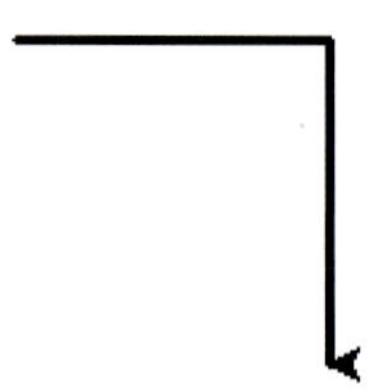

```
import turtle
turtle.pensize(3)
turtle.speed(1)
turtle.forward(100)
turtle.right(90)
turtle.forward(100)
turtle.right(90)
```

1 Create a new file in Python.
   - Copy and complete the program above so that it draws a square.
   - Save this program as **TurtleSquare.py**.
2 Create a new file in Python.
   - Import the turtle library at the start of your program.
   - Draw an equilateral triangle using the pseudocode below to help.
   - Save this program as **TurtleTriangle.py**.

```
IMPORT turtle library

pensize = 3

speed = 1

MOVE forward 100
```

```
TURN right 120
MOVE forward 100
TURN right 120
MOVE forward 100
```

3 - Create a new file in Python.
- Import the turtle library.
- Using the appropriate Python commands, create the drawing shown here. Each square is 100 × 100 in size and there is a gap of 50 between each square.
- Save this program as **TurtleSquares.py**.

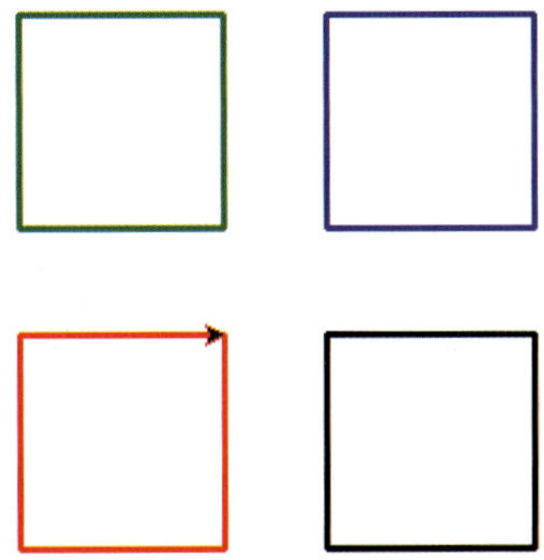

Challenge yourself

Now that you are familiar with using the turtle library, decompose this graphic into its smaller parts and then recreate it in Python.

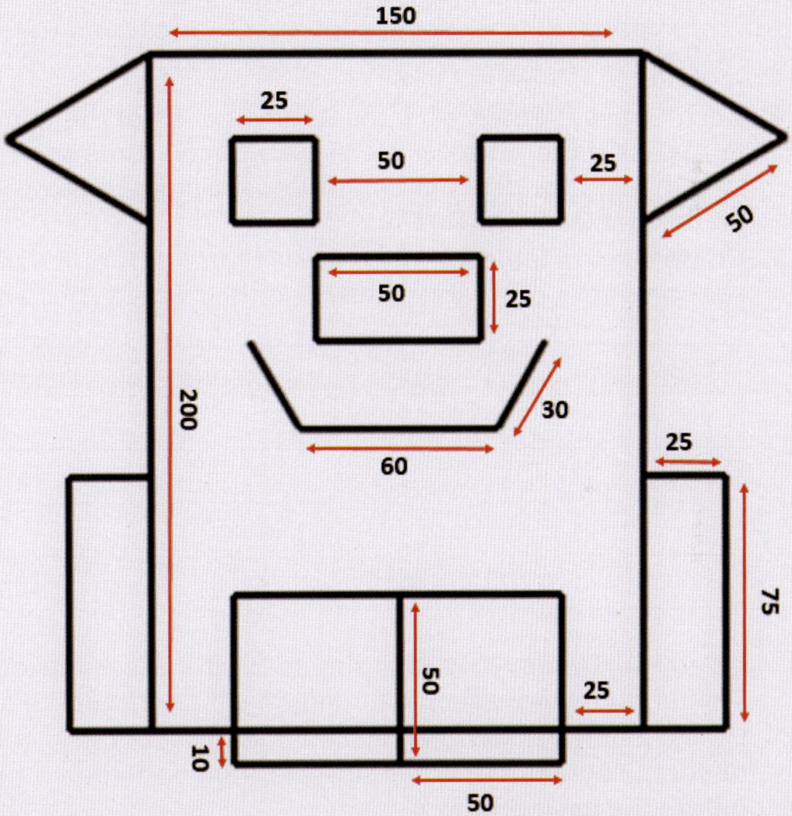

1. Make a list of the different shapes that create this image.
2. Give each shape a number to represent the order in which you will draw each shape.
3. Compare this with your partner. Is it the same or different? Discuss with them the reasons for your choices.
4. Open a new file in Python.
5. Recreate this drawing using the different turtle commands you have learned. Remember to run and test your program regularly to identify any issues as you develop it.
6. Create your own drawing similar to the one above for someone else to recreate in Python. Make sure that you include:
   - the dimensions of each shape
   - the angles of any shapes (if they are not obvious)
   - the distance between the shapes to get the positioning correct.
7. Swap your drawing with your partner. Are you able to recreate their drawing in Python?

Final project

Look back to the start of this unit to remind yourself of the Scenario. You are now going to finish the development of your adventure game by completing a number of tasks.

The final room in the quiz game is the Mental Maths Room. This room requires the player to complete a set of mental-arithmetic maths tasks. There should be an addition, a multiplication and a division question.

The addition and multiplication questions should be generated using two random numbers between 1 and 10.

The division question should be generated using one random number between 2 and 10, which the player should divide by 2.

The program should allow the player to answer each question in turn and, if they are correct, then it should provide two letters from the secret code and award 20 points. If they are wrong, then it should subtract 5 points from their score.

Complete the following tasks.

1 Decompose the Mental Maths Room section of the game into smaller sub-problems to make it easier to solve. Refer back to the 'Breaking things down' section early in this unit and create a decomposition diagram to show the different parts that make up the Mental Maths Room.

2 Complete the table below to identify the different variables you will need for this section of the program. Determine their data types and justify your choices.

Variable name	Data type	Justification

3 Open **QuizGameV6.py** (this should be the latest version of your adventure game). The random library should already be imported at the start of your program.

4 Define a new sub-program called 'mentalMaths' and code the Mental Maths section of your program. Write this sub-program underneath the 'world' sub-program and before the main program.

5 Add to the code near the end of your main program to call the 'mentalMaths' sub-program if the player selects room3.

```
if room == 1:
    score = anagram()
elif room == 2:
    score = world()
else:
    score = mentalMaths()
```

6 Develop the program code for the first question in the Mental Maths Room using the pseudocode below as a guide.

```
points = 0
OUTPUT "You will be asked three mental arithmetic questions"
num1 = random (1,10)
num2 = random (1,10)
correctAnswer = num1 + num2
OUTPUT Question1 "What is", num1, "plus", num2"
INPUT answer1
IF answer1 == correctAnswer THEN
    OUTPUT "Well done. You have gained 20 points and the letters ON from
    the secret code."
    points = points + 20
ELSE
    OUTPUT "Sorry. That's not correct. Lose 5 points."
    points = points - 5
ENDIF
```

7 Develop your program code further, by generating two more random numbers to use when asking a multiplication question.
If the answer is correct, then the player should gain 20 points and another two letters from the secret code. If the player answers incorrectly, then they should lose 5 points.

8 Next, develop the division question. This question needs only one random number to be generated, between 2 and 10, and the player should be asked to divide the random number by 2. Think carefully about the data type to use for this question when asking the player for their answer.
If the answer is correct, then the player should gain 20 points and another two letters from the secret code. If the player answers incorrectly, then they should lose 5 points.

9 Add a comment to your program, immediately below the line of code `import random` to explain what importing the random library has enabled you to do. Add the comment by typing a hash sign (#) at the start of the line.

10 Save this file as **QuizGameV7.py** and test your program.

11 The final part of the game should give the user an opportunity to enter the secret code to open the treasure chest and then provide an appropriate message.

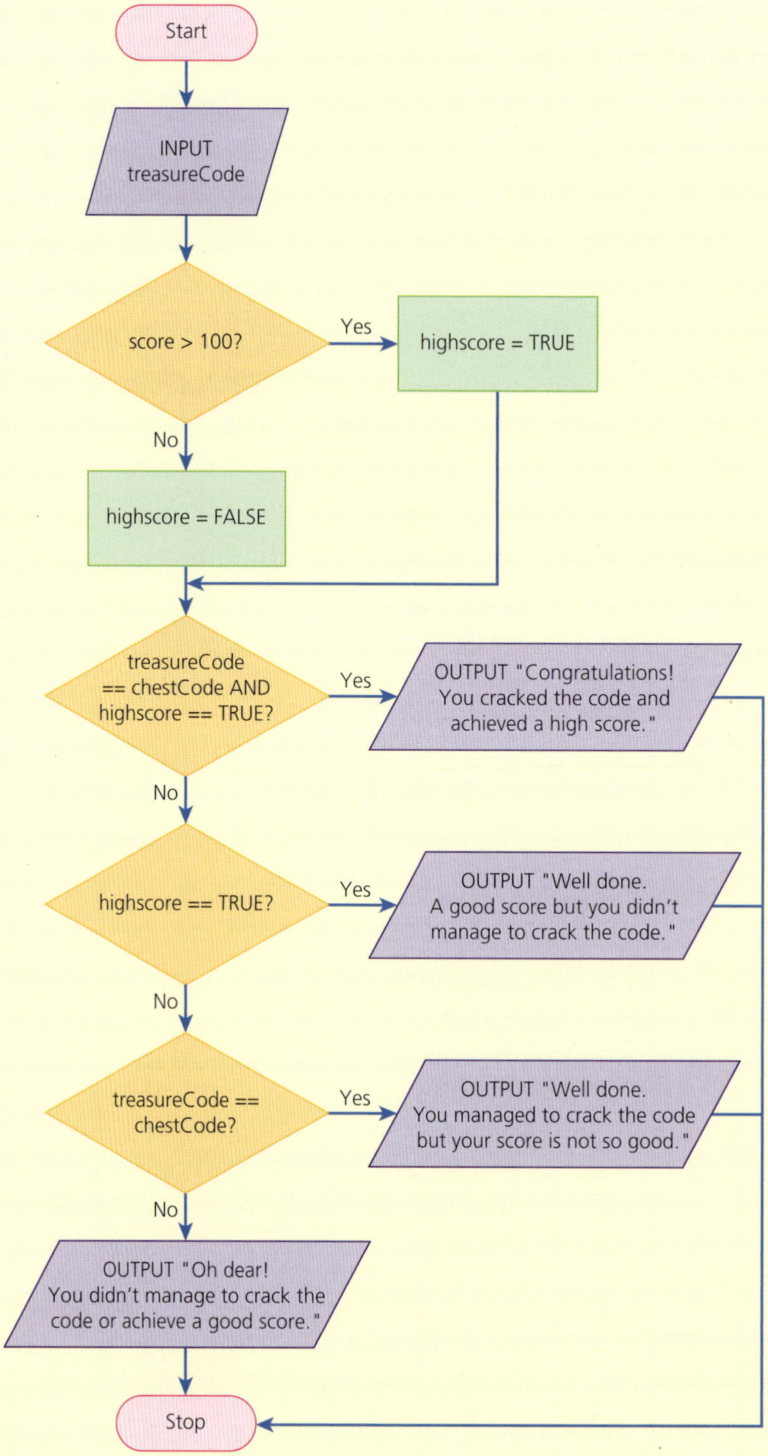
Start
INPUT treasureCode
score > 100?
Yes
highscore = TRUE
No
highscore = FALSE
treasureCode == chestCode AND highscore == TRUE?
Yes
OUTPUT "Congratulations! You cracked the code and achieved a high score."
No
highscore == TRUE?
Yes
OUTPUT "Well done. A good score but you didn't manage to crack the code."
No
treasureCode == chestCode?
Yes
OUTPUT "Well done. You managed to crack the code but your score is not so good."
No
OUTPUT "Oh dear! You didn't manage to crack the code or achieve a good score."
Stop

12 Follow the flowchart on the previous page, and predict the outcome of the algorithm for the data provided in the table below.

secretCode	userGuess	Score	Output
comp	comp	150	
comp	comp	50	
comp	science	70	
comp	science	120	

13 Using the flowchart above as a guide, implement the final part of the program in your quiz game. Write it as the final part of the main program.

14 Use the table below to create a test plan for the final stage of the game to check that it works as intended. Use a range of test data to ensure that the program works for all possible routes.

Test number	Test data	Expected outcome	Pass/fail
1			
2			
3			
4			

15 Save this file as **QuizGameV8.py**.

Evaluation

1. Swap programs with your partner and play each other's game. Comment on the following:
   - Does their game cover all the requirements?
   - Is their game easy to use?
   - Are the questions easy to understand?
   - Does the game calculate the score correctly depending on the number of right answers?
2. Now open your own program and look at the code. Reflect on what you could do to improve your game. You might want to consider the following.
   - How difficult is it to get a score of more than 100 points to achieve a high score? How could you make this easier?
   - How difficult is it to crack the secret code? How could you make this easier?
   - Is the length of the game appropriate? How could you make the time players spend in each puzzle room longer?
3. Based on these evaluations, make a list of recommendations to improve your game.

What can you do?

Read and review what you can do.

- ✔ I can follow and understand an algorithm presented as pseudocode.
- ✔ I can predict the outcome of algorithms to check that they meet the expected outcomes.
- ✔ I can decompose a problem into smaller sub-problems to make it easier to solve.
- ✔ I can explain why programming languages use libraries.
- ✔ I can identify and use library functions in Python programs.
- ✔ I can identify and describe the data types in a Python program.
- ✔ I can create a Python program that uses the conditional statement IF-ELSE.
- ✔ I can create a program in Python that uses a range of different data types.
- ✔ I can explain and use the rules AND, OR and NOT to create logic within an algorithm.
- ✔ I can develop a Python program that uses rules involving AND, OR and NOT.
- ✔ I can develop a Python program using an iterative process.
- ✔ I can develop and apply a test plan to ensure that a Python program works correctly.
- ✔ I can explain why a range of test data is important when developing a test plan.

Unit 8.5 Data input: Data collection and validation

Get started!

Have you ever wondered how data is gathered and used to predict what the weather will be like tomorrow?

Discuss with your partner times when you or a family member had to collect and analyse a large amount of information to help you to make an important decision. Think about how difficult it was to manage so much information. What did you do to make it easier to understand?

In this unit, you will build on what you learned in Stage 7 about the use of spreadsheets and databases to create models of real-life situations. You will look at the importance of accurate data when making decisions, and learn how you can reduce the chance of making a mistake when collecting data for those important decisions. Decisions made using the wrong data can lead to unpleasant outcomes. Imagine using an old train timetable when going to the airport for your summer holiday, only to find that your train left the platform 30 minutes before you arrived!

Sometimes, having too much data can disrupt decision-making. In this unit, you'll look at how you can use spreadsheets and databases to model the important data items in a real-life situation to help in the decision-making process.

Learning outcomes

In this unit, you will learn to:

- explain the difference between a **data model** and a **simulation** and understand the key features of both
- identify the **data** needed for a **spreadsheet** application
- identify the data needed for a **database** application
- design a **data-capture form** to collect the data for a model of a real-life scenario
- create formulae in a spreadsheet application to make meaningful links between **data items** in a data model
- explain and use formulae to help investigate the links between the data items in a spreadsheet model
- apply data **validation** to data in a spreadsheet application
- add a range of validation methods, including **input masks**, to a database structure
- evaluate the design of an existing database structure to ensure that it meets all the **data requirements** of a user modelling a real-life situation
- evaluate the suitability of data that has been collected in a database model of a real-life scenario
- use a spreadsheet model of a real-life system and **what-if** questioning techniques to make predictions and compare different scenarios.

KEYWORDS

data model: a digital data representation of a real-life scenario; the scenario is broken down into individual attributes, which are represented as data items in the model

simulation: a computer program that represents a real-life scenario using formulae and can be used to predict outcomes

data: raw facts and figures

spreadsheet: an application that uses rows and columns to organise data and carry out calculations using that data

database: an application that is used to organise data that can then be stored, processed and accessed electronically

data-capture form: a predefined document (electronic or paper based) that contains headings and instructions to collect appropriate data for a specific purpose

data item: a single piece of data

validation: an automatic check to reduce the chance of errors being made when data is entered into a computer system

input mask: controls how data is entered into a database by defining a particular layout or format for the data

data requirements: a list of the data items required to produce an accurate model or simulation of a real-life scenario

what if: changing the values in a spreadsheet cell to investigate the impact on other cells in the spreadsheet

Warm up

In Stage 7, you explored the concept of a data model and a simulation. You also learned the difference between a spreadsheet and a database application. Can you remember the difference between the applications?

Part 1

Look at the images below.

Image 1 is a computer-generated graphical representation of a car.

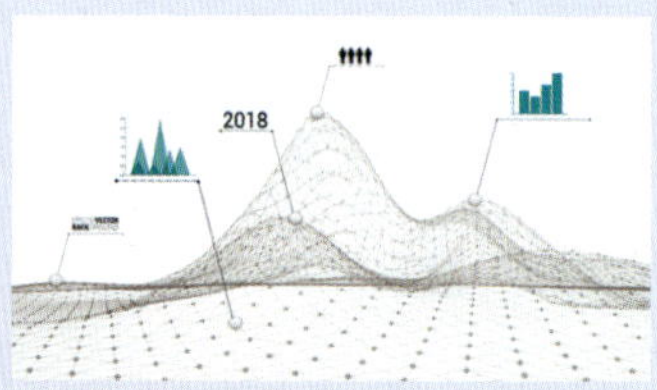

Image 2 shows the number of cars sold in particular periods of time.

1 Which do you think is an example of a simulation and which is an example of a data model? Give a reason for your answer.
2 Work with your partner to list the key differences between a simulation and a data model.

Part 2

Databases and spreadsheets can both be used to create data models.

1 List four important features of a database application. Name a database application that you have used.
2 List four important features of a spreadsheet application. Name a spreadsheet application that you have used.

Part 3

Discuss each of the following tasks with your partner and decide whether you would use a database or a spreadsheet application to create a model for each situation. Give a reason for your answer.

1 Monitoring the books on loan from a school library.
2 Storing and updating students' contact details.
3 Recording students' scores in exams across a school year and working out the average score for each student.
4 Recording individual members' times in an athletics club and calculating the difference between members' fastest and slowest times in the same event on different dates.

SCENARIO

Your school's music department offers lessons to students in a wide range of musical instruments. They have many tutors who offer lessons during school time and also **online** via video calls in the evenings. Students must pay tutors for their lessons, and the database records those who have paid their fees and the date on which they paid them. Each tutor can assess a student and assign them a music grade, but students must book a slot with the tutor at a convenient time and they must tell them in advance whether they will use the slot for a lesson or for an examination.

The data recorded by the department on a Microsoft Access data table includes:

- students' lesson/examination dates and times
- the instrument each student plays and their current grade
- the tutor assigned to each lesson/examination
- examination grade levels
- payment received for each examination or lesson.

The school would like to introduce a system where they offer students a music scholarship based on the grades they have achieved: the higher the grade, the greater the discount on fees.

The music department will **subsidise** the students' fees, and they need to monitor how much money is paid to their tutors as this will be taken out of their own **budget**. The data table they use at the moment to record students' lessons was poorly constructed; many errors have been made when collecting data and sometimes not all the data needed has been entered. This has led to some tutors being double-booked for lessons and some students not being entered for the correct examination grade. In this unit, you will help the music department to improve the database model so that it meets their data requirements. You will also help them to develop a database model that can be used to organise the distribution of tickets for the school's summer music festival.

There is currently no spreadsheet application in place to help the music department calculate potential discounts in fees for students, and they have asked you to create a suitable spreadsheet data model to help them with this task.

KEYWORDS

online: connected to the internet

subsidise: contribute payment towards a fee to help reduce overall cost

budget: a particular amount of money set aside for a task, department or organisation

Do you remember?

Before starting this unit, you should be able to:

- ✔ explain what is meant by a data model
- ✔ describe real-life situations where data models and simulations are used to help to make decisions
- ✔ evaluate data-capture forms used to collect data for a data model
- ✔ create and use rules to highlight important data in a data model
- ✔ identify and select appropriate primary key fields in a database model
- ✔ identify appropriate data types for data in a data model
- ✔ insert data and labels into spreadsheet models of real-life scenarios
- ✔ select appropriate data types for data items in a spreadsheet model
- ✔ add formulae to cells in a spreadsheet model (using SUM and AVERAGE functions, in addition to arithmetic operators)
- ✔ apply conditional formatting to cells in a spreadsheet model.

DID YOU KNOW?

Scientists often use data models and simulations to allow them to do things that would be impossible or dangerous in real life, for example testing new medicines.

Before starting this unit, you will need to make sure that you can access Microsoft Access and Microsoft Excel (or a similar database and spreadsheet software application) on your own personal device.

Databases: Getting the data structure right

Learn

Databases built to model any real-life situation are not only needed to store data but also to help the user meet certain needs or requirements. **User requirements** are a detailed list of what the user expects the data model to do. User requirements help the database designer to understand the data requirements of the data model.

KEYWORD

user requirements: a detailed list of what the user expects the data model to do

A well-designed database accurately reflects the structure of a real-world problem and meets the user's requirements by:

1. making sure that the data model can store all the data items needed to create a full model of the real-life situation
2. ensuring that all the data required is entered into the model
3. ensuring that no unnecessary data is stored as part of the data model
4. ensuring that the data stored is correct, by reducing the chances of errors being made when the user enters the data into the data model
5. providing users with an easy-to-understand way of adding data to the data model
6. providing users with an easy way of interacting with the data model.

Points 1–4 in the list above are very important when making sure that a database model is structured correctly and that the data entered is correct. If all the required data is not entered into a data model, then the data model is incomplete. When data is incomplete, there is a high chance that the results of any processing will also be incomplete or inaccurate.

One of the most important things to consider when designing a database structure is how the data is stored. The data is organised into fields and each field has a label called a *field heading* that describes the information it holds. The fields and their headings provide a structure that helps the database user create a full model of the situation, so they need to be well thought out.

Database tables store data in **entities**. Entities are the people or things represented in a database. All the data about one entity is stored in a single record. For example, a student is the entity and a record in a database stores all the data about that student.

To ensure a database model collects all the data required, it is best practice to break down the data items into the smallest units possible.

KEYWORD

entities: the people or things represented in a database

Computational thinking – decomposition

Look at the database extract below from a table storing details about students in a Stage 8 class.

Student name	Student address	Age	Stage
Keirin	Giza	thirteen	8
Samira Kahn	10 Elmessaha Street, Cairo	13	Stage 8
Anand Adel	Cairo	Thirteen	8

Discuss this database extract with your partner.

1 Identify the problems with the way in which the data has been recorded for each of these students.
2 How could you break down the 'Student name' and 'Student address' data items to enable users to enter all of the data required by the data model?

When you break down data items into the smallest unit like this, you are creating an **atomic data structure**.

3 What problems might users of this database experience if they tried to search for all the students with 'Age = 13' or 'Stage = 8'?
4 Make recommendations, based on what you know about **data types** in databases, to ensure that a user enters data in the correct format under the headings of both 'Age' and 'Stage'.

Now that you have a new database structure with fields that are broken down to the smallest units possible (they are atomic), identify a field that would make a suitable **primary key field** in this database.

Some of the **main data types** used in MS Access are shown in the following table.

Data type	Use
Text	Stores data that is a mixture of text and numbers; normally stores data that is not part of a calculation
Number	Stores data that may be used as part of a calculation; one of the most common number types available is **integer**
Date/Time	Different date and time formats are available so that a field can record a date such as `12 October 2021` or a time such as `10:04PM`
Currency	Stores money values in different currency formats such as Dollar or EGP
Autonumber	Automatically assigns a number to each record in a database – the application creates a new number for each record added to the data table; once a number has been assigned to a record it cannot be used again, even if that record is deleted
Yes/No	Data can have only one of two values, such as YES/NO or TRUE/FALSE
Lookup	Provides users with a list of all the possible data values that can be entered into a database under a specific field heading

Database developers, just like programmers, have to think carefully about the data type they assign to a data item. If the wrong data type is assigned to a data item, it can have an effect on how that data can be **processed**. For example, if you identify a field as a text data item, you cannot carry out calculations using that data item. It is very important that database developers select the correct data type at the design stage. Database developers will use a **data dictionary** to describe the data items they wish to use in a database table.

An example data dictionary is shown below.

Field name	Data type	Field length
StudentID (primary key field)	Autonumber	
StudentSurname	Text	25
StudentFirstname	Text	25

KEYWORDS

atomic data structure: a data structure where the data items are broken down into the smallest unit possible

data type: the set type of data that is being stored, e.g. number, string, date

primary key field: a field in a database that is unique and can be used to distinguish one entity from another

integer: a whole number

lookup: a lookup list provides the user with a list of options to choose from when entering data under a particular field heading in a database

process: carrying out an operation on data, e.g. querying a database or doing a calculation using data in a spreadsheet

data dictionary: a table that outlines the field headings, data types and other key features of each of the fields

Practise

The head of the music department has identified the following requirements for the database that you are helping them to redevelop.

User requirements

The database should record all the following:

- The full name and Stage of every student taking music lessons
- The type of instrument the student is playing and the grade they currently hold
- The date and time of any lessons or examination slots the student has booked
- Whether each slot a student has booked is an examination or a lesson
- The grade the student is to be examined on if the slot is an examination; students must work through the grades in order (1, 2, 3, 4, 5, 6, 7, 8)
- The full name of the tutor for each lesson
- Whether each lesson is online or in person
- The fee for each lesson/examination session
- Whether payment has been made for each lesson/examination session.

Part of the database the school is currently using to store this data is shown below.

Name	Stage	Instrument	Curr ent grad e	Lesson time	Examination time	Examination grade	Tutor name	Online or in person?	Fee payable	Fee paid ?
S Kahn	8	Drums	3		12 Jan, 9am	4	Uma Fouad	In person	20	Yes
Anand Amall	8	Guitar	4		12 Jan, 6pm	5	Ur Youssef	Online	$20.00	No
Satya Karr	8	Voice	4	13 Jan, 10am			Omari Fawzy	In person	$15	Y
Reem Ragab	8	Drums	5		13 Jan, 11am	6	Dalila Atef	In person	$20.00	Y
Ali Essan	8	Voice	1	13 Jan, 1pm			Dalila Atef	In Person	15	Y
Dina Amer	8	Guitar	6	14 Jan, 9am			Uma Fouad	In person	15	No

Part 1

Discuss this database structure with your partner and answer the following questions.

1 Are all the fields in this database broken down into the smallest unit possible? If not, which ones can be broken down further? What new fields and field headings would you add to break down the data items?
2 Some of the field headings have no data items recorded underneath them. How would you restructure the data to prevent this from happening?
3 As students must progress through their grades in a fixed order, does the table need to record both the current grade and the examination grade?
4 Discuss with your partner how you could restructure this database based on your answers to questions 1–3.
5 Make a list of the new fields and field headings that you would use to restructure this database.
6 When you have finished listing the new fields and field headings, complete the data dictionary below for your new structure. The first row has been completed for you.

How would you record the lesson/examination times differently? What if the table referred to them as a session type where the user entered a value of either 'Exam' or 'Lesson'? How might this affect the structure of the database?

Field name	Data type	Field length
LessonID (primary key field)	Autonumber	

Think carefully about the **field lengths** when you are designing your database. Discuss with your partner the impact this might have on the file size of a large database and therefore the time it would take to process the data.

To help you to complete this task, refer to the main data types used in MS Access as explained in the Computational thinking box on page 132.

As a class, discuss your data dictionary for the music department database before moving on to the next activity. You may need to make some changes to your data dictionary before you progress to Part 2.

KEYWORD

field length: the number of characters a field in a database application allows to be stored

You may not have used a lookup list before.

When using a lookup list, think carefully about all the potential values that you may need to enter under a field heading. For example, in the music department database, you may choose to use a lookup list for the instrument field, especially if there is a limit to the number of instruments taught in the school.

- Can you think of any advantages to using a lookup list to help the user when they are entering data into the database?
- Can you think of any additional fields where a lookup list might be appropriate?

When using a lookup list with a field in a data dictionary, always provide a list of all the possible values available to the user. For example, when setting the data type for the instrument field in the data dictionary, record this under data type as 'lookup – values to include guitar, drums, voice, piano'.

Part 2

Your teacher will provide you with a database called **MusicSchool.accdb**.

The database contains a table and data that the music department will use to monitor lesson and examination bookings for this year.

Use your updated data dictionary to complete the following tasks.

- Select the correct data type for each field in the database.
- Set the field lengths to match your data dictionary.

1 Open MS Access and open the database called **MusicSchool.accdb**.
2 Open the data table **bookingsTBL**.
3 View **bookingsTBL** in Design view to amend the data types for each of the fields in the new database table.

Remember: To view the table in Design view, click on View and then Design View:

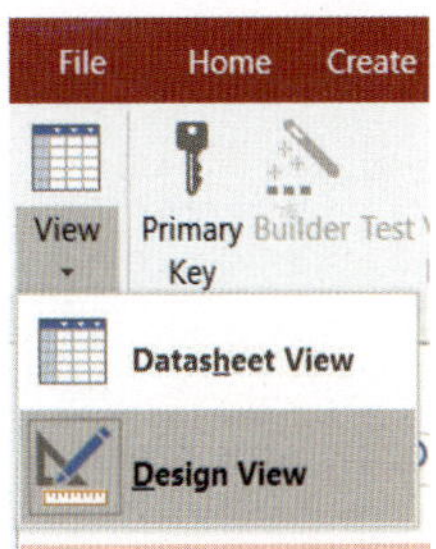

4 Amend the data types and field sizes for the following fields in **bookingsTBL**.

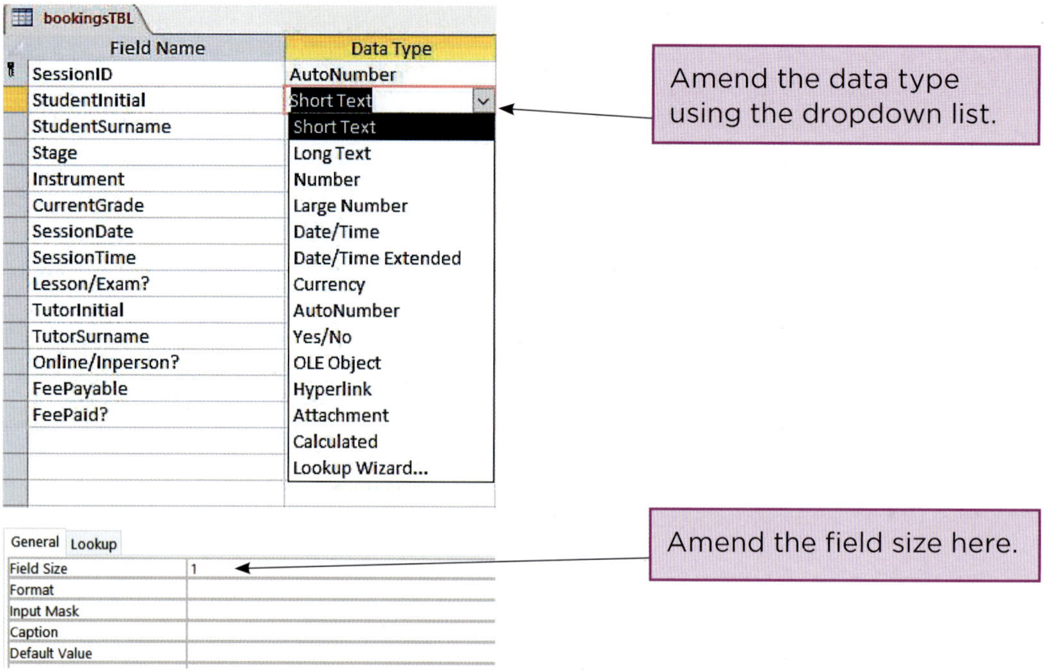

5 Now use the Lookup Wizard to set up a list of options for the user to select from when adding an instrument for a new booking.
With **bookingsTBL** still open in Design view:

- select the Instrument field name and select Lookup Wizard from the data type dropdown list
- select 'I will type in the values that I want' and click on Next

Lookup Wizard

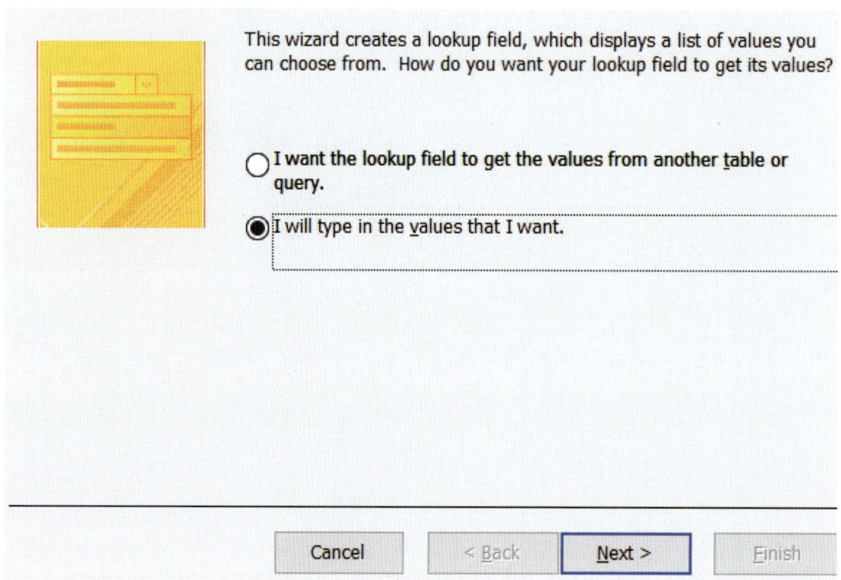

- enter the list of all possible instruments available (limited to the four shown below) and click on Next

Lookup Wizard

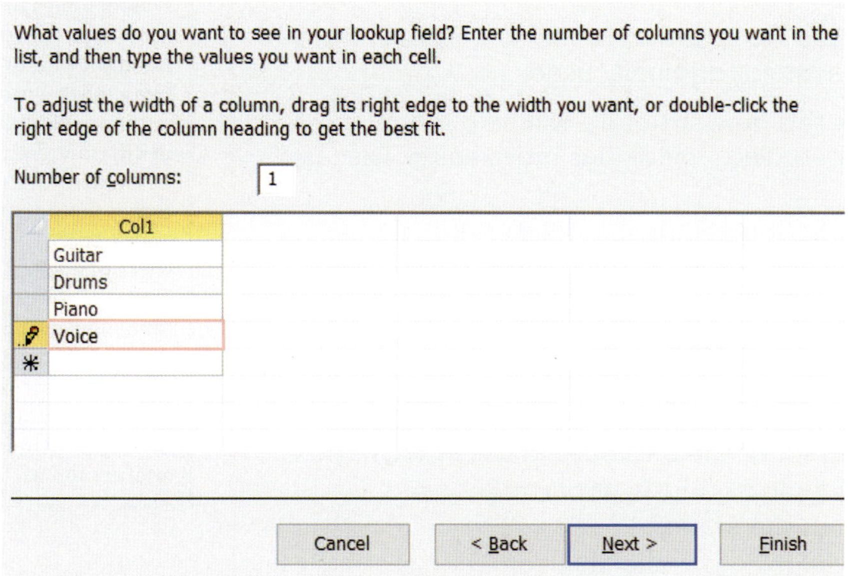

- when asked 'What label would you like for your lookup field?', this should already say 'Instrument', so you can click on Finish to complete the process.
  - Switch from Design view back to Datasheet view to see how you can use this new data type to add data to **bookingsTBL**.
  - Click on the Instrument field for any student in **bookingsTBL** to see the dropdown list that is now available.

You will have to save your database table before switching to Datasheet view.

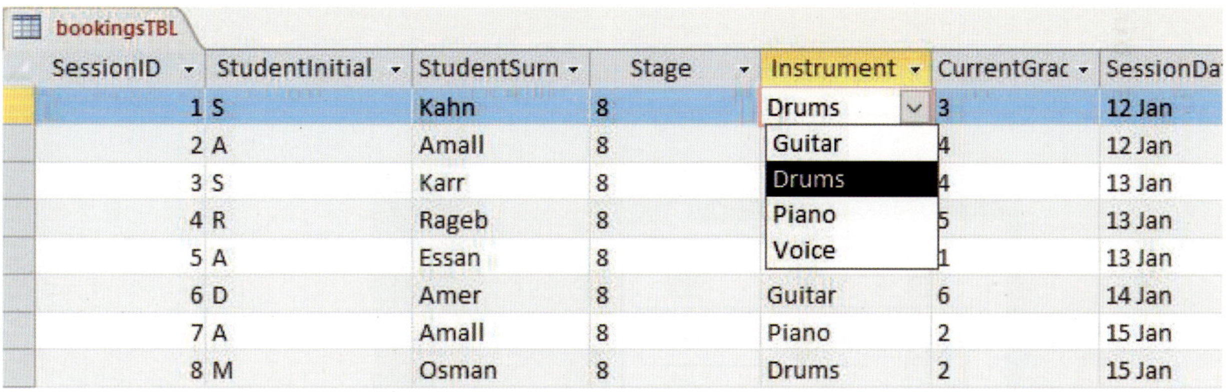

bookingsTBL

SessionID	StudentInitial	StudentSurn	Stage	Instrument	CurrentGrac	SessionDa
1	S	Kahn	8	Drums	3	12 Jan
2	A	Amall	8	Guitar	4	12 Jan
3	S	Karr	8	Drums	4	13 Jan
4	R	Rageb	8	Piano	5	13 Jan
5	A	Essan	8	Voice	1	13 Jan
6	D	Amer	8	Guitar	6	14 Jan
7	A	Amall	8	Piano	2	15 Jan
8	M	Osman	8	Drums	2	15 Jan

6 Use the Lookup Wizard to set up lookup lists for the following fields with the following values.

Field heading	List of lookup values
CurrentGrade	1, 2, 3, 4, 5, 6, 7, 8
Lesson/Exam?	Lesson, Exam

Computational thinking – abstraction

Examine the way in which data is recorded in **bookingsTBL** and compare this with the database extract in the Practise box.

The table in this database has a structure that is different from the one the music department originally used.

As a class, discuss how this new structure will help the music department to monitor students' bookings more easily. Discuss, in particular:

- why a primary key is so important in a database
- why students' names and tutors' names were broken down into initials and surnames
- why the field headings were renamed
- the way data relating to lessons/examinations is now recorded
- why the headings for these data items have been updated – think back to the extract of the database in the Practise box.
  - Was the structure that the music department used previously easy to understand?
  - Would it have been easy to make an error when storing details for a lesson or an examination session?
- how the data structure in the new **MusicSchool.accdb** database is an improvement.

DID YOU KNOW?

In some database models, the data is separated into several tables that are connected together using the primary key. If you have a very large database about lots of different entities, it is more efficient to create separate tables and connect them via relationships. For example, the database for a medical practice might store details about patients in one table and details about their appointments in another table.

Make no mistakes

Learn

It is easy to make mistakes when entering data into a database. Database applications allow the user to set rules that automatically check the data to make sure that it is reasonable or sensible. This process is known as data **validation**.

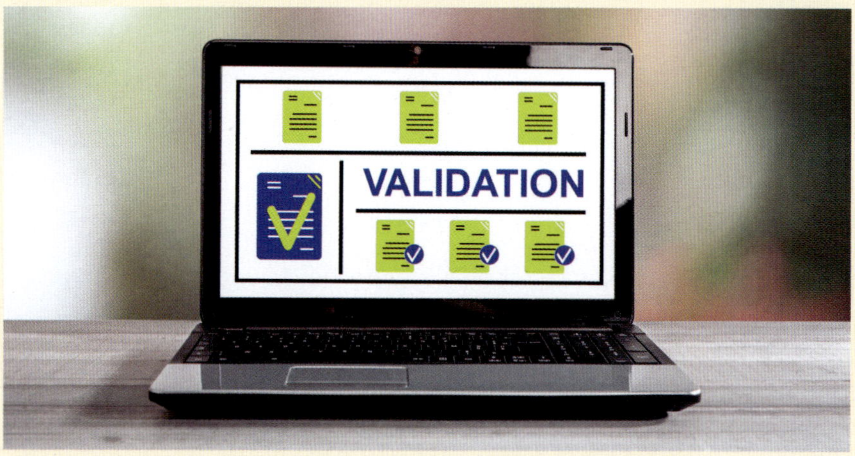

Data **validation rules** are assigned to each field in a data table when the table is created. Data that does not follow the rules for a particular field is rejected and an **error message** is displayed. The person entering the data can use the information in the error message to work out why the data is rejected and re-enter it, after correcting their mistake.

Good error messages:

- alert the user that something has gone wrong
- tell the user what has gone wrong
- if possible, give the user some information to help them to solve the problem.

A number of different types of validation checks can be added to an MS Access database table.

Some of the following validation checks could be used in the **MusicSchool.accdb** database.

Validation check	Description	Example
Presence check	Ensures that an important data item is not omitted	When making a booking in the **MusicSchool.accdb** database, all data items are completed and no essential field is left blank
Length check	Ensures that a data item has the correct number of characters	Student and tutor initials, instead of full names, are entered; a length check on both of these fields would ensure that one character only was entered
Range checks	Ensures that data is within an upper and lower limit	Students can be awarded grades 1–8 only; a range check would ensure that a value higher or lower than this could not be entered
Format checks	Ensures that data matches a fixed pattern	When entering a student's or tutor's surname, a format check would ensure that an uppercase letter is used at the beginning, followed by lowercase letters for the remaining characters
Type check	Ensures that data matches the data type assigned to a particular field	Fee payable must be entered in currency format, using the correct currency

Remember: While validation checks reduce the chance of errors when data is entered into a database, they cannot guarantee that the data is correct. Look at the following example.

bookingsTBL

SessionID	StudentInitial	StudentSurn	Stage	Instrument	CurrentGrac	SessionDate
1	S	Kahn	8	Drums	3	12 Jan
2	A	Amall	8	Guitar	4	12 Jan
3	S	Karr	8	Voice	4	13 Jan
4	R	Rageb	8	Drums	5	13 Jan
5	A	Essan	8	Voice	1	13 Jan
6	D	Amer	8	Guitar	6	14 Jan
7	A	Amall	8	Piano	2	15 Jan
8	M	Osman	8	Drums	2	15 Jan
9	A	Amall	8	Piano	-2	16 Jan

In the example extract of the **MusicSchool.accdb** database above, a new record was added for student A Amall. The student's current grade has been entered as -2. The number -2 is a valid number but this could not be a correct data entry for 'CurrentGrade' as music grades can be only positive numbers in the range 1 to 8.

Adding validation checks to the database helps to reduce the chance of **invalid data** being entered into the database, but may not rule it out completely.

KEYWORDS

validation: an automatic check to reduce the chance of errors being made when data is entered into a computer system

validation rule: a rule that specifies the characteristics of a valid data item in a database field

error message: information, hints or instructions to help a user resolve a problem

invalid data: data that does not comply with validation rules applied automatically by a computer application

condition: a set of rules to test a data item

validation text: a message displayed when the data a user enters under a field heading in a database does not match the validation rules for that field

DID YOU KNOW?

In MS Access, users are able to ignore the content of a lookup list and type their own data. It is always a good idea to add validation checks, even when a field has a lookup list!

DID YOU KNOW?

Data that is well validated is known as *clean data*. Organisations rely on clean data to make good decisions. For example, imagine that your school was trying to calculate which students should attend a reward trip at the end of the school year, but they were using data based on assessments that the students took two years ago!

Practise 1

MS Access uses validation rules to set **conditions** to test each data item that a user enters. Validation rules can be used in addition to lookup lists to reduce the chance of errors in data.

1 Open MS Access and **MusicSchool.accdb**.
2 Open **bookingsTBL** and view the table in Design view.
3 Follow the steps in the boxes below to add a selection of validation checks to **bookingsTBL** (presence check, length check, range check, format check and type check).

You add validation checks to fields in MS Access tables by using the validation rule and **validation text** properties.

DID YOU KNOW?

Some data types, such as Autonumber, do not support data validation. The database application enters data automatically into Autonumber fields, so validation is not required.

Practise 2

Presence check

Remember: A presence check ensures that a field cannot be left blank.

1 Select the StudentInitial field by clicking on it.
2 Scroll down to the General properties for this field.
3 Set the Validation Rule and Validation Text properties for the StudentInitial field as shown below.

General | Lookup

Field Size	1
Format	
Input Mask	
Caption	
Default Value	
Validation Rule	Is Not Null
Validation Text	Please enter a value from A-Z as the students initial
Required	No
Allow Zero Length	Yes
Indexed	No
Unicode Compression	Yes
IME Mode	No Control
IME Sentence Mode	None
Text Align	General

Is Not Null means 'is not blank'; this prevents the user from leaving this data item empty (or null).

This message appears if the user tries to add a new record without adding an initial for the student.

Text added here displays on screen to advise the user if the values they have entered do not pass the validation rule; this message should include some information to help the user to correct their mistake.

4 Repeat steps 1–3 to add the same validation rule and similar validation text to the field TutorInitial.
5 Test your validation rules by adding one more record to **bookingsTBL** (see below).

Tip: When adding the data, try to add StudentSurname before adding data to the StudentInitial field. The following message should appear.

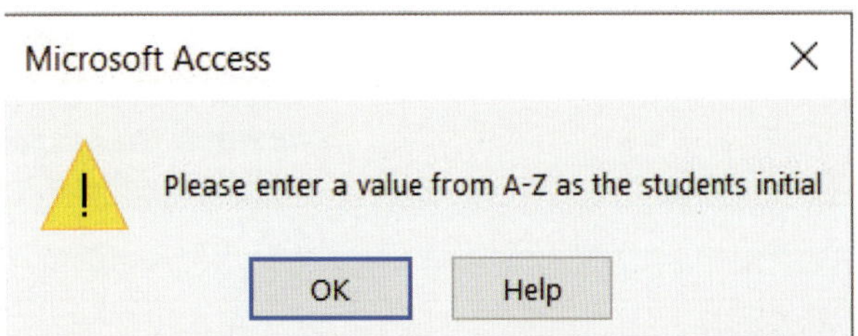

Session ID	Student Initial	Student Surname	Stage	Instrument	Current Grade	Session Date	Session Time	Lesson/ Exam	Tutor Initial	Tutor Surname	Online/ Inperson	Fee Payable	Fee Paid
10	S	Kahn	8	Drums	4	17 Jan	11:00	Lesson	U	Fouad	InPerson	$15.00	Y

6 Now try adding TutorSurname before you add TutorInitial. Does your error message appear?

DID YOU KNOW?

In the General properties for each field, there is an option to set a field to be a 'Required field'; this is the same as using Is Not Null. The advantage of using Is Not Null is that you can add your own error message to help the user to correct their error.

Practise 3

Length check

Remember: A length check ensures that the correct number of characters is entered into a field. This could be a minimum or maximum number of characters that is acceptable, or a precise number of characters that is required for that field.

You could use a length check to limit the data entered into some of the fields in the database, for example the StudentSurname field.

1 View **bookingsTBL** in Design view again and update the General properties of the StudentSurname field as shown.

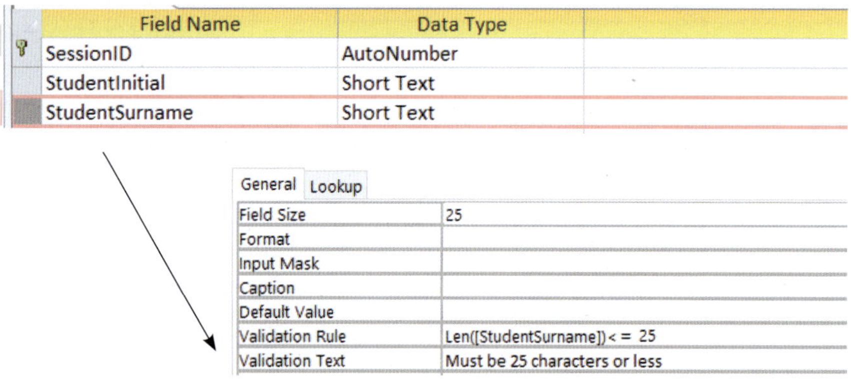

Field Name	Data Type
SessionID	AutoNumber
StudentInitial	Short Text
StudentSurname	Short Text

General | Lookup

Field Size	25
Format	
Input Mask	
Caption	
Default Value	
Validation Rule	Len([StudentSurname])< = 25
Validation Text	Must be 25 characters or less

2 Save your updated database and view the table in Datasheet view.

3 Test your validation rule by trying to edit one of the students' surnames so that it contains more than 25 characters. Does your error message appear?

Computational thinking – logic and evaluation

Recall the following operators and expressions.

Operator	Meaning	Check your understanding with this example – say whether the output from each statement is TRUE or FALSE, where A = 7, B = 10, C = 2 and D = FALSE
=	Equal to	A = C
>	Greater than	B > C
<	Less than	C < A
>=	Greater than or equal to	B >= C
<=	Less than or equal to	C <= A
<>	Not equal to	A <> B
AND	Both conditions must be TRUE for the output from a statement to be TRUE	A < B AND C < A
OR	Only one of two conditions must be TRUE for the output from a statement to be TRUE	A < B OR C < A
NOT	The output from a conditional statement is the opposite of the input	NOT D

Practise 4

Range check

Remember: A range check ensures that data entered into a database falls within specified values.

Look at two fields in **bookingsTBL** where you could add a range check.

- **Stage:** In this example, assume that students in Stages 7 to 11 can all take music lessons. This means that the only values that can be entered into this field are 7, 8, 9, 10, 11.
- **SessionDate:** Sessions cannot be booked for dates in the past, so any date entered into the field SessionDate must be either today's date or a date in the future.

Stage validation

1 Open **bookingsTBL** in Design view.
2 Edit the validation rule and validation text for Stage to read as shown below.

Make sure that you have formatted the Stage field to short integer before you add this validation check!

Validation rule	Between 7 And 11
Validation text	Stage must be between 7 and 11.

Between is a special function in MS Access. It takes an upper and lower limit and checks that any value entered into the field is between those two values.

3 Test your validation rule by trying to change one student's Stage to the following values.

Test value	Expected result
5	The error message should appear.
7	The user should be able to enter these values for the Stage.
9	
11	
15	The error message should appear.

Remember the original Stage value so that you can change it back again when you have finished your validation checks!

SessionDate validation

Some range checks rely on only one value. For example, when booking a session with a music tutor you would not book a session for a date in the past.

Make sure that you have formatted the SessionDate field to short date and time before you add this validation check!

MS Access allows the use of conditional statements with **conditional operators** when creating validation checks.

Now use some conditional expressions in your validation checks.

1 Open **bookingsTBL** in Design view.
2 Edit the validation rule and validation text for SessionDate as shown.

Validation rule	>=Date()
Validation text	Sessions cannot be booked for dates that occur in the past.

Date() is a special function in MS Access. It inserts today's date into a conditional statement.

In this statement, today's date is compared with the SessionDate that the user enters. An error message displays if the user enters a date that is before today's date.

3 Test your validation rule by adding a new booking for any of the existing students in the database. Try to add a SessionDate that occurs in the past.
4 Does your error message appear as expected?
5 Try adding today's date. The error message should not appear.
6 Now try adding a date in the future. The error message should not appear.

KEYWORD

conditional operator: symbol such as >, < and =; used to carry out comparisons between two values

DID YOU KNOW?

Computer programmers use range checks in the same way as you have done for the Stage validation. It is important to test the rules of the validation check using normal (correct) data (9), extreme data (7 and 11) and invalid data (5 and 15). Programmers predict what the output will be when each value is entered and then check that their program generates the results they expect.

Practise 5

Format check and type check

Remember: Type checks make sure that the user enters the correct type of data into a field, for example only digits are added to number fields or only text is added to a short text field. Format checks make sure that the data is entered in a specific pattern.

MS Access can use two methods of ensuring that users enter data in the correct format.

Method 1: Validation rules that accept only very specific data items

For example, students can book sessions that are classified as either 'Online' or 'InPerson'.

1 Open **bookingsTBL** in Design view.
2 Edit the validation rule and validation text for Online/InPerson? as shown below.

Validation rule	Online OR InPerson

You can enter the validation rule as it is shown here. MS Access automatically formats the rule to display as `"Online" Or "InPerson"`.

Note the use of the OR **Boolean operator**. The database now accepts only the words 'Online' or 'InPerson' as a value for this field.

Validation text	Please enter either Online or InPerson.

3 Test your validation rule by amending the values in this field for an existing booking, for example change a booking to 'On-line'.
4 Does your error message appear as expected?

Method 2: Input mask

A tool called an **input mask** implements both format checks and type checks in a database table.

Input masks use special characters to define the layout of a data item when a user enters it into a field. Some of these special characters are shown below.

Input mask character	Formatting rule
L	A–Z accepted; a letter must be entered
?	A–Z accepted; a letter may be entered (i.e. not all spaces have to be filled)
>	All characters after this symbol will be converted to uppercase
<	All characters after this symbol will be converted to lowercase

1 Open **bookingsTBL** in Design view.
2 Add an input mask to the field TutorSurname.
3 Select the TutorSurname field by clicking on it.
4 In General properties, click on the Input Mask row.
5 Enter the following input mask for the field.

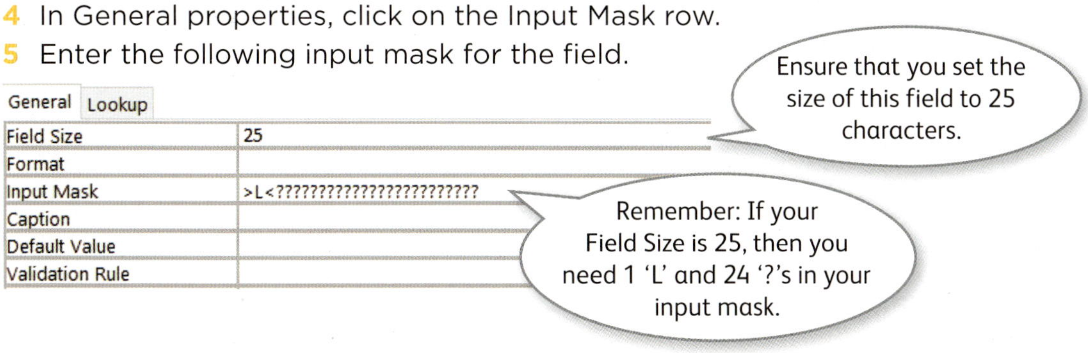

6 Test your input mask by opening **bookingsTBL** in Datasheet view and trying to make the following changes.

Changes to existing data in SessionID	Expected outcome
Try to change TutorSurname from 'Fouad' to 'fouad'	The surname automatically updates to Fouad with an uppercase 'F'
Try to change TutorSurname from 'Fouad' to 'FOUAD'	The surname automatically updates to Fouad with an uppercase 'F' and lowercase 'ouad'
Try to change TutorSurname from 'Fouad' to '1234'	The database should not accept numerical values
Try to change TutorSurname from 'Fouad' to a random set of 26 or more letters	The database should stop accepting letters after 25

KEYWORDS

Boolean operator: the three main Boolean operators are AND, OR and NOT

input mask: controls how data is entered into a database by defining a particular layout or format for the data

DID YOU KNOW?

MS Access does not provide a way for error messages to be displayed if data does not match the rules of an input mask. Database designers must therefore try to give users as much help as possible in the forms collecting the data. You will look at this in more detail in the next Learn box.

Collecting the data

Learn

Data-capture forms can be used to enter new data, **modify** existing data or even view the contents of an existing record in a database.

Data entered into a form is automatically stored under the correct field headings in the user's database (see the example below). This form collects details about individuals ordering cupcakes.

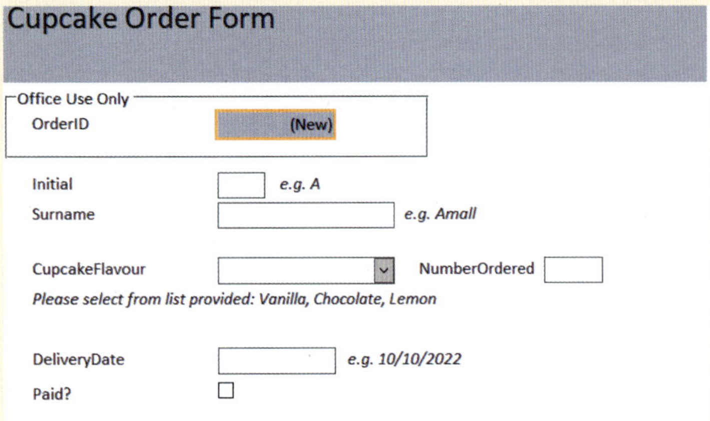

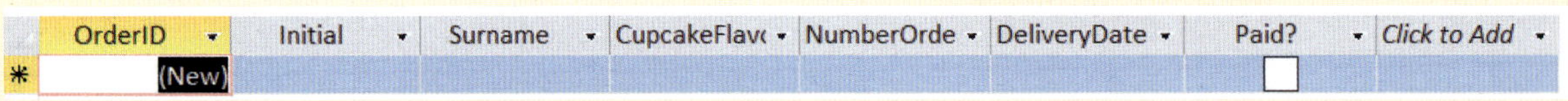

Data-capture forms can contain a number of different **elements**, including:

> The OrderID field in this form is linked to a primary key field, which is an autonumber data type. Discuss with your partner why this is shaded a different colour from the other text boxes and why it is labelled 'office use only'.

- labels that help the user to understand what information they need to add to the form and where, for example 'Initial', 'Surname'
- text boxes, for example the boxes beside 'Initial' and 'Surname', for users to type the data into
- dropdown lists, where the user can select from options, for example for Cupcake Flavour in the form above (dropdown lists are often linked to lookup lists such as the ones you created to help data entry for Lesson/Exam in the 'Databases: Getting the data structure right' Practise box)
- **radio buttons**/**check boxes**, for example beside 'Paid?' where the user can select from a number of options; this form element is often used with fields that collect data with a YES/NO (Boolean) data type.

Labels can be used in data-capture forms to provide the user with some additional instructions to help them to complete the form. Other form elements are often linked to a field in a database application. When the user has finished completing the form, the data recorded in each form element is inserted into the correct field in the database.

A well-designed data-capture form should:

- present the user with labels that help them to understand easily what data they need to enter into each section

- include **atomic field headings** to ensure that all the required data is collected
- provide examples and hints to help the user to complete the form and reduce the chance of them making mistakes
- provide options for the user to select from, where possible
- provide the user with correctly sized text boxes to help them to understand how much detail they are expected to provide for each field.

Practise

1 Use what you have learned about data-capture forms to design a data-capture form similar to the one in the Learn box above, but for the **bookingsTBL** in your **MusicSchool.accdb** database.

When you are designing your form:

- ensure that the user knows which fields they do not have to complete (for example, OrderID in the example from the Learn box)
- provide examples to help the user to complete fields that must be entered in a specific format
- provide details of the options for any dropdown lists
- include as many instructions as possible to help the user to avoid making mistakes (resulting in validation text displaying on screen)
- include each of the form elements shown in the Learn box:
  - labels describing the information required
  - text boxes for users to type the data into
  - dropdown lists of options
  - radio buttons/check boxes showing options.

2 When you have completed your form design, ask your partner to evaluate it alongside your **bookingsTBL** and the validations you have included.

a Ask your partner the following questions.
  - Have I included all the fields from **bookingsTBL** in my data-capture form?
  - Are my field labels clear and easy to understand?
  - Are the fields in the correct order in my data-capture form?
  - Have I included enough examples and instructions to help a user to complete the form correctly?
  - Do the text boxes match the field length of each field in my database?

b If your partner suggests any improvements to your form design, make changes with a different-coloured pen or pencil.

KEYWORDS

modify: update or change

form element: an object in an electronic data-capture form

radio buttons: a list of options on a form for the user to choose from; the user can select only one of the options available to them

check boxes: a list of options on a form for a user to choose from; the user can select multiple options

atomic field heading: a field heading that describes atomic data items in a database

linear search: searching for an item in a list by comparing each item in turn with the searched-for item

Computational thinking – algorithms

Primary key fields are an important part of any database table. The primary key identifies specific records in the data model. For example, if two people with the same name completed the form in the previous Learn box, the primary key would distinguish one customer from another. Many databases use tools such as the autonumber data type to assign values to primary key fields because the primary key field is so important.

Primary key fields are also useful when the user is searching a database. For example, in the database extract below, consider how easy it is to locate the details of booking number 10. When you know the value of the primary key field, it is easy to carry out a **linear search** of all the primary key fields by comparing the search value with each of the key fields in turn, until you locate the value that you are searching for.

bookingsTBL

SessionID	StudentInitial	StudentSurn	Stage	Instrument	CurrentGrac	SessionDate	SessionTime	Lesson/Exar
1	S	Kahn	8	Drums	3	12 Jan	09:00	Exam
2	A	Amall	8	Guitar	4	12 Jan	18:00	Exam
3	S	Karr	8	Voice	4	13 Jan	10:00	Lesson
4	R	Rageb	8	Drums	5	13 Jan	11:00	Exam
5	A	Essan	8	Voice	1	13 Jan	13:00	Lesson
6	D	Amer	8	Guitar	6	14 Jan	9:00	Lesson
7	A	Amall	8	Piano	2	15 Jan	20:00	Exam
8	M	Osman	8	Drums	2	15 Jan	9:00	Lesson
9	A	Amall	8	Piano	2	16 Jan	10:00	Lesson
10	S	Kahn	8	Drums	4	17 Jan	11:00	Lesson

1 What are the steps involved in a linear search?
2 Why is a linear search a suitable search method for this database example?
3 Discuss the disadvantage of using a linear search on a large database of information.

Data models and simulations

Learn

Data models are used to create models of real-life scenarios; they do this using individual data items (or attributes) to represent important factors in a real-life situation.

Once they have been developed, data models can be used to experiment with a real-life situation; this is called using the data model as a **simulation**. It is possible to do this when some of the data items in the model are linked in some way.

Advantages of data modelling and simulations

- It is safer and cheaper to interact with a model or simulation.
- It is easy to test a situation before it happens in real life.
- Businesses can use models and simulations to test products before they build them.
- It is possible to ask 'what-if' questions (see the next Learn box).

KEYWORDS

data model: a digital data representation of a real-life scenario; the scenario is broken down into individual attributes, which are represented as data items in the model

simulation: a computer program that represents a real-life scenario using formulae and can be used to predict outcomes

Some models use numbers, text and formulae to create a model of a real-life situation. Other models that use complex graphics and specialised **hardware** can be used to create simulations that mimic real life in a more realistic fashion:

- An **augmented-reality (AR)** simulation is where the user interacts with computer-generated images that are superimposed into the real-world environment. Interactions happen in real time and the user can interact with the graphic images as though they are real.

- **Virtual-reality (VR) simulations** provide the user with a completely **immersive**, **3D** interaction with another environment. Often the user needs to wear a special headset or gloves to allow them to interact with the simulation.

Augmented-reality and virtual-reality simulations have many uses in society today. These include:

- Gaming: AR and VR gaming applications are becoming very popular.
- Training: It is safer to train pilots and doctors, for example, in a simulated environment than in the real world, where errors could be dangerous for passengers and patients.
- Tourism: Travellers can explore a new location before they visit it in real life, or visit locations that may be too dangerous or expensive, for example the depths of the ocean or outer space.
- Education: Students are able to visit dangerous or unusual locations or, for example, experience a music recital in Carnegie Hall or the Sydney Opera House, without leaving their own home or school.

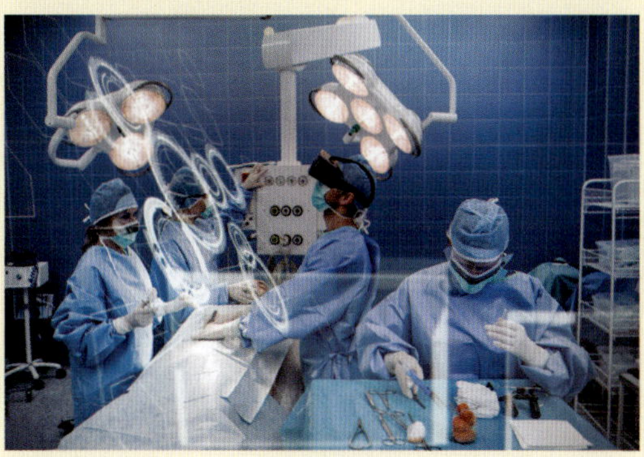

KEYWORDS

hardware: the physical parts of a computer that you can touch and see, e.g. the processor, storage devices, input devices, output devices

augmented-reality (AR): a simulation that superimposes digital images into the user's real-world environment and allows the user to interact with those images

virtual-reality (VR) simulation: a digital experience that allows the user to feel and interact with a digital world

immersive: a feeling of being physically present in a virtual world

3D image: an image that appears to have depth, as opposed to a flat printout; may be generated digitally and can sometimes be animated

Practise

1 Research online how businesses and other organisations use simulations and data models. For example, businesses can use data models such as databases to keep track of customers' orders. Include examples of businesses using AR simulations and VR simulations. For example, some shops allow customers to try products in their own homes using AR apps on their phones, while VR can allow **clients** to view a model of a new building as a walk-through using VR goggles.

2 Make a list of advantages and disadvantages of using AR and VR simulations to model a scenario.

3 In pairs, discuss the data that would be needed to model one of the following scenarios:
- the changes in weather in your town over a period of one month
- the details a SatNav needs to calculate a (walking) route from one location to another, for example from your home to your school, and how long your journey might take.

KEYWORD

client: the person a product is being developed for

What-if you ...?

Computational thinking – decomposition

So far in this unit, you have looked at how databases can be used to build a digital model of a situation. Spreadsheet applications can also be used to create a model of a real-life situation.

With spreadsheet applications, it is easy to create links between the different data items using mathematical formulae.

Your school is holding a cake sale to raise funds for charity.

With your partner, design a spreadsheet that the school could use to help them to keep track of how many of each flavour of cupcake they have sold, and how much profit they have made overall from the sale. The ingredients for each cupcake cost $0.20. The cupcakes are sold for $1.60 each.

Cupcake flavour	Number made
Vanilla	350
Strawberry	225
Chocolate	200
Lemon	120

Show the headings you need in your spreadsheet design. Include the data in each cell and show the formula you would need to calculate:

- the overall cost of producing each type of cupcake
- the income made from selling each flavour of cupcake
- the total cost of making all the cupcakes
- the income made from selling all the cupcakes
- the overall profit made from the sale of the cupcakes.

(Assume that all the cupcakes are sold at the cake sale.)

Learn

The spreadsheet below creates a model that represents all the students in a music class and their scores in assessments across the academic year.

	A	B	C	D	E	F	G	H	I	J
1			**Test 1**		**Test 2**		**Test 3**		**Average**	
2	**Student Initial**	**Student Surname**	**75**	**%**	**90**	**%**	**80**	**%**	**Score**	**%**
3	S	Kahn	68	91	75	83	77	96	**73**	**90**
4	A	Amall	70	93	78	87	80	100	**76**	**93**
5	S	Karr	69	92	89	99	58	73	**72**	**88**
6	R	Rageb	66	88	78	87	79	99	**74**	**91**
7	A	Essan	74	99	68	76	75	94	**72**	**89**
8	D	Amer	70	93	78	87	68	85	**72**	**88**
9	M	Osman	67	89	88	98	76	95	**77**	**94**
10			**Max %**	**99**	**Max %**	**99**	**Max %**	**100**		
11			**Min %**	**88**	**Min %**	**76**	**Min %**	**73**		
12										

The attributes in this model are linked using formulae. Formulae are used to calculate percentage (%) scores in each test, average scores, average percentage and maximum (max) and minimum (min) percentages in each test. By changing a formula in a spreadsheet model, you are changing the rules that control some of the factors in that model. By changing the value of some data items linked together using formulae, you can start to experiment with the data model to help you to make decisions. For example, what would happen in the model above if you changed S Kahn's score from 68 in Test 1 to 75? Some of the other cells in this model are linked to cell C3. If you change the contents of C3, the linked cells also update.

Changing data in a spreadsheet in this way to investigate the impact it will have on the output from the spreadsheet is known as **what-if analysis**. What-if analysis involves using current data and past experiences to investigate different scenarios using a data model.

What-if analysis is something you do regularly when you are making decisions. For example, suppose that you meet some friends for a day out and you need to decide what you are going to do. Friend 1 would like to go to an amusement park, Friend 2 would like to go to the cinema and you would like go out on your bike. When you calculate how much money you have as a group, you realise that you have $15.00 each, plus $5.00 for snacks. Biking will cost nothing; the cinema will cost $10.00 each before you purchase any snacks; and going to the amusement park will cost $20.00 each. You have to decide how you will spend your time and whether you have enough money to buy snacks based on these facts. What you are doing as you make your decision is an example of what-if analysis.

What-if analysis is important for organisations as it allows them to make decisions based on predictions. They can make predictions using current data and past experience, which they can use to create the rules that link data items together in the data model. By experimenting with the data in a model, it is possible to make predictions about how changing one input value can affect another one.

While data modelling and simulations are important tools for organisations as they make predictions about the future, remember that a model may not consider everything that can possibly happen in a scenario and sometimes the predictions can be inaccurate!

KEYWORD

what-if analysis: using current data and past experiences to investigate different scenarios using a data model; in a spreadsheet, this involves changing values in a cell to see how this will affect the outcome of formulae in the spreadsheet

Practise

Part 1

With your partner, discuss the formulae used in the spreadsheet in the Learn box on page 151.

In the Learn box, you saw how you can use a spreadsheet to model a real-life scenario. When a user makes changes to the input in a model to experiment with the data and the links between data items, the model becomes a *simulation*.

1 a Write down the formulae that have been used in cells D3, I3 and J3.
  b What do the terms *absolute cell referencing* and *relative cell referencing* mean? You may need to revisit Stage 7, Unit 4 to help you answer this question.
  c Which type of cell referencing will the formulae from question **a** use?
2 What would happen to the contents of cell E8 if D Amer's score in Test 2 increased from 78 to 82?
3 What other cells would be affected by this change?
4 Open MS Excel and open **Student Test Score.xlsx** provided by your teacher.
  a Examine the formulae in cells D3, I3 and J3 and compare these with your answers to question 1.

  The model you looked at in the Learn box uses formulae to create links between the data.
  b Make a list with your partner of any other cells in the spreadsheet **Student Test Score.xlsx** that are linked by a formula to cell C3.

Part 2

Now practise some what-if questioning using the file **Student Test Score.xlsx**.

Discuss with your partner how you can use your model to answer the following questions.

1 What if R Rageb scored 71 in Test 1 instead of 66?
  a What would their new percentage (%) be for Test 1?
  b What would their new Average Score and Average % be for all three tests?
2 What if A Essan obtained full marks in Test 2?
  a How would updating this score affect this student's Average Score and %?
  b How would it affect the contents of cell F10 on the spreadsheet?

The teacher realised that they made an error in assessing a question in Test 3. Each student's score out of 80 has now been reduced by 3.

3 Describe how this change affects other values in the model. You may want to take a screenshot of your model to help with this task. Use annotations to describe the changes to the model.

Changing the scenario

Learn

In the previous section, you carried out what-if analysis by changing values manually in your spreadsheet. This is fine if you want to make changes only once to the values in a spreadsheet model. In real life, however, organisations often use the same models many times. When this is the case, it is important they save the what-if values so that they can be applied in exactly the same way each time.

MS Excel provides a special tool that allows a user to create and save what-if models so that they can be used at a later stage.

Practise

Your teacher will provide you with a file called **Test Score Model.xlsx** to allow you to complete this task.

This model has been developed to include additional formulae to help the teacher work out:

- whether a student has passed or failed an assessment, based on a pass mark recorded in cells B15, B16 or B17
- the number of students who have passed Test 1, Test 2 and Test 3
- the average score in each of the three tests
- the number of tests each student obtained a pass mark in.

You may examine the formulae used in this model if you want to, but that is not necessary to complete this task.

1. Open your copy of **Test Score Model.xlsx**.
2. Click on the Data tab, and in the Forecast group click on What-if Analysis. From there, select Scenario Manager.

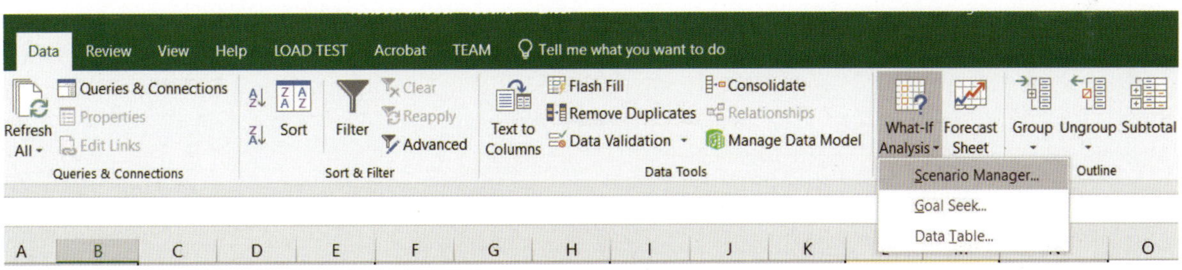

3. A new dialogue box called the 'Scenario Manager' will appear. Click on Add to create a new scenario.
4. Give the scenario a name, for example Test 1 % Pass 90, and click on the spreadsheet cell that you want to change the value of; in this case, B15. Click on OK.

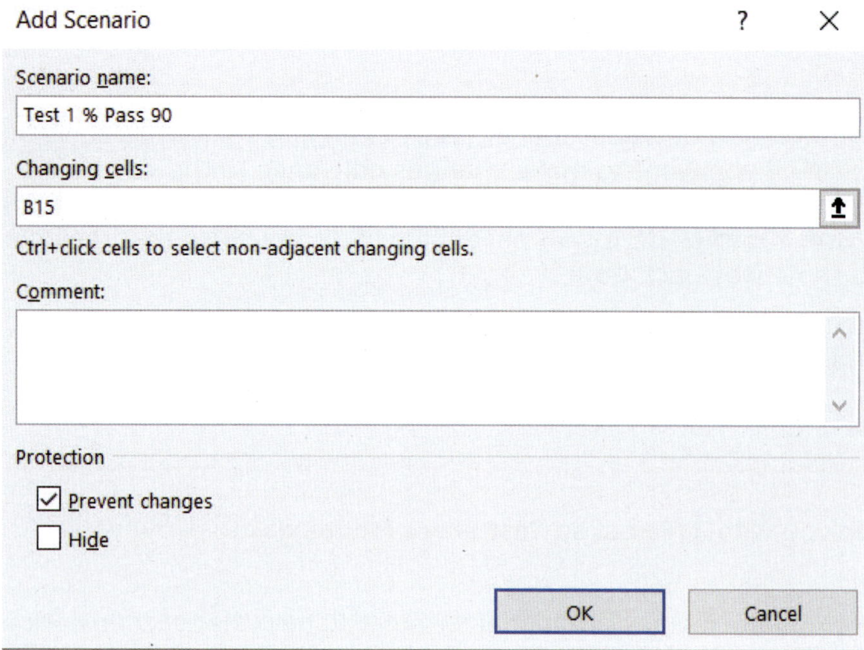

5 Change the content of cell B15 to 90.

6 Your new scenario should now appear in your Scenario Manager.

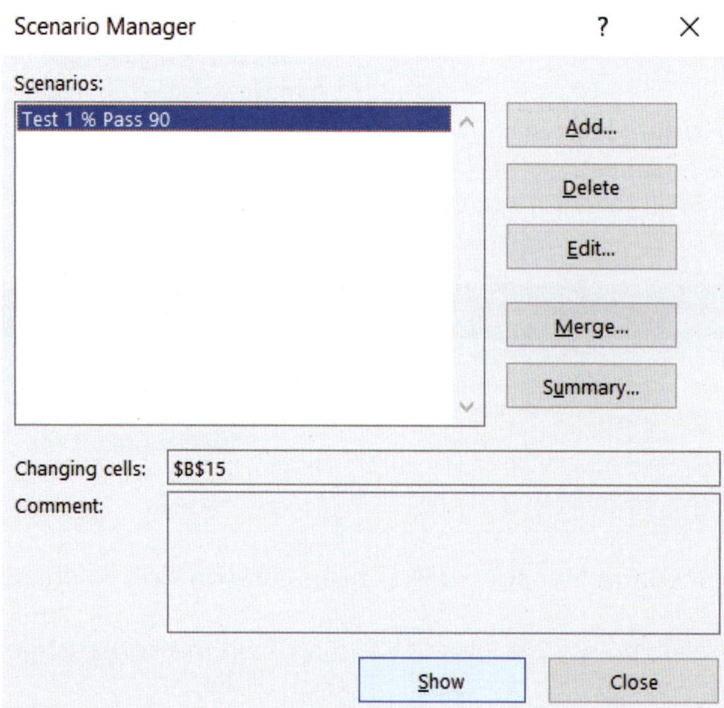

Click on the scenario and click on Show to see how this affects the contents of your data model.

7 Experiment with the model by running each scenario until you have a situation where all seven students have passed all three tests.

Go further

Databases

The 'Make no mistakes' section introduced you to the concept of data validation and input masks.

You have already added the following validation checks and input masks to your own version of **bookingsTBL** in **MusicSchool.accdb**.

- **StudentInitial** – presence check to ensure that this field is not left blank
- **StudentSurname** – length check to ensure that the user enters no more than 25 characters
- **Stage** – range check to ensure that the user enters a stage value between 7 and 11 only
- **SessionDate** – range check to ensure that the user does not try to book a session for a date that has occurred in the past
- **Online/InPerson?** – validation rule to ensure that only the values Online or InPerson are entered into this field
- **TutorSurname** – input mask to ensure that the tutor's surname is entered with an uppercase letter followed by lowercase letters only.

Do you remember using Len in the Practice panel on page 142 when adding a length check to a field in a database? Using an input mask is another way of ensuring that the user does not enter more characters than they should. The input max used with TutorSurname, for example, does not allow the user to enter any characters beyond those specified by the 'L' and the '?' symbols in the input mask.

1 Use what you have learned in the 'Make no mistakes' section to add some additional validation checks and input masks to the **bookingsTBL**, this time to a version of the database called **MusicSchoolGoFurther.accdb**, provided by your teacher.
  The following rules about the data for each field will help you.
  - Data must be entered for all fields when a booking is made.
  - StudentSurname should start with an uppercase letter.
  - The only instruments available are Guitar, Drums, Piano and Voice.
  - CurrentGrade can be only 1, 2, 3, 4, 5, 6, 7 or 8.
  - Only Lesson or Exam can be entered for Lesson/Exam?
  - Only one character should be entered for TutorInitial.
  - FeePayable must be between $15 and $20.

2 Create a **test plan** similar to the one below to plan the additional validation checks or input masks that you would like to add to your database and how you will test whether they are working correctly. Some examples have been completed for you.

Field name	Validation check/input mask	Testing
All fields	Set all fields to be a required field	Try entering a new record and not adding a StudentInitial, for example
StudentSurname	Input Mask – >L	Try to add a lowercase letter; it should automatically change to an uppercase letter

3 Now edit the table **bookingsTBL** in your copy of **MusicSchoolGoFurther.accdb** to include the validation checks and input masks that you have designed. Remember to test your validation checks and input masks as you add them.

Spreadsheets

Validation is an important element of any model. Spreadsheet applications also provide facilities for data validation. You can use data validation to help reduce the chance of the teacher making a mistake when they are entering student assessment scores.

Use your copy of **Test Score Model.xlsx** to complete the following data-validation tasks.

1 Open MS Excel and open **Test Score Model.xlsx**.

2 Highlight all the student scores (not their %) for Test 1.

3 Select the Data tab and then Data Validation.

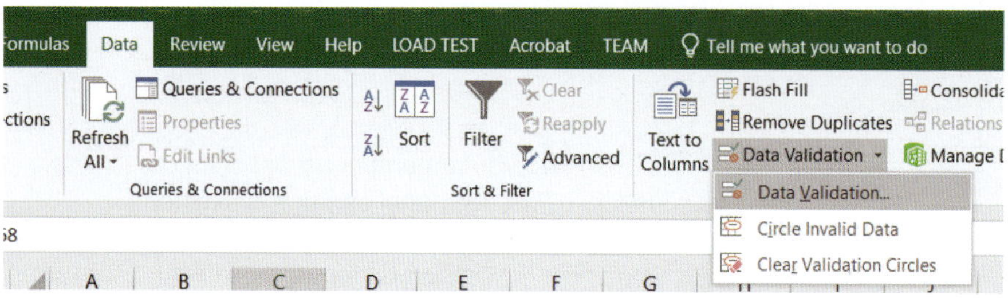

4 Add the following data validation rule by using the tabs 'Settings', then 'Input Message' and finally 'Error Alert'.

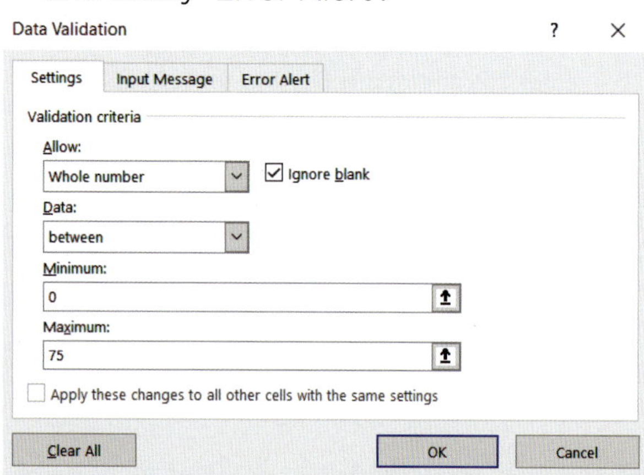

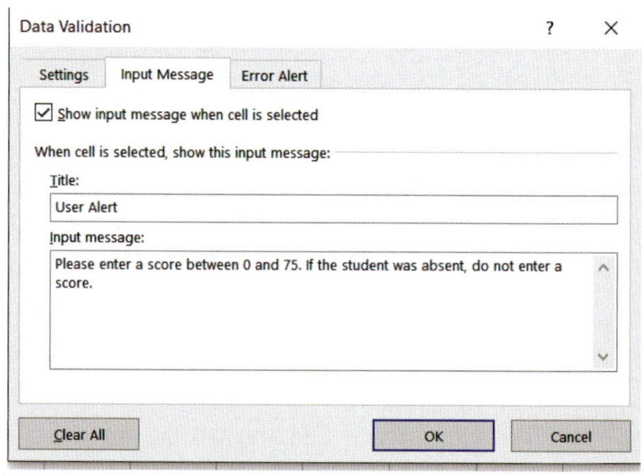

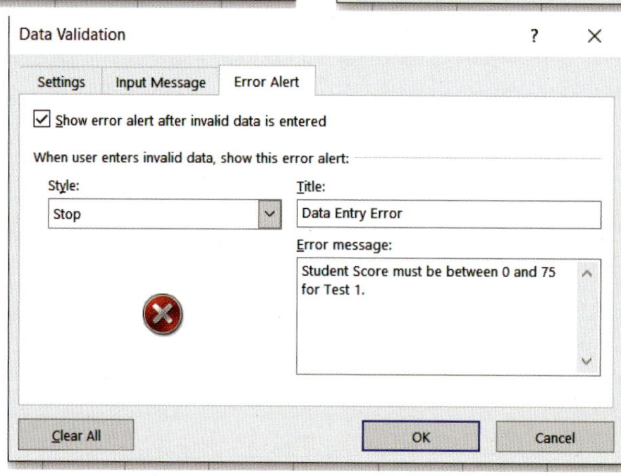

5 Now test your validation check by adding an incorrect result for student S Kahn, for example 900.

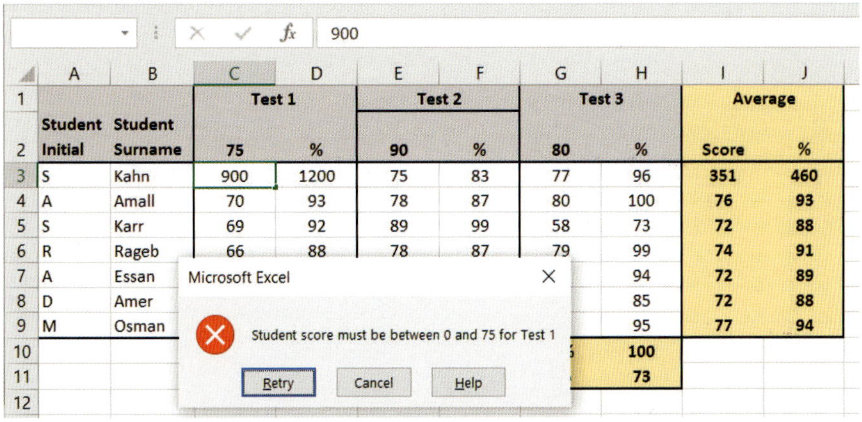

	A	B	C	D	E	F	G	H	I	J
1			Test 1		Test 2		Test 3		Average	
2	Student Initial	Student Surname	75	%	90	%	80	%	Score	%
3	S	Kahn	900	1200	75	83	77	96	351	460
4	A	Amall	70	93	78	87	80	100	76	93
5	S	Karr	69	92	89	99	58	73	72	88
6	R	Rageb	66	88	78	87	79	99	74	91
7	A	Essan						94	72	89
8	D	Amer						85	72	88
9	M	Osman						95	77	94
10								100		
11								73		
12										

6 Add similar validation checks for the student scores in Test 2 and Test 3. Remember to test your validation checks by entering an invalid value.

7 Save **Test Score Model.xlsx** and close MS Excel.

KEYWORD

test plan: a document that details the tests to be carried out when a program is complete and whether or not they are successful

Challenge yourself

Even if you do not set validation rules for a database field when you are creating the data table, MS Access will still allow you to validate data in the data-capture form that collects the data from the user.

You can do this using the same validation rules, but this time on an electronic data-capture form.

Your teacher will provide you with a file called **MusicSchoolChallengeYourself.accdb** to enable you to complete this task.

1 Open MS Access and open the file called **MusicSchoolChallengeYourself.accdb** provided by your teacher.

2 Double-click on the **database object** called **bookingsFRM**.

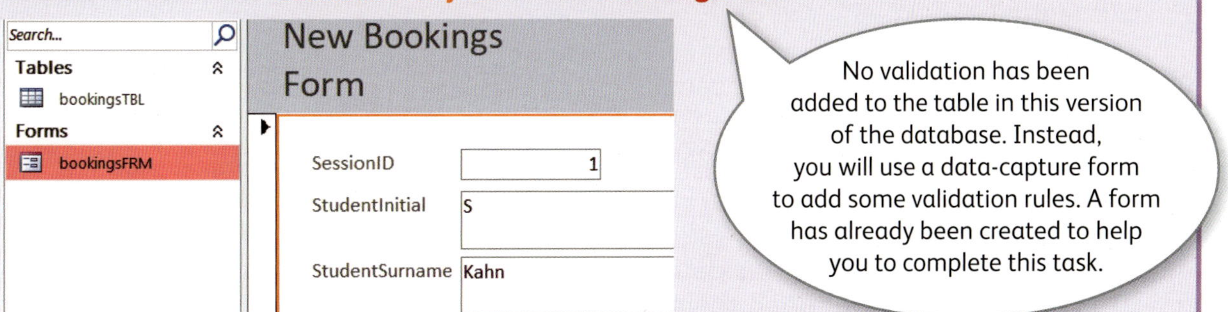

3 Open the form in Design view (in the same way as you would open a table in Design view). The form should look similar to the one on the next page.

The database form is made up of form labels and text boxes.

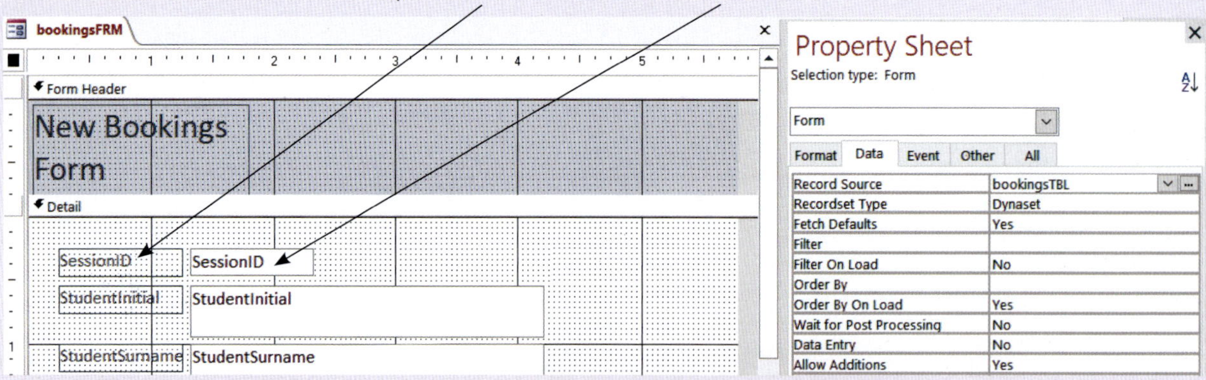

The form Property Sheet appears on the right-hand side of the screen. This means that the properties being displayed at the moment relate to the entire form.

- Form labels provide information that help the user to complete the form.
- Text boxes are usually linked to fields in a database table. Data entered into a text box will eventually be stored in a field in the database.

4 Click on the text box for the database field 'StudentInitial'. The Property panel for the StudentInitial text box should now be displayed.

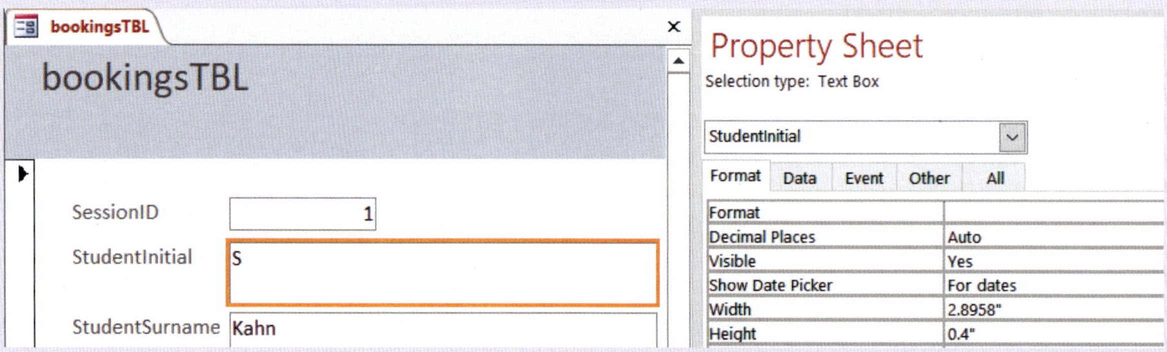

5 Notice also that you can add an 'Input Mask', a 'Validation Rule' and 'Validation Text'.

6 Refer back to the validation checks and input masks that you added to your original **MusicSchool.accdb** database. Try adding the >L input mask to the form for the StudentInitial field.

7 Switch from Design view to Form view and test your input mask by deleting the initial of the first student who appears in the form, S Kahn.
   - Try retyping the student's initial in lowercase.
   - What happens?
   - Is this similar to the way validation rules operated when you added them to the database table?

Remember to test each validation check after you have added it. With your partner, discuss and use an appropriate test data item to test each validation check.

> **KEYWORD**
> **database object:** a single item inside an MS Access database, e.g. a database table or a data-capture form

Final project

Part 1: Database

The music department are so pleased with the database that you have created to keep track of the students' bookings for examinations and lessons that they have now asked you to create a database to monitor ticket allocations for the school summer music festival. The head of the music department has provided the following information about the festival and ticket allocations.

- The festival runs over a series of three days.
- Parents can order tickets for any or all of the three days.
- Tickets are ordered using the student's name.
- Each student can order a maximum of four tickets for each day.
- Students must provide the name and telephone number of a parent or guardian when they purchase the tickets.

The school have already set up a basic database to keep track of ticket allocations. Part of this database is shown below.

Student Name	Stage	Day 1 (Num Tickets)	Day 2 (Num Tickets)	Day 3 (Num Tickets)	Contact Name	Telephone Number	Tickets Collected?	Date Collected
S Kahn	8	2	2	3	Samira Kahn	01056985654	Yes	13 May
Anand Amall	8	2		2	P Amall	01278654782	No	
Satya Karr	8		4	4	A Karr		Yes	15 May

The school have asked you to improve the design of their existing database system. They have also asked that you apply the following validations to the data. They are happy for you to add any others that you think are needed!

- Each student's Stage must be between 8 and 11.
- Add presence checks where possible to make sure that all important data is included in the database.
- The number of tickets purchased for each day must be between 1 and 4, but tickets do not need to be ordered for every day.
- The telephone number must be a mobile number, so it should be 11 digits long and it must start with 01.
- The DateCollected cannot be a date in the future.

1 Create a data dictionary similar to the one you completed in the Practise box for the 'Databases: Getting the data structure right' section at the start of this unit. In your data dictionary, show how you can improve the database design by including a primary key field and by making the field headings atomic.

Also develop your data dictionary to show what validation checks you will include in the updated database table. For example:

Field name	Data type	Field length	Validation check/input mask
BookingID (primary key field)	Autonumber		
StudentInitial	Short Text	1	>L

2 Your teacher will provide you with a copy of a file called **EventBooking.accdb**. Use the information in your data dictionary to update the design of the school's EventBooking database to:
- ensure that the correct data types and field lengths have been applied for each field
- include the validation checks that you have identified in your data dictionary.

Remember: If you are using a validation rule, you should include the validation rule and validation text in your data dictionary.

3 On paper, design a form to collect all the data in the database. On your form, show the location of each label and text box that will collect data. Include a range of instructions and hints to help the user to complete the form correctly.

Part 2: Spreadsheet

Part of the school's **initial data requirements** focused on the need for a data model that would allow them to keep track of a new scholarship system. The scholarship system offers students a discount on the fees they pay for music lessons. The higher the student's current grade, the higher the discount on their fees for each lesson.

The school have a small budget ($500.00) set aside to allow them to provide students with this discount. They have asked you to set up a spreadsheet model to work out how much discount they can offer students this year.

To help you to create the model, the school have provided you with the following information.

- Students will have one lesson per week for 35 weeks of the school year.
- The student's grade at the start of the academic year is used to calculate their discount level for the entire year.
- The head of the music department hopes to offer the following discounts:
  - Grades 1 to 4 = 5% discount on fees
  - Grades 5 to 8 = 10% discount on fees.

1 Open the file **Final Project.xlsx** provided by your teacher.

2 Edit the model to include details such as:
- a record of the number of lessons each student should have each year
- a validation check to ensure that the number entered in the 'Stage' column can be between the numbers 7 and 11 only

Remember: This will be the same for every student, so should this be saved once and accessed as an absolute cell reference, or should it be saved for every student?

- a formula to calculate the total fees each student will need to pay for the entire school year
- a method of working out how much discount each student should receive
- a formula to calculate the total discount each student should get each year
- a calculation to add up the total value of the discounts the school has paid to all students.

3 Use your model to compare the total value of the discounts the school has paid to all students with the budget available.

4 Use what-if questioning to work out in cell K2 how many lessons the music department could give a discount for before it goes over budget.

Can you remember how to use conditional formatting? Use conditional formatting to highlight this value in green if it is under budget and red if it is over budget.

Part 3: Modelling and simulation in school

Other departments are very keen to try to incorporate data modelling and simulations into their lessons. Some have also said that they are interested in using AR and VR in their lessons.

1 Write a short report to explain to the heads of department the differences between a data model and a simulation. Include the key features of a data model and a simulation in your report.

2 Use the internet to carry out additional research into how at least two other departments in the school could use AR and VR simulations to enhance learning.

KEYWORD

initial requirements: the idea and starting plan for a project

Evaluation

Part 1: Database

Swap databases with your partner.

1 Ask your partner to test the validation methods that you have included in your database table by trying to add a new record to your table that has as much invalid information as they can think of.

2 Ask your partner to make a note of the examples of invalid data that they were able to add into your database.

3 Update your validation checks to prevent this from happening again.
   a Use the feedback from your partner to evaluate the data-capture form you designed. Is there any additional advice that you could provide on the form to help someone using the database to understand exactly what data you need them to enter for each field?
   b Update the design of your data-capture form to take into consideration any new validation checks that you have added to your data table.

Part 2: Spreadsheet

Examine with your partner your spreadsheet solutions to Part 2 of the Final project.

1 Discuss how each of you met the requirements outlined in the Final project.
2 Where do your field headings or formulae differ?
3 Which approach do you think is better and why?

Part 3: Modelling and simulation in school

Discuss with your partner your recommendations for AR and VR simulations in school. Include the following in your discussion.

1 Are there any school subjects that you think would really benefit from the use of these types of simulations in the classroom? Why?
2 Are there any new subjects that you think the school could introduce into the curriculum if they had access to AR and VR simulations to support teaching and learning?

What can you do?

Read and review what you can do.

- ✔ I can explain the difference between a data model and a simulation and understand the key features of both.
- ✔ I can identify the data needed for a spreadsheet application.
- ✔ I can identify the data needed for a database application.
- ✔ I can design a data-capture form to collect the data for a model of a real-life scenario.
- ✔ I can create formulae in a spreadsheet application to make meaningful links between data items in a data model.
- ✔ I can explain and use formulae to investigate the links between the data items in a spreadsheet model.
- ✔ I can apply data validation to data in a spreadsheet application.
- ✔ I can add a range of validation methods, including input masks, to a database structure.
- ✔ I can evaluate the design of an existing database structure to ensure that it meets all the data requirements of a user modelling a real-life situation.
- ✔ I can evaluate the suitability of data that has been collected in a database model of a real-life scenario.
- ✔ I can use a spreadsheet model of a real-life system and what-if questioning techniques to make predictions and compare different scenarios.

Unit 8.6 Iterating through a solution: Software design and development

Get started!

Have you considered how to approach a project or programming task so that it flows from start to finish? Discuss with your partner:

- How do you normally start a new programming project?
- What planning do you do?
- When do you check for errors in your program?

Working on a project requires you to develop the initial idea through to the planning and development of the final program. This is a cycle of development that you will look at in detail throughout this unit.

You will see how to work through a project from start to finish in an effective way. You will develop your use of pseudocode to plan your algorithm and use your programming skills to create a quiz-based Python program.

Learning outcomes

In this unit, you will learn to:

- develop a Python program using an iterative process
- identify and explain the key characteristics of pseudocode
- follow and understand an algorithm presented as pseudocode
- explain and use the rules AND, OR and NOT to create logic within an algorithm
- follow flowcharts and pseudocode algorithms that use conditional statements
- predict the outcomes of algorithms that use pseudocode
- create a Python program that uses conditional statements
- create a program in Python that uses a range of different data types
- develop a Python program that uses rules involving AND, OR and NOT
- decompose a problem into smaller sub-problems to make it easier to solve
- explain what a program library is used for in Python and give an example of how libraries are used
- identify and use library functions in Python programs
- identify and describe the data types in a Python program
- develop and apply a test plan to ensure that a Python program or algorithm works correctly.

Warm up

In pairs, think about the stages you work though when creating any product. What is included in each of the stages? How do you know when you are ready to move on to the next stage?

Discuss a project that you have been involved with, for example writing a story, creating a working program or designing a poster. Consider how you worked through it from start to finish.

- How did you start the project?
- What was involved in the planning for the project?
- How did you create the final product?
- How did you know whether the final product was a success?
- How did you develop the product from the initial idea?

A good product will **evolve** as you work through its development, but does not lose sight of the initial idea. How can you ensure that you keep the requirements of the product in mind while you develop the solution?

KEYWORDS

evolving: changing and improving

iterative process: how a project develops throughout stages

SCENARIO

Quiz questions are integrated into a wide range of academic and social activities. You may have completed quiz questions in school, in a magazine, through a website or via social media. All quiz questions have correct and incorrect answers.

You will also have undertaken a wide range of projects throughout your education that require you to plan before you create. Following a clear process from start to finish is an essential tool to a product's success.

When creating a quiz program, you can develop program code in sections through an **iterative process** to ensure that the final program is the best it can be and free from errors. An iterative process is about continuously developing the idea as you work through both the algorithm and programming to develop it further.

Your challenge is to create a program for your local community to inform the user whether or not a specific item can be recycled. You will use a quiz-style program to ask three questions; once the user has answered all three questions, your program will tell them whether the item can be recycled. You will use an iterative process throughout the planning, development, testing and evaluation stages.

Do you remember?

Before starting this unit, you should be able to:
- ✔ follow an algorithm presented in pseudocode
- ✔ follow pseudocode algorithms that use conditional statements
- ✔ discuss how to develop a program in Python
- ✔ use a pseudocode algorithm to develop a program in Python
- ✔ develop programs in Python that use conditional statements.

In this unit, you will use the Python programming language.

Python's Integrated Development and Learning Environment (IDLE) provides features for creating, editing and running programs. Before using Python, you will need to install IDLE on your own personal device.

For more information about IDLE, see the 'Making choices' section in Unit 8.4.

1 Go to **www.python.org/downloads**
2 Select `Download Python`.
3 Once downloaded, double-click on the file to open it and then choose `Install Now`.
4 Once IDLE has installed, it should appear in your Start menu.

What is an iteration?

Learn

You have looked in previous units at a range of projects and have developed them from the initial plan through to **program** completion. How you approach and work through a project is important. The development needs to follow a clear process to allow you to make improvements and detect and fix errors. The whole process of development allows the final delivered program to meet the **initial requirements** of the project.

Waterfall model

One way to work through a project is called the **waterfall model**.

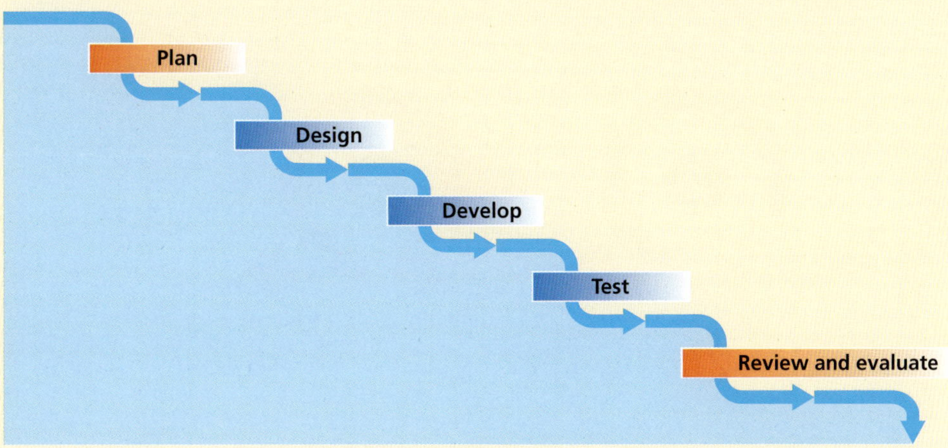

In a waterfall, water falls from the top down to the bottom. A waterfall model works in the same way: the project starts at the top and moves down each individual step in turn.

When a waterfall model is used, the **client** delivers the project requirements and then sees the final product only at the end of the process. They have little involvement throughout the process and so more time is spent on the planning stage before moving to development.

The waterfall model usually has the following stages.

- The **planning** stage involves gathering and understanding all the client's requirements. The project is broken down into its sub-tasks in a process known as **decomposition**, and the requirements for each of these sub-tasks are written down, along with timelines and success criteria.
- The **design** stage differs depending on the product being created. If an **interface** is required, this would usually be sketched out ready to be used when the creating starts. If program code is required, this is where the **algorithm** would be planned and represented as either a **flowchart** or **pseudocode**. The algorithm would be tested and there would be input from others to gain feedback and ideas for improvement.
- The **development** stage is when the product is created. If the product requires programming, this is the stage when it is written and developed.
- Throughout the **testing** stage, the product is checked and more feedback is gathered. If programming has been used, then this is checked for errors and a structured **test plan** with a range of test data is used to identify and fix any errors. The client and other users are involved in this stage to give feedback.
- **Reviewing** is a key area as, throughout the testing and feedback, the product is **evaluated** and improved before the final solution is launched. Once a product has been released, further improvements may be made.

Iterative process

Another way to approach a project is to follow an **iterative process**. This involves splitting the project into smaller sections, which are looked at in order of priority. There is reduced planning as the client is involved at the completion of each stage to help to refine and develop the project, and ensure that it stays on track and meets the requirements.

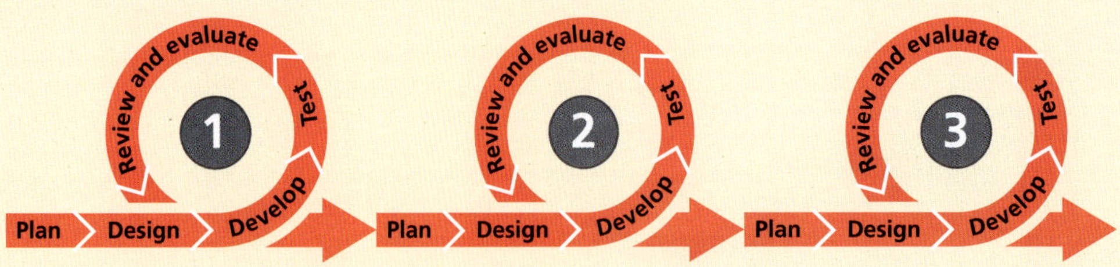

The diagram at the bottom of page 166 shows that the iterative process is made up of a number of cycles. **Iteration** means 'repetition'. The different stages of the project are developed in repeated sections.

The iterative process is also known as an **agile** approach, and each section is called a **sprint**. It allows the project to be developed and refined throughout the process to ensure that the final project is released on time and meets the initial requirements.

The iterative model usually has the following stages.

- The project has an initial **plan** that is put together from the requirements the client provides.
- The next step is to move into the **design** stage. Depending on the project, this could be a flowchart or pseudocode to plan the algorithm required.
- The **development** stage includes writing the program code to create the program.
- The **test** stage requires a test plan to check the functionality of the program, so as to identify and fix errors and ensure that it works as expected and meets the requirements.
- The **review** and **evaluation** stage is when other users check the program code and provide feedback. The client is also brought in to check that they are happy with this part of the product before the next part begins.

Once a section is complete, the project moves to the next section to start the cycle all over again.

Here is a comparison of the two project processes.

Waterfall process	Iterative process
• More time is spent on the planning stage before moving to development. • The client delivers the project details and then sees the final product at the end. • The project starts and moves down to the next step as each individual step is completed.	• The client is involved in each stage to help to refine and develop the product. • The process develops as the project does. • The project is split into smaller sections and the sections are looked at in order of priority.

KEYWORDS

program: the instructions that tell a computer system how to complete a task

initial requirements: the idea and starting plan for a project

client: the person a product is being developed for

decomposition: the process of breaking a problem down into smaller sub-problems to make it easier to solve

interface: how a user interacts with a product

algorithm: step-by-step instructions to solve a particular problem

flowchart: a visual representation of an algorithm

pseudocode: a textual representation of an algorithm

test plan: a document that details the tests to be carried out when a program is complete and whether or not they are successful

iteration/iterate: repetition/to repeat

Practise

1 Work in pairs to follow the iterative process throughout this task, with one student playing the part of the client and the other being the developer.
   a The client should think of a new style for a mobile phone and describe it to the developer. **Decompose** the different elements that you need to consider in the design of a mobile phone, for example:
      - the inputs, such as buttons (e.g. on/off and volume), microphone and camera
      - the outputs, such as screen and speaker
      - the overall size, shape and colour.
   b The developer needs to sketch out the design from this initial description and then present their initial design to the client.
   c The client should observe the development and offer feedback on areas that need adjusting to meet their requirements.
   d Continue this process until the client is happy with the requirements.
2 Discuss with your partner how the iterative process differs from the waterfall process.

Why iterative?

Learn

As you have seen in the previous section, the iterative process is about developing a project by breaking it down into smaller parts and working through each section in stages.

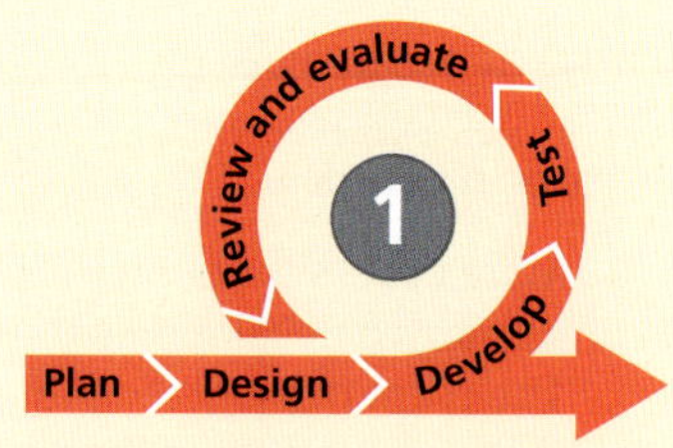

If you were developing the program code for a large project, you would break down the code you need to write into sections, and develop and test one section at a time before adding more to the program code. This makes it easier to find and fix errors as they occur, while developing a working program. If you test a small amount of code and find an error, you can usually fix it quickly and easily. If you complete the program and then discover an error, it may take longer to find and fix.

Look at how the iterative process can be applied to developing a new mobile-phone app. The client has given the following details.

> The app is going to be a resource for students learning to program in Python. The interface needs to use a font that looks like a programming language. The app needs to have a programming area where students can add the program code and another area to show the output when they run the program. There also needs to be a place where the user can see suggestions of Python code that they can use.

This initial outline can be broken down into three areas of focus: the **app layout**, the **programming interface** and the **glossary**. A glossary is an alphabetical list on a particular subject; here, it is used to list suggestions of Python code.

KEYWORDS

decompose: break down

glossary: an alphabetical list of words on a particular subject, like a dictionary

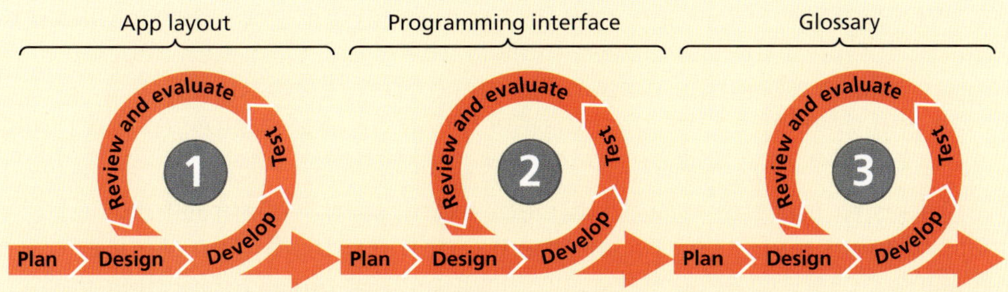

The first stage of the project is to create a design for the layout of the app, either as a sketch or by using shapes on drawing software.

When considering the app layout, developers may need to break this stage down further to consider the layout of the different screens needed for each part of the app. The table below outlines the iterations for developing the first screen of the app.

Design 1	Design 2	Design 3
The initial design may have only basic sections identified to help the client see the potential layout and where specific aspects are going to be positioned, without any images. There is some detail to allow the client to see the aim of each section.	The next design takes on board the feedback from the client and develops the layout. There may be more detail added to develop the design of the screen layout.	The next design again incorporates the feedback and develops the design further.
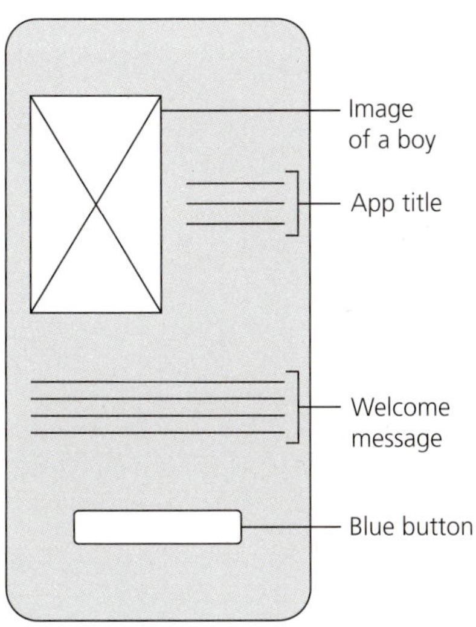		
Feedback from the client: *I like the layout but I need to be sure that it appeals to all genders. Could you use a character instead? The app is aimed at 8- to 12-year-olds. Could the colour be a neutral one?*	Feedback from the client: *I like the animals as they will appeal to all within the age range. The font works well but could there be more colour added to the design to attract the younger age range?*	Feedback from the client: *Happy with the design; like the colours, the layout and the characters.*

As you can see from the development of the very first screen layout, the client is refining their own ideas as well as those of the developer. Initially, the client wanted a neutral colour but then changed this to a brighter colour. The developer responded to the feedback at each stage and developed the design until the client was happy. At this point, they can move on to the next section and begin the iterative process again.

There are some advantages to this way of working. For example, the client is fully involved and the final product meets their requirements for the project. The client and the developer are working closely to ensure that no misunderstandings make their way into the design. The disadvantage is that the client's vision may change as the product develops, requiring more iterations to develop the product.

Advantages of iteration	Disadvantages of iteration
• Ideas are developed and are flexible to changes. • There is less chance of errors or misunderstandings. • Errors are detected and rectified quickly. • It can be a quicker process.	• There are fixed deadlines. • The client is involved throughout and gives regular feedback, which can slow down development. • The client's vision may change as the product develops.

The iterative process works well when a new product is being developed, especially one that uses new technology, as the client and developer need to work closely to find out what is possible. Developments in how new technology can be used can lead to innovative ideas.

Practise

Part 1

1. Using the information in the Learn box above, create your own infographic to explain the iterative process.
2. Annotate your diagram to describe the steps that are involved.
3. Discuss with your partner the advantages and disadvantages of an iterative process when applied to developing a new recipe to serve at school.

Part 2

A new company wants to create an app to keep track of people's contact details.

1. Discuss with your partner the different features that the app would need, for example storing the details of a new contact or searching for someone and identify the **data** it would need to store about each person.

KEYWORD

data: raw facts and figures

2 Work with your partner to design the layout of the screen to display the information for one contact. Use an iterative process, as described in the Learn box above, with one person describing what they would like the screen to look like and the other person creating and **modifying** the design.

3 Discuss with your partner the benefits of decomposing a large problem into smaller problems.

4 Discuss with your partner how you could use an iterative process to develop the rest of this app.

KEYWORDS

modify: update or change

conditional statement: a statement or expression that uses conditional operators and produces results that are either TRUE or FALSE

Analysis and requirements

Learn

When developing a program using an iterative process, there may be times when two developers can work on different sections at the same time. This can reduce the time it takes to develop the program.

If developers were creating a program for an eco quiz, there may be two different difficulty levels that could be split into separate tasks for two developers. An eco quiz would contain questions around environmental matters.

They would start by breaking down what is required for the program.

- The user needs to select a difficulty level.
- The choice the user makes determines the next section of the program to run.
- Each difficulty level will have a series of questions for the user to answer.
- Each question will have a set answer and the user will be told whether their answer is correct or incorrect.

From this, there are key areas that the developers can focus on and develop iteratively:

- a program to ask the user to select the difficulty level
- a set of questions for the easy level using **conditional statements**
- a set of questions for the difficult level using conditional statements.

This information can be used to create a visual structure of the quiz. The first step is to consider what comes first when the quiz is run.

1 The user is going to select a difficulty level from the menu.

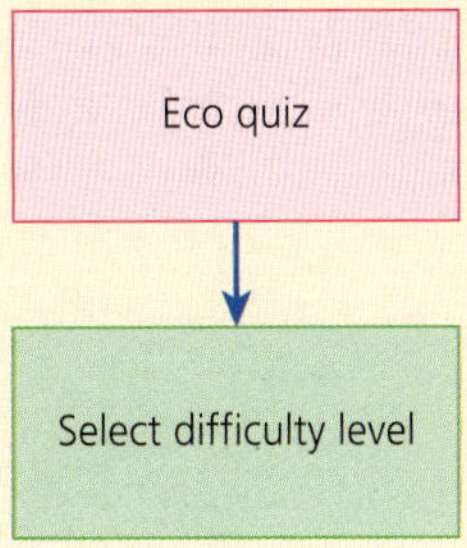

2 Next, consider what the two options are going to be: **easy** and **hard**. This can be demonstrated in the diagram as two pathways.

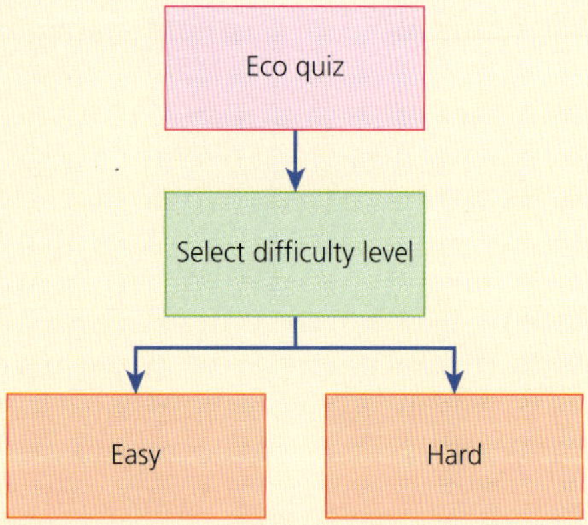

3 Finally, what will be available in each level? The set of questions for the user to answer.

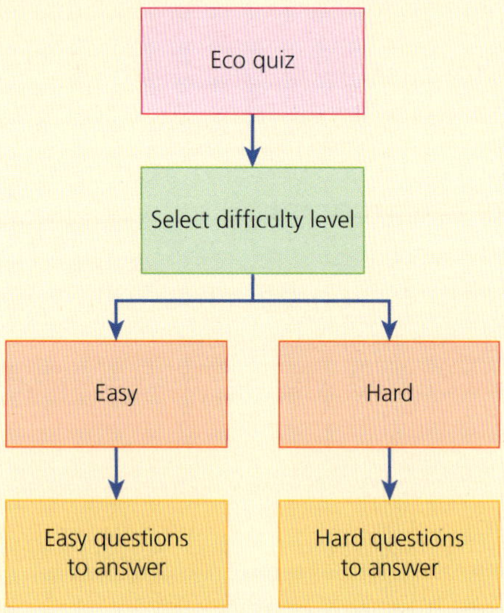

The structure diagram sets out the sub-tasks that need to be completed and how they relate to one another. This structure can be developed further to plan out each question, and identify what happens if the answer that the user provides is correct or incorrect.

Practise

You will now use the structure explained in the Learn box to plan out some questions for the eco quiz. In pairs, each person will plan a section of the program.

1. First, work with your partner to make a list of the requirements of the eco quiz program.
2. Decide who will plan the easy level and who will plan the hard level of the program.
3. Research and write up two environmental questions for the level you are planning; one question with a text answer and one with a numerical answer.
4. Plan the structure for each question and answer, using the diagrams in the Learn box as a template. Make sure that you include a message telling the user whether their answer is correct or incorrect.
5. Once you have created the structure, swap plans with the other developer and follow their structure. Check that the questions are suitable for the quiz and offer any feedback.
6. Act on feedback you receive from your partner, to develop and improve the structure.
7. What are the advantages of working in an iterative process with your partner? Discuss your thoughts.
8. How does decomposing a larger problem into smaller sections benefit the program development?

Design

Learn

As you have already seen, an algorithm (step-by-step instructions to solve a problem) can be represented visually using a flowchart or textually as pseudocode.

To recap the key characteristics of pseudocode: the main aim is for it to be precise so that it can be used as a clear plan to develop the program.

The pseudocode is usually laid out with one instruction per line and with a clear START and STOP to define the whole algorithm. Although pseudocode is not a programming language like Python, there are certain aspects that align with expectations in programming. For example, **variables** are **declared** at the top of both the program and the pseudocode.

```
START
score = 0
STOP
```

Another similarity with Python is the use of `PRINT`, which is sometimes used in pseudocode to define the output instead of `OUTPUT`.

```
START
score = 0
PRINT score
STOP
```

However, commas, colons, brackets and so on are not required when creating pseudocode.

To use a **conditional statement** in pseudocode, you define it follows.

```
IF set the condition THEN
   indent the output if true
ENDIF
```

```
START
score = 0
IF score > 10 THEN
    PRINT "You win"
ENDIF
STOP
```

The conditional statement here is: **if** the value stored in the variable 'score' is greater than 10. If this is TRUE, **then** output the message 'You win'. `ENDIF` is used to show the end of the use of **selection** in this section of the pseudocode, so the programmer knows to return to the continuation of the main program code.

There are different **data types** used in the example above. The use of quotation marks shows a **string** and the value **assigned** to the variable 'score' is an **integer** as it is a whole number. The output to the conditional statement is **Boolean** as it can be only one of two states: TRUE or FALSE.

The pseudocode is developed until the final algorithm is complete and is ready to be given to the programmer to write the program code and start a new iterative cycle.

Look at an example question for the eco quiz, and a plan of the algorithm for asking a question as both pseudocode and a flowchart. Question 1 of the quiz is going to be:

Is a long-term change in weather patterns a sign of climate change?

1 First, consider any variables that the program requires. There is going to be a score for each question that a user answers correctly.

   The score variable will have the name 'score', be an integer data type and be assigned the starting value of 0.

```
START
score = 0
STOP
```

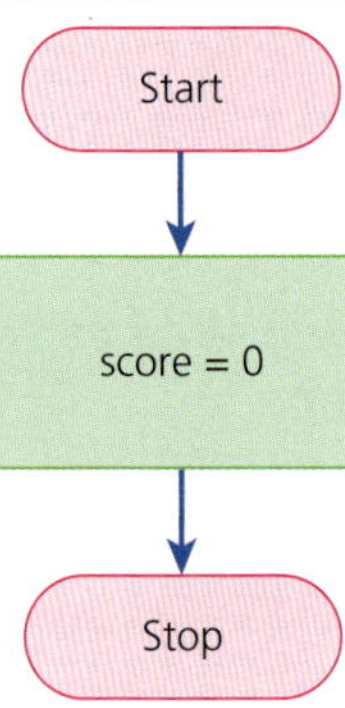

2 Next, the user needs to be asked the question and then input their answer, which must be stored in a variable.

The variable will have the name 'question1'. When an input function is used in Python, the answer is automatically stored as a string.

```
START
score = 0
question1 = INPUT "Is a long-term
change in weather patterns a sign
of climate change?"
STOP
```

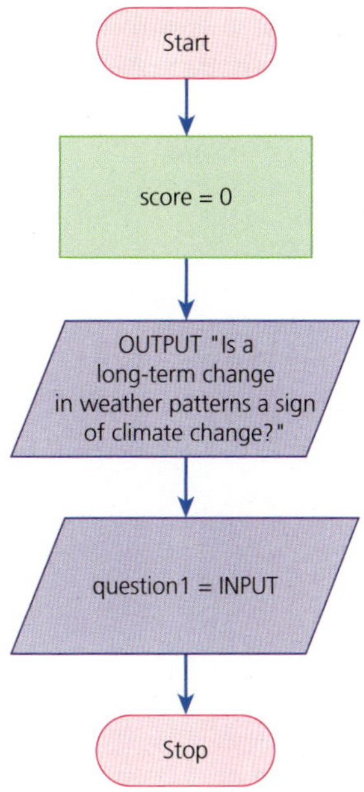

KEYWORDS

variable: a named temporary storage location within a program; it can hold one value and this value can be changed or used at any point in the program

declared: where a variable has been set up with its initial value

selection: a choice in a program that is based on a question; the answer determines the next instruction to be run

data type: the set type of data that is being stored, e.g. number, string, date

string: a sequence of characters that can be text, numbers or symbols; quotation marks around the characters define them as a string

assigned: giving a variable a value when it is created

integer: a whole number

Boolean: can store only one of two values: TRUE or FALSE

3 You now have the variables set, the question has been asked and the user has had the opportunity to input their answer. With the answer stored, you now need to test whether the answer is correct, using a conditional statement.

```
START
score = 0
question1 = INPUT "Is a long-
term change in weather patterns
a sign of climate change?"
IF question1 == "Yes" THEN
   PRINT "Correct"
ELSE
   PRINT "Incorrect"
ENDIF
STOP
```

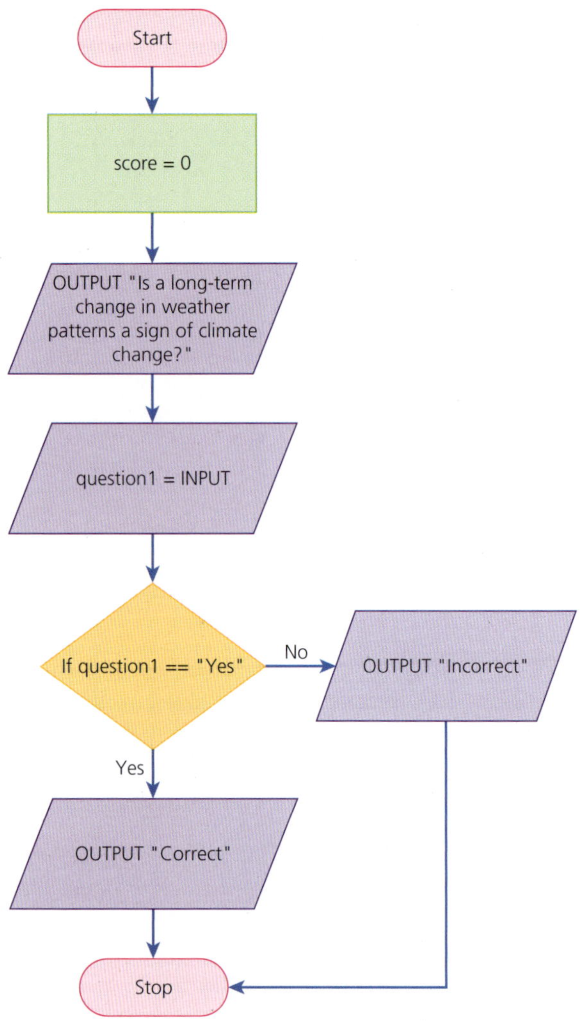

4 The final step is to incorporate the increase in the score if the user answers correctly. This needs to be part of the program that is followed if the **condition** is TRUE, so needs to be **indented** underneath in the pseudocode.

```
START
score = 0
question1 = INPUT "Is a long-
term change in weather patterns
a sign of climate change?"
IF question1 == "Yes" THEN
   PRINT "Correct"
   score = score + 1
   PRINT score
ELSE
   PRINT "Incorrect"
ENDIF
STOP
```

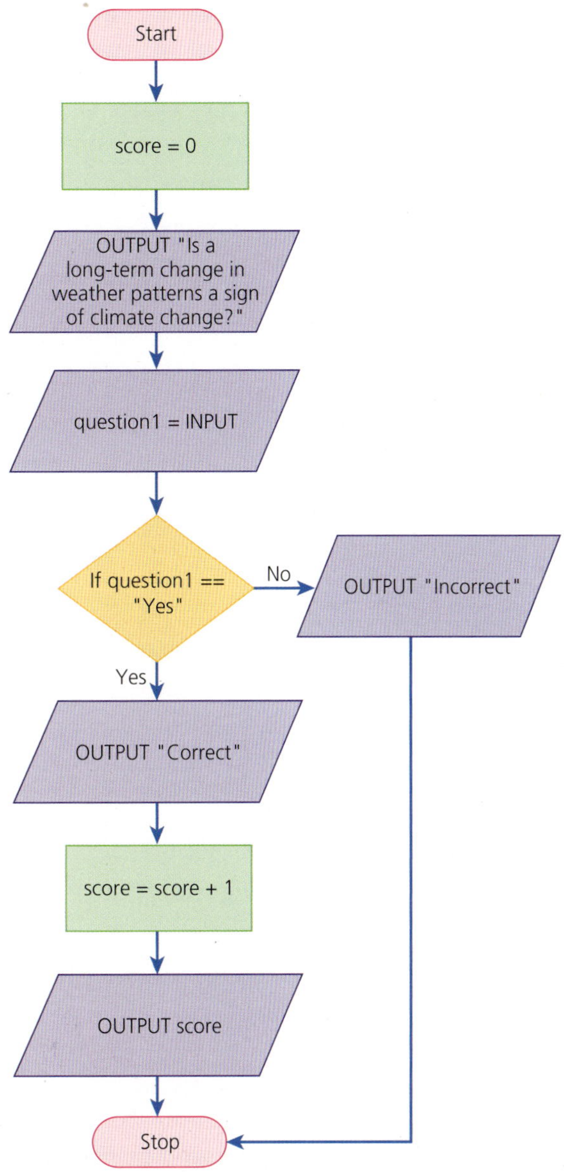

After each addition to the algorithm, whether as a flowchart or pseudocode, you need to check that it is correct. To do this, you need to follow the pseudocode or flowchart through from the start to the finish using a range of inputs to make sure that the program flow and outputs are correct. If you find any errors, you will need to correct them and check the algorithm again. Once this process is complete, your algorithm will be ready for you to pass to the programmer for the next stage.

For this algorithm, you may want to consider how the user will enter the correct answer. The conditional statement is looking for 'Yes' but the user may enter their response all in lowercase letters: 'yes'.

You can add this alternative correct answer to the algorithm to show the programmer what inputs to accept. This will require a **Boolean operator** to state that either of these inputs is acceptable to return the output 'Correct'. The correct Boolean operator to use is **OR**.

```
START
score = 0
question1 = INPUT "Is a long-
term change in weather patterns
a sign of climate change?"
IF question1 == "Yes" OR "yes"
THEN
   PRINT "Correct"
   score = score + 1
   PRINT score
ELSE
   PRINT "Incorrect"
ENDIF
STOP
```

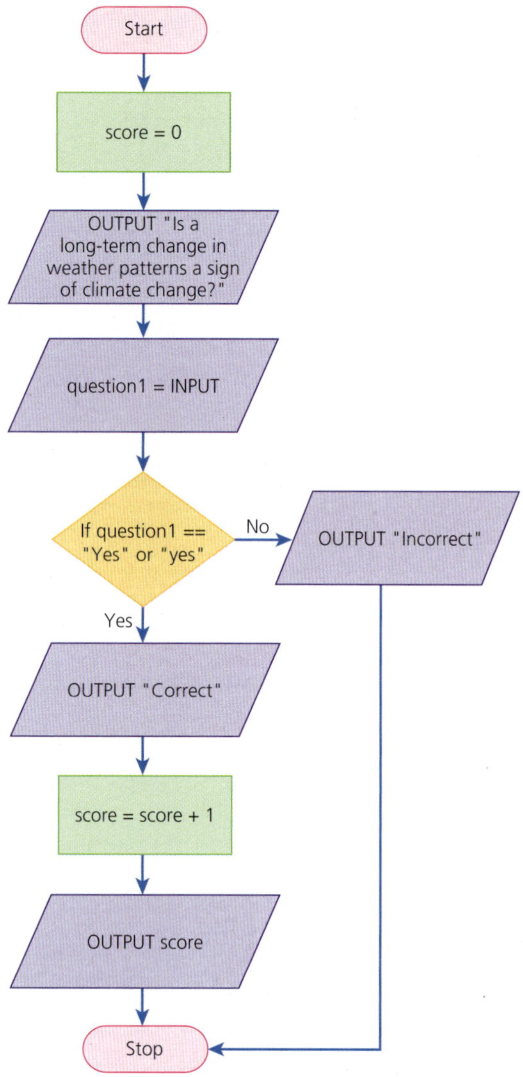

KEYWORDS

condition: the question that is asked to determine the next instruction in a program

indented: describes a line of code that has been moved away from the left-hand margin to represent the code that will run if a condition is met

Boolean operator: the three main Boolean operators are AND, OR and NOT

Practise

```
START
score = 0
OUTPUT "Q1: How long does it take for a plastic bottle to decompose, 200 or
450 years?"
question1 = INPUT
IF question1 == 450 OR "450 years" THEN
      OUTPUT "Correct"
      score = score + 1
      OUTPUT score
ELSE
      OUTPUT "Incorrect"
      OUTPUT score
ENDIF
OUTPUT "Q2: What percentage of drinks cans are made from aluminium?"
question2 = INPUT
IF question2 == 90 THEN
      OUTPUT "Correct"
      score = score + 1
      OUTPUT score
ELSE
      OUTPUT "Incorrect"
      OUTPUT score
ENDIF
STOP
```

1 Look at the pseudocode above. Discuss with your partner what this program will do.

2 Three users have answered the questions in this program.
   - User 1 answered the first question with the answer 450 and the second question with 80.
   - User 2 answered the first question with the answer 200 years and the second question with 100.
   - User 3 answered the first question with the answer 450 and the second question with 90.

   a What outputs will each of them see?

   b What will be their final scores?

3 Discuss with your partner what variables and data types are used in this pseudocode.

Variable representations

Learn

When starting to create a program, one aspect you need to consider is the use of variables. A variable is a temporary storage location within the program; it can hold one value and this value can be changed or used at any point in the program.

Recall that a variable is given a name and that a value is **assigned** to it using an equals sign (=).

The example below shows the variable 'name' with the value 'Sophie' assigned to it. The value has been placed in quotation marks to define it as a **string**. The variable is then called upon in the output by adding the 'name' variable to the output sentence.

```
name = "Sophie"
print("Hello",name)
```

You can see that, to use a variable in the output, you need to place a comma after the string, then follow it with the name of the variable.

Variables are used in many places in programs such as games. Considering the data type of variables is important. Look at an example of a game and where variables could be used within it. The image below shows a game where the main character must move through the setting and collect the coins and hearts.

The player has 0 coins or hearts at the start of the game. When the player's character moves over a coin or heart, they collect it and the value stored in the variable increases.

As you know, a variable stores a value that can be edited and used throughout the program. The name of the variable is essential, to make clear what it is storing.

Look at how variables are used in two example programs.

Program code 1

```
variable1 = 0
print("Is a long-term change in weather patterns a sign of climate change?")
variable2 = input("Y / N: ")
if variable2 == "Y" or variable2 == "y":
    print("Correct")
    variable1 = variable1 + 1
    print(variable1)
else:
    print("Incorrect")
```

'variable1' is not a sensible name; you would not know what it is storing or how to use it. Further through the program development, you would lose track of what you are using each variable for, especially when creating a program like a quiz that requires multiple variables.

Program code 2

```
score = 0
print("Is a long-term change in weather patterns a sign of climate change?")
question1 = input("Y / N: ")
if question1 == "Y" or question1 == "y":
    print("Correct")
    score = score + 1
    print(score)
else:
    print("Incorrect")
```

This program code is clear, and it is easy to know what each variable contains.

One way to check whether the program code is easy to understand is to ask another person to read through the program and ask them what they think the different variables contain.

How will you name the variables in your program?

So far, in the examples above, a string and an **integer** data type have been used. There are other data types that can be useful too.

Integer	A whole number
String	A sequence of characters that can be text, numbers or symbols; quotation marks around the characters define it as a string
Real/float	A number with a decimal point
Boolean	Can store only one of two values: TRUE or FALSE

A **Boolean** data type returns TRUE or FALSE. When you use conditional statements in selection, a TRUE, or FALSE outcome is generated, and if the comparison is TRUE, then the indented code below the condition will be run.

You do not usually see the Boolean outcome from the comparison when your program is run, but it is possible to print it out.

In the example below, the program asks the user to enter one value, which it stores in a variable called 'recycled', and another value, which it stores in a variable called 'rubbish'. The program then compares the two values and prints the output to the screen using the `print` function.

```
recycled = int(input("Enter number of recycled items: "))
rubbish = int(input("Enter number of non-recycled items: "))

print(recycled>rubbish)
```

If the values entered are `recycled = 5` and `rubbish = 2`, then the outcome you will see is TRUE, because the number of recycled items is greater than the number of rubbish items.

```
Enter number of recycled items: 5
Enter number of non-recycled items: 2
True
```

You can use Python to tell you the data type of a value stored in a variable. Using the code `print(type(recycled))` will tell the user the data type of the value stored in the variable 'recycled'.

```
recycled = int(input("Enter number of recycled items: "))
rubbish = int(input("Enter number of non-recycled items: "))

print(recycled>rubbish)
print(type(recycled))
print(type(rubbish))
```

```
Enter number of recycled items: 5
Enter number of non-recycled items: 2
True
<class 'int'>
<class 'int'>
```

A program can store a number as an integer or as a decimal number (a real/**float** number). In Python, this is referred to as a *floating-point number* or *float*. You can set an input to be stored as a real number in Python by adding `float` before the input, in the same way that you add `int` for an integer.

```
recycled = float(input("Enter number of recycled items: "))
rubbish = float(input("Enter number of non-recycled items: "))
```

It is important that you consider the data you will use throughout the development of a program. This can help to ensure that you use the correct data type. What data will you use for the Scenario at the start of this unit?

KEYWORDS

assigned: giving a variable a value when it is created

string: a sequence of characters that can be text, numbers or symbols; quotation marks around the characters define them as a string

integer: a whole number

Boolean: can store only one of two values: TRUE or FALSE

float: a number with a decimal point

Practise

1. Create a table with the headings 'Variable', 'What the variable is used for', 'Data type' and 'How will it change?'
2. Think about your eco quiz and make a list of the variables you might need and what they will be used for.
3. Add the data type that you will need to use for each of the variables.
4. Consider how the variable will change, and complete the last column defining how the content may change during the program.
5. Compare your list with your partner's and discuss similarities and differences.
6. Discuss with your partner where you may develop or use a Boolean data type.
7. Develop your list based on your findings.
8. How have you developed your list iteratively?

Development

Learn

You now have a plan for a section of the program for a quiz question. Next, you need to develop the algorithm into a Python program.

Use the pseudocode, which has been planned, to develop the program code.

1 Declare the variables at the start of the program.

Pseudocode	Python
START score = 0 STOP	score = 0

2 Set the question for the user, allow the user to answer and store the answer in a variable.

Pseudocode

```
START
score = 0
question1 = INPUT "Is a long-term change in weather patterns a sign of
climate change?"
STOP
```

Python

```
score = 0
question1 = input("Is a long-term change in weather patterns a sign of climate change? ")
```

3 When including a question for a user to answer, it is sensible to add a couple of spaces after the question but still within the quotation marks. This will display a space when the program is run before the user adds their answer.

With a space	`Is a long-term change in weather patterns a sign of climate change? Yes`
Without a space	`Is a long-term change in weather patterns a sign of climate change?Yes`

4 Add the conditional statement to compare the user's answer with the expected answer, making sure that you incorporate the different ways in which a user could enter their answer into the program code.
Ensure that the value stored in the variable 'score' increases by 1 when a user enters the answer correctly.

Pseudocode

```
START
score = 0
question1 = INPUT "Is a long-term change in weather patterns a sign of
climate change?"
IF question1 == "Yes" OR "yes" THEN
      PRINT "Correct"
      score = score + 1
      PRINT score
ELSE
      PRINT "Incorrect"
ENDIF
STOP
```

Python

```
score = 0
question1 = input("Is a long-term change in weather patterns a sign of climate change? ")
if question1 == "Yes" or question1 == "yes":
    print("Correct")
    score = score + 1
    print(score)
else:
    print("Incorrect")
```

Practise

1 Write the Python code for one of your questions. Save it as **EcoQuizV1.py**.
2 Discuss with your partner how you have considered the user's input in the question structure.
3 Discuss with your partner what variables and data types you have used.
4 Compare with your partner the different questions you have both written and how this has affected the variables and data types you have each used.
5 How did you work iteratively to develop the program code?

Testing

Learn

Testing is an important part of any program development. Once a section of the program has been written, it is tested. It is easier to find and fix errors in a small amount of code, rather than waiting until the whole program has been developed.

So far, you have seen the development of a section of the program code for one question of the eco quiz. To ensure that this section of the program works, you need a wide range of inputs to check that the program works as expected.

For example, the quiz-style question needs to consider the different ways in which a user can enter the correct answer to the question. If the answer is a yes/no type, then considering how the user may enter the word is part of the test data. This test data is used to create a test plan, which is used to test the program to make sure that it works correctly and gives the expected outputs.

Test	Test data	Expected outcome	Pass/fail
1	Yes	`"Correct"`	
2	yes	`"Correct"`	
3	YES	`"Correct"`	
4	Y	`"Correct"`	
5	y	`"Correct"`	

Practise

1 In pairs, discuss what makes a good test plan. Consider how the test plan for the eco quiz would develop as different questions are added.
2 Develop a test plan for **EcoQuizV1.py**. Use a range of test data to check that the program always gives the correct outputs.
3 Ask your partner to check your program using your test plan.

Review and evaluate

Learn

The testing on the eco quiz has been completed and this has shown areas that need to be addressed in the next iteration of development. In the previous section, the test plan highlighted that if the user enters 'Yes' or 'yes' then the outcome is correct. However, if the user enters 'Y', 'y' or 'YES', then the outcome is not as expected.

Reviewing and evaluating are important elements in any product development, and can follow on from testing. The tests are reviewed and evaluated individually to identify any improvements that need to be made, and lead into the next iterative cycle of development.

Test	Test data	Expected outcome	Pass/fail
1	Yes	"Correct"	Pass
2	yes	"Correct"	Pass
3	YES	"Correct"	Fail
4	Y	"Correct"	Fail
5	y	"Correct"	Fail

To correct the problems shown above, the easiest solution is to add extra detail to the question to explain to the user how to enter their response.

Python

```
score = 0
question1 = input("Is a long-term change in weather patterns a sign of climate change? Y / N ")
if question1 == "Y" or question1 == "y":
    print("Correct")
    score = score + 1
    print(score)
else:
    print("Incorrect")
```

Now the program asks the user to answer the question with a 'Y' or 'N' answer. The conditional statement can then be altered to accept the answer as either an upper or lowercase letter.

This is an example of using testing, reviewing and evaluating to find a potential error or problem in the code and editing the code to create a solution that works.

The program is then tested again to find any other errors. This time, when the program is run, the question is so long that it is spread over two lines. This makes it harder for the user to read.

```
Is a long-term change in weather patterns a sign of climate change? Y /
N
```

The way the program is output to the user is important. This part can be rewritten so that the question is an output using the `print` function and the answer options are displayed as part of the `input` prompt.

```
score = 0
print("Is a long-term change in weather patterns a sign of climate change?")
question1 = input("Y / N: ")
if question1 == "Y" or question1 == "y":
    print("Correct")
    score = score + 1
    print(score)
else:
    print("Incorrect")
```

```
Is a long-term change in weather patterns a sign of climate change?
Y / N:
```

Now, both the question and details of what the user can enter – 'Y' or 'N' – are clear.

The program is tested until no errors are detected and no areas of improvement are identified. The next stage in the review and evaluation stage is to check against the initial program requirements. It is important to refer back to the initial brief and to use this as a checklist to confirm that all areas are covered.

Practise

1 Look at the testing that you completed in the previous Practise box and identify areas for improvement from reviewing and evaluating the outcomes in the test plan.
2 Discuss with your partner the areas for improvement that you have identified by reviewing each other's programs.
3 Open **EcoQuizV1.py**. Develop your program to make any necessary improvements, and save it as a new iteration named **EcoQuizV2.py**.
4 Test your program again to make sure that it now works correctly.
5 Refer to the list of program requirements that you wrote for the eco quiz (for the Practise box in the 'Analysis and requirements' section) and identify which ones you have met.
6 Discuss with your partner where testing, reviewing and evaluating take place in an iterative process.

More questions

Learn

So far, you have followed the process of planning, designing, developing, testing and reviewing to write a program to ask one question for your eco quiz. The next cycle in the iterative process is to develop the program to incorporate more questions.

As this is a new cycle in the iterative process, you need to revisit all the stages.

1 Revisit the requirements of the program.
2 Develop the algorithm to show the flow for the next question.
3 Develop the program code for the next question.
4 Test the program using a structured test plan.
5 Review and evaluate the findings of the test plan and any feedback from others. Use this to identify areas for improvement.

Practise

1 Write a list of requirements for the second question of your eco quiz.
2 Create a structure diagram for your second quiz question to show what happens for correct and incorrect answers.
3 Open **EcoQuizV2.py** and develop the program code for your second eco quiz question. Save it as **EcoQuizV3.py**.
4 Develop a test plan for your second eco quiz question.
5 Swap programs with your partner and ask them to test your program using your test plan.
6 Review the feedback from your partner and identify any areas for improvement.
7 Open **EcoQuizV3.py** and make any changes or improvements that you and your partner have identified, and then save your file.
8 Test your program again to make sure that it works correctly and is complete.
9 Make sure that you have met all the requirements that you identified at the start of this Practise box.

Go further

Program libraries

When you start to write a program in Python, you can use a range of standard commands and in-built functions. If you want to expand the **library** of code that you have available, you have to import it so that you can use it. In real life, a library refers to a location that stores a wide range of books. In programming, a library stores a range of extra programming commands that you can use, all linked to the title of the library.

A popular Python library is 'time'. The command `time.sleep()` pauses the program for a set amount of time before continuing to the next line in the code.

The amount of time to wait is defined in the brackets.

`time.sleep(1)`	Delays the next instruction by 1 second
`time.sleep(2)`	Delays the next instruction by 2 seconds
`time.sleep(5)`	Delays the next instruction by 5 seconds

You can use this type of program code to create a countdown. The pseudocode for the program is shown below.

```
START
OUTPUT "Countdown 3 to 1"
OUTPUT "3"
wait one second
OUTPUT "2"
wait one second
```

```
OUTPUT "1"

wait one second

OUTPUT "Go"

STOP
```

1 Use this pseudocode to create a countdown program in Python.
   - What data types will you need?
   - Import the 'time' library.
   - Use `time.sleep()` to add a pause between each number in the countdown.

2 Discuss with your partner:
   - how you could test the program to check for errors and make sure that the time delay is correct
   - how you could develop the program.

KEYWORD

library: an additional set of functions that can be imported into a Python program

Challenge yourself

Another example of a Python library is 'random', which adds code so that the program can use randomly generated values.

The program code below will generate a random integer between 1 and 10.

```
import random
number = random.randint(1,10)
print(number)
```

It is also possible to generate a random decimal number between 0 and 1 using `random.random()`.

```
import random
number = random.random()
print(number)
```

```
0.13515642125016847
```

The number can be rounded to a number of decimal places using the `round` function. In the program below, 'number' is rounded to two decimal places.

```
import random
number = random.random()
print(number)
number = round(number,2)
print(number)
```

When the program is run, it outputs the random decimal number followed by the rounded number.

```
0.13515642125016847
0.14
```

1 Open a new Python program file and copy and edit the code above to write a program that generates a random decimal number and then rounds the number to one decimal place.
2 Add to your code to allow the user to guess the number and assign the input to a variable. Make sure that you use the correct data type for storing the input.
3 Add a conditional statement to check whether the guess matches the rounded number, and output appropriate feedback if it does.
4 Add another conditional statement to see whether the guess is larger than the rounded number, and output appropriate feedback if the guess is larger.
5 Add appropriate feedback if the guess is smaller than the rounded number.
6 Test your program to check that it works correctly.

Final project

The skills you have learned in this unit are all about developing a project iteratively from the planning stage through to the final product. You have learned about the use of an iterative process to develop a section of a program through planning, designing, developing, testing and reviewing/evaluating the program code. You have looked at the importance of testing to ensure that errors are detected early on in smaller sections of code instead of in a large complete program. You have developed the use of data types, conditional statements, variables and program libraries.

You are going to create your own program for the local community to decide whether or not a specific item can be recycled.

Plan

1 Reread the Scenario from the start of the unit.
2 Decompose the problem and write a list of the program's requirements.

Design

Base the program code on the following pseudocode algorithm.

```
START
recycle = FALSE
OUTPUT Question1
question1 = INPUT
IF <condition1> THEN
      recycle = True
ENDIF
OUTPUT Question2
question2 = INPUT
IF <condition2> THEN
      recycle = True
ENDIF
OUTPUT Question3
question3 = INPUT
IF <condition3> THEN
      recycle = True
ENDIF
IF recycle == True THEN
      OUTPUT "Your item can be recycled"
ELSE
      OUTPUT "Your item cannot be
recycled"
ENDIF
STOP
```

3 Identify the important characteristics of this pseudocode.

4 Explain what will be output at the end of the program if none of the conditions is met.

5 Complete the first two columns of the table below to plan three questions that your program needs to ask to find out whether an item is suitable for recycling, for example the type of material it is made from or whether it has a recycling logo on the packaging.

Question	Answer if suitable for recycling	Conditional statement to be used in program	Reason for using any Boolean operator

6 Complete the rest of the table to plan the conditional statements that you will use in your program, making sure that you use suitable conditional operators. Add a comment to explain why any Boolean operator that you use is needed.

7 Create a table to list the variables that you are going to need in your program. Ensure that you have chosen suitable names and make a note of the data types that you will need to use for each one.

Develop

8 Open a new Python program file and develop the program code for your first question, making sure that it follows the pseudocode algorithm on page 192.

9 Save your program as **FinalProjectV1.py**.

Test

10 Create a test plan, using a range of suitable data to test your program.

11 Use your test plan to check that your program works correctly, and document the outcomes of a range of test data.

Review and evaluate

12 Make any necessary adjustments to your program based on the testing, and resave your program.

13 Check that your program meets all the design requirements for the first question.

Iteration 2

14 Check the requirements for the second question and begin the second development iteration to add the code for the second question. Save your program as **FinalProjectV2.py**.

15 Create a test plan and use it to check that your new code works correctly.

16 Correct any problems, and review and evaluate your program to make sure that it meets the requirements.

Iteration 3

17 Check the requirements for the third question and begin the third development iteration to add the code for the third question. Save your program as **FinalProjectV3.py**.

18 Create a test plan and use it to check that your new code works correctly.

19 Correct any problems and review and evaluate your program, to make sure that it meets the requirements.

Iteration 4

20 Check the requirements for giving feedback on whether the item can be recycled.

21 Add the final outputs to your program to give feedback to the user.

22 Using the 'time' library, add a pause in between each question. Save your program as **FinalProjectV4.py**.

23 Create a test plan and use it to check that your new code works correctly.

24 Review your program to make sure that it meets all the program requirements identified in the original planning stage.

Evaluation

1 Swap programs with your partner and test their program. Comment on the following.
   - Does it cover all the requirements?
   - Is the solution easy to use?
   - Are the questions suitable?
   - Do the inputs work as expected?
   - Does the program generate a suitable output to tell the user whether the item can be recycled?
   - Are the variables clear to understand?
   - What extra features has your partner added, such as Python libraries, and what impact does this have on the final program?

2 Now open your own program and look at the code. Reflect on what you could improve in your own program.

3 Based on your partner's feedback and your own evaluation, make a list of recommendations to improve your final program.

What can you do?

Read and review what you can do.

- ✔ I can develop a Python program using an iterative process.
- ✔ I can identify and explain the key characteristics of pseudocode.
- ✔ I can follow and understand an algorithm presented as pseudocode.
- ✔ I can explain and use the rules AND, OR and NOT to create logic within an algorithm.
- ✔ I can follow flowcharts and pseudocode algorithms that use conditional statements.
- ✔ I can predict the outcome of algorithms that use pseudocode.
- ✔ I can create a Python program that uses conditional statements.
- ✔ I can create a program in Python that uses a range of different data types.
- ✔ I can develop a Python program that uses rules involving AND, OR and NOT.
- ✔ I can decompose a problem into smaller sub-problems to make it easier to solve.
- ✔ I can explain what a program library is used for in Python and give an example of how libraries are used.
- ✔ I can identify and use library functions in Python programs.
- ✔ I can identify and describe the data types in a Python program.
- ✔ I can develop and apply a test plan to ensure that a Python program or algorithm works correctly.

Glossary

3D image: an image that appears to have depth, as opposed to a flat printout; may be generated digitally and can sometimes be animated

adware: a type of spyware that increases the number of adverts a user has on their computer system, often displaying adverts as banners or pop-ups inside software and sometimes enticing users to click on links to insecure or malicious websites or downloads

algorithm: step-by-step instructions to solve a particular problem

anti-spyware: software that detects and removes spyware from a computer

antivirus: software that detects and removes viruses from a computer

applications software: the software that users access to carry out tasks

artificial intelligence (AI): the study of machines and algorithms designed to carry out tasks in a way that is similar to humans

ASCII (American Standard Code for Information Interchange): a 7-bit binary code that represents all the keys on a standard keyboard

assigned: giving a variable a value when it is created

atomic data structure: a data structure where the data items are broken down into the smallest unit possible

atomic field heading: a field heading that describes atomic data items in a database

augmented reality (AR): a simulation that superimposes digital images on the user's real-world environment and allows the user to interact with those images

augmented-reality (AR) glasses: glasses or goggles that add information, normally in the form of 3D images or videos, to the user's real-world environment by placing a computer-generated image over the user's real-world image viewed through the glasses

authenticate: allowing a computer or a human to verify that the user is who they say they are

autonomous programming: computer hardware and complex AI software working together to solve a problem without any human interaction

bandwidth: a measure of the maximum number of bits that can be transmitted over a network or cable in a specified amount of time

base 10: another term for the 'denary number system' as it is based on 10 digits

binary: the number system that uses just two digits: 0 and 1; also known as 'base 2'

binary number format: using 1s and 0s to represent numbers

bit flip: when a single bit changes from 0 to 1, or 1 to 0, during transmission

Bluetooth: a wireless technology that allows data transmission using radio waves

Boolean: can store only one of two values: TRUE or FALSE

Boolean operator: the three main Boolean operators are AND, OR and NOT

boot-up program: the program that locates the computer's operating system in secondary storage and loads it into RAM so that the processor can provide the user with a way of using the digital device; another name for this program is the 'BIOS' (Basic Input/Output System)

brute-force attack: a type of cyber-attack that uses a dictionary to try to discover passwords automatically

budget: a particular amount of money set aside for a task, department or organisation

character set: all the letters, numbers, punctuation symbols and special symbols that can be represented on a device

check boxes: a list of options on a form for a user to choose from; the user can select multiple options

circuit board: a small board with electrical circuits attached

client: the person a product is being developed for; or a computer device that requests access to a service that a server provides

combinational logic: logic circuits made up of more than one logic gate

compression: reducing the size of a file by removing some data items

condition: the question that is asked to determine the next instruction in a program; or a set of rules to test a data item

conditional operator: symbol such as >, < and =; used to carry out comparisons between two values

conditional statement: a statement or expression that uses conditional operators and produces results that are either TRUE or FALSE

constant: a named place in memory that stores a value that does not change while the program is running

cyber-attack: the collective name for all types of attacks on a computer or computer network

data: raw facts and figures

database: an application that is used to organise data that can then be stored, processed and accessed electronically

database object: a single item inside an MS Access database, e.g. a database table or a data-capture form

data-capture form: a predefined document (electronic or paper based) that contains headings and instructions to collect appropriate data for a specific purpose

data dictionary: a table that outlines the field headings, data types and other key features of each of the fields

data item: a single piece of data

data model: a digital data representation of a real-life scenario; the scenario is broken down into individual attributes, which are represented as data items in the model

data requirements: a list of the data items required to produce an accurate model or simulation of a real-life scenario

data set: a collection of data items that are all related

data-transmission time: the amount of time from the beginning to the end of a message being sent

data type: the set type of data that is being stored, e.g. number, string, date

debugging: finding and fixing errors

declared: where a variable has been set up with its initial value

decompose: break down

decomposition: the process of breaking a problem down into smaller sub-problems to make it easier to solve

denary format: a number system that uses the digits 0, 1, 2, 3, 4, 5, 6, 7, 8, 9 to represent every numerical value

entities: the people or things represented in a database

error message: information, hints or instructions to help a user resolve a problem

ethernet cable: a popular type of copper cable used to transmit data between devices

evolving: changing and improving

execute: to run

field length: the number of characters a field in a database application allows to be stored

firewall: software or hardware that prevents unauthorised access to a network

float: a number with a decimal point

flowchart: a visual representation of an algorithm

form element: an object in an electronic data-capture form

glossary: an alphabetical list of words on a particular subject, like a dictionary

hardware: the physical parts of a computer that you can touch and see, e.g. the processor, storage devices, input devices, output devices

hardware specification: a document that details the main components of a digital device

immersive: a feeling of being physically present in a virtual world

indented: describes a line of code that has been moved away from the left-hand margin to represent the code that will run if a condition is met

initial requirements: the idea and starting plan for a project

input mask: controls how data is entered into a database by defining a particular layout or format for the data

integer: a whole number

interactive graphics: graphic images (often animated) that a user can interact with using a device such as a mouse, keyboard or joystick

interface: how a user interacts with a product

interference: what happens when something interrupts the transmission of a signal; this could be a physical obstruction such as a wall, or other radio waves

invalid data: data that does not comply with validation rules applied automatically by a computer application

iteration/iterate: repetition/to repeat

iterative development/process: how a project develops throughout stages

least significant bit (LSB): the digit at the right-hand side of a number; the bit with the smallest place value

library: an additional set of functions that can be imported into a Python program

linear search: searching for an item in a list by comparing each item in turn with the searched-for item

live video stream: continual images and sound that are broadcast via the internet as they are being filmed

Local Area Network (LAN): a type of network that communicates over a small geographical area, such as a single building

logic gate: an electronic switch used in digital devices, which produces an output of 1 or 0 (TRUE or FALSE)

lookup: a lookup list provides the user with a list of options to choose from when entering data under a particular field heading in a database

machine learning: when AI systems are able to use data to make a decision without the help of a human

malicious: describing something that intends to cause harm

microprocessor: a mini-computer able to execute and store one program

MicroPython: the programming language used on the micro:bit

modify: update or change

most significant bit (MSB): the digit at the left-hand side of a number; the bit with the largest place value

network: a collection of computing devices connected to each other, either wired or wirelessly

network administrator: a person responsible for the maintenance and security of a network

non-volatile: describes a type of memory (ROM) that does not lose the data in it when the computer is switched off

online: connected to the internet

operating system: the systems software that manages hardware and software, giving the user an interface to operate the computer

parallel transmission: 8 bits (or 1 byte) of data are transferred simultaneously

Personal Area Network (PAN): a type of network that communicates over an area of no more than 10 metres, usually connecting smart devices within the immediate area of a user

physical computing device: a device that can be programmed using block- or text-based programming languages

place value: the numerical value a digit has as a result of its position in a number, e.g. the number 24_{10} represents $(2 \times 10) + (4 \times 1)$

platform: the combination of hardware and software used to complete a digital task

power surge: a temporary increase in power, often caused by lightning, which can damage computer hardware

primary key field: a field in a database that is unique and can be used to distinguish one entity from another

primary memory: storage to hold programs and data currently in use on a digital device

process: carrying out an operation on data, e.g. querying a database or doing a calculation using data in a spreadsheet

program: the instructions that tell a computer system how to complete a task

pseudocode: a textual representation of an algorithm

quarantine: moving a file to a safe place where it cannot contaminate other files on the computer

radio buttons: a list of options on a form for the user to choose from; the user can select only one of the options available to them

random access memory (RAM): a form of memory that stores tasks that are currently running, which the operating system controls

read-only memory (ROM): stores the data and instructions needed to start up a digital device

real: a data type consisting of numbers containing decimal points, e.g. 7.68

run-length encoding (RLE): a specialised algorithm used to support the compression of image files

secondary storage device: any storage device used to store programs or data for a long period of time to allow the user to access them at a later stage

selection: a choice in a program that is based on a question; the answer determines the next instruction to be run

serial transmission: data is transferred one bit at a time

server: a computer that offers a service to other devices on a network, such as file-sharing services and printer-sharing services

simulation: a computer program that represents a real-life scenario using formulae and can be used to predict outcomes

software: the programs or set of instructions that tell a computer what to do to complete a task; aspects of a device you cannot touch

spreadsheet: an application that uses rows and columns to organise data and carry out calculations using that data

string: a sequence of characters that can be text, numbers or symbols; quotation marks around the characters define them as a string

subsidise: contribute payment towards a fee to help reduce overall cost

switch: a network device that forwards data from one device to another

syntax: the defined rules required for a programming language

systems software: the software that helps a user run the computer

telecommunication: the transfer of information in the form of video and/or sound using cables, radio or satellite

test plan: a document that details the tests to be carried out when a program is complete and whether or not they are successful

text-based programming: programming that requires the programmer to type text, e.g. Python

text-based quiz game: a game in which the player types in answers to questions or puzzles

transistor: a tiny switch that can be activated by electrical signals – if the transistor is ON, it represents 1; when it is OFF, it represents 0

trojan: software that pretends to be something that it is not; trojans track keystrokes and mouse movements – even sometimes webcams

truth table: a table used to evaluate the outcome of a logical expression

unauthorised: not allowed

user requirements: a detailed list of what the user expects the data model to do

utility program: a program used to help maintain a digital device

validation: an automatic check to reduce the chance of errors being made when data is entered into a computer system

validation rule: a rule that specifies the characteristics of a valid data item in a database field

validation text: a message displayed when the data a user enters under a field heading in a database does not match the validation rules for that field

variable: a named temporary storage location in a computer; it can hold one value and this can be changed at any point in a computer program

virtual-reality (VR) simulation: a digital experience that allows the user to feel and interact with a digital world

volatile: describes a type of memory (RAM) that loses the data in it when the computer is switched off

web server: a computer that stores web pages that can be accessed by other devices using the internet

what if: changing the values in a spreadsheet cell to investigate the impact on other cells in the spreadsheet

what-if analysis: using current data and past experiences to investigate different scenarios using a data model; in a spreadsheet, this involves changing values in a cell to see how this will impact on the outcome of formulae in the spreadsheet

Wide Area Network (WAN): a type of network that communicates over a large geographical area, such as across a city or country

WinZip: compression software designed for use with Windows, macOS, iOS and Android operating systems

Wireless Access Point (WAP): enables devices to connect to a network using Wi-Fi

Index

N

O

P

Q

R

S

Acknowledgements

The Publishers would like to thank the following for permission to reproduce copyright material.

Photo credits

p. 8 © Mike Mareen/stock.adobe.com; **p. 11** *t* © Yuriy Golub/stock.adobe.com, *b* © SeventyFour/stock.adobe.com; **p. 12** © Andrea Danti/stock.adobe.com; **p. 14** *t* © Ridjam/stock.adobe.com, *b* © Xfilephotos/Shutterstock.com; **p. 15** © Teerasan Phutthigorn/stock.adobe.com; **p. 16** *t* © Sunshine Studio/Shutterstock.com, *b* © Olly/stock.adobe.com; **p. 18** © Gorodenkoff/stock.adobe.com; **p. 20** © Vitalii Stock/stock.adobe.com; **p. 21** *t* © Pixelrobot/stock.adobe.com, *b* © Aisvector/Shutterstock.com; **p. 23** © Minerva Studio/Shutterstock.com; **p. 24** © VikiVector/stock.adobe.com; **p. 25** *t* © Daisy Daisy/stock.adobe.com, *m* © RoSonic/Shutterstock.com, *b* © Rawpixel.com/Shutterstock.com; **p. 27** © Jamdesign/stock.adobe.com; **p. 28** © Alexmillos/stock.adobe.com; **p. 30** © GoodStudio/stock.adobe.com; **p. 32** © Warmworld/stock.adobe.com; **pp. 40, 41** *apple* © Eva Speshneva/Shutterstock.com, *banana* © Ivan Lukyanchuk/Shutterstock.com; **p. 43** © Micro:bit Educational Foundation microbit.org; **p. 51** © Lano Lan/Shutterstock.com; **p. 61** © Mmaxer/Shutterstock.com; **p. 63** *t* © Metamorworks/stock.adobe.com, *b* © Andrey Popov/stock.adobe.com; **p. 67** *tl* © Robertosch/stock.adobe.com, *tr* © Yaraz/Shutterstock.com, *b* © cristi180884 - Fotolia.com; **p. 69** © Stockphoto-graf/stock.adobe.com; **p. 73** © Spainter_vfx/stock.adobe.com; **p. 76** © Cookiecutter/stock.adobe.com; **pp. 76, 77** © Frozen Design/stock.adobe.com; **p. 78** *t* © Daniel Krasoń/stock.adobe.com, *m* © Markd800/stock.adobe.com, *b* © Artem Merzlenko/stock.adobe.com; **p. 80** *t* © BullRun/stock.adobe.com, *b* © Premio Stock/Shutterstock.com; **p. 82** © Wachiwit/stock.adobe.com; **p. 83** © Phonlamai Photo/stock.adobe.com; **p. 84** *t* © Freer/stock.adobe.com, *bl* © Matthew Corley/Shutterstock.com, *br* © Tartila/stock.adobe.com; **p. 85** © Taka/stock.adobe.com; **p. 86** © Nazarkru/stock.adobe.com; **p. 93** © MicroOne/stock.adobe.com; **p. 94** © MicroOne/stock.adobe.com; **p. 96** © Moving Moment/stock.adobe.com; **p. 100** © MicroOne/stock.adobe.com; **p. 111** © Respiro888/stock.adobe.com; **p. 113** © Gstudio/stock.adobe.com; **p. 116** © Zephyr_p/stock.adobe.com; **p. 127** © Sergey Nivens/stock.adobe.com; **p. 128** *l* © Gorodenkoff/stock.adobe.com, *r* © ShpilbergStudios/stock.adobe.com; **p. 129** © Kawee/stock.adobe.com; **p. 130** © Skyelar/adobe.stock.com; **p. 138** © Thodonal/stock.adobe.com; **p. 149** *t* © Zapp2Photo/stock.adobe.com, *b* © Vectorfusionart/stock.adobe.com; **p. 163** © Julia Lazebnaya/Shutterstock.com; **p. 164** © Viktoria Kurpas/stock.adobe.com; **p. 180** © Jessica/stock.adobe.com.

Text credits

The following brands mentioned in this book are trademarks or registered trademarks:

- 3G
- 4G
- 5G
- Adaware
- Android
- Avast Mobile Security
- Bitdefender Internet Security
- Bluetooth
- Google Maps
- iOS
- Lempel–Ziv–Welch (LZW) algorithm
- Linux
- MacOS
- MicroPython
- Microsoft Access
- Microsoft Excel
- Microsoft Windows
- Norton 360
- Pokémon GO
- Python
- Python's Integrated Development and Learning Environment (IDLE)
- Radio Silence
- Snapchat
- WiFi
- WinZip

BBC micro:bit images and screenshots © Micro:bit Educational Foundation microbit.org

Google and Google Maps are trademarks of Google LLC and this book is not endorsed by or affiliated with Google in any way.

Microsoft product screenshot(s) used with permission from Microsoft.

Every effort has been made to trace all copyright holders, but if any have been inadvertently overlooked, the Publishers will be pleased to make the necessary arrangements at the first opportunity.

Although every effort has been made to ensure that website addresses are correct at time of going to press, Hodder Education cannot be held responsible for the content of any website mentioned in this book. It is sometimes possible to find a relocated web page by typing in the address of the home page for a website in the URL window of your browser.